MW01493720

MY FATED LIFE

CHERRY HINKLE

MY FATED LIFE

Copyright © 2023 Cherry Hinkle.

All rights reserved. No part of this book may be used or reproduced by any means, graphic, electronic, or mechanical, including photocopying, recording, taping or by any information storage retrieval system without the written permission of the author except in the case of brief quotations embodied in critical articles and reviews.

iUniverse books may be ordered through booksellers or by contacting:

iUniverse
1663 Liberty Drive
Bloomington, IN 47403
www.iuniverse.com
844-349-9409

Because of the dynamic nature of the Internet, any web addresses or links contained in this book may have changed since publication and may no longer be valid. The views expressed in this work are solely those of the author and do not necessarily reflect the views of the publisher, and the publisher hereby disclaims any responsibility for them.

Any people depicted in stock imagery provided by Getty Images are models, and such images are being used for illustrative purposes only. Certain stock imagery © Getty Images.

ISBN: 978-1-6632-5514-3 (sc)
ISBN: 978-1-6632-5516-7 (hc)
ISBN: 978-1-6632-5515-0 (e)

Library of Congress Control Number: 2023914277

Print information available on the last page.

iUniverse rev. date: 07/29/2023

CONTENTS

1

NASHVILLE ENCOUNTER – THE REAL THUNDERBIRDS

I had one of my rare days off, my teenage daughters Monica and Sabrina were on a weekend with friends on a racehorse farm in Mt. Juliet, Tennessee. My three-year-old daughter, Mystique, was spending the night with her dad, leaving my son Marc and me alone to share the day. My son was precocious, and an advanced seven-year-old boy, his idea of a day with mom must mean include many hours inside a natural forest, and backpacking deep in that forest, fishing for our dinner and enjoying a bedroll at night. For a seven-year-old kid, he always knew exactly what he wanted to do. He heard from older friends at school that that primitive forest north of Nashville was dangerous. More than one strange beast reached the newspaper report regarding those trees. It didn't surprise me when Marc said that was exactly where he wanted to go that day.

Before 11am, Marc and I were deep into that dense forest. I had parked the car near the edge of a logging road, making sure a loaded truck of cut logs had plenty of room to get past my car. As always, I left a visible note on the dash of my car. The note stated time we left the car, the direction we plan to hike, and when we plan to return. Just the usual precautions just in case something unexpected happened.

Marc found a stream with icy cold water, and he hoped to find a few fish, but the fish had other plans, so instead of fresh fish for dinner, we enjoyed sliced Spam fried sandwiches, ice tea to drink and munched fresh apples for desert. About after a couple hours of dinner, those bedrolls sure felt great, and we fell asleep in no time.

We set up our bedrolls right beside a brief sheltering outcrop of rocks. You might say it was more like a short cliff, maybe twelve feet high, but the outcrop of rocks was enough to shelter us from a rain, as long as the rain fell straight down.

It was near dawn when we suddenly woke up to the odd crashing sounds very near us. From the sounds they made, something in the dark was fighting, and whatever it was, it was large and not more than thirty feet away!

Marc and I left our bedrolls and pressed ourselves harder against the rocks, I pushed Marc behind me. Picked up my large old folding knife opened it, and silently pressed it into Marc's hand. I quickly picked up my revolver; ready for whatever it was that was that seems to be fighting. I admit I worried they were fighting for us – and one of them planned to eat us for breakfast.

It felt like twenty minutes, but when you are in fear for your child's life, and fearing for the worse any minute, time loses all proper meaning. All you know is the sky is getting a little brighter and it won't be long and I'll be able to see the creatures that were fighting.

Suddenly – the crashing stopped, and all I could hear was the sound of my heart pounding and then I heard Marc's gasp. I turned to look at my son's face – and my eyes followed his gaze – about a short twenty feet I saw what looked like an over-grown buzzard. It was still too dark to make out any details, but I swear I was looking at a ten-foot buzzard, and at his feet was his dead companion.

Marc and I watched as the huge bird first stood on top the dead bird, and then we watched – in amazement – as it struggled hard to take off, bringing that dead bird in his talons! It took his a few times, but he finally lifted up, cleared the treetops and headed towards the rising sun.

Marc and I just hugged each other, not saying a word. We just sat there, hugging each other until the sun broke the edge of the near mountain.

We packed up our gear, walked over to the area were we witnessed the fighting birds. I reached in my waist pack and grabbed a small metal measuring tape. I measured one of the bird's footprints – 32-1/4 inches long by 28-1/2 inches. That bird has a footprint that was almost three feet long – can you image the size of the bird?

Marc and I didn't waste any time in that forest – we were afraid that huge bird might still be around – and hungry.

About one year after that event, I drove to the northeast part of Nashville again. I was looking for a house to buy. I noticed a sign near the edge of the road, it said "house for sale, buyer anxious to leave." I drove up the long driveway, and noticed a small foundation; I stopped and walked to the small cement area. My mind visualized a nice gazebo. As I walked on the cement I looked on the right side and noticed what looked like a giant bird nest, my heart froze, I glanced around, and there they were – more of those giant bird footprints! I ran to the car, and left the area and never again thought about the north part of Nashville. I know the real Thunderbirds exist, and they live north of Nashville Tennessee!

2

IDAHO ENCOUNTER

One strange night, many years ago, when I was at the age almost ten years, a humanoid visited me and kept me terrified all night. Some nights are carved in our memories for one reason or another this night, is the night I recall, vividly.

Although I was almost ten years old, I looked much younger. I wore the dress of a six year old child. Being petite, I was always smaller than my class-mates at school.

That night happened many decades ago, but I clearly remember the face of that humanoid, he almost looked like a man. There is no two ways about it; this petite humanoid could pass as human, except he was so very small. I recall don't his actual size, but although I was a kid, and I still knew was very small for a man. Looking back I suspect he may have been about less than four feet tall.

There is no other way to describe him - he appeared to be delicate, with well matched even facial features. He had smooth little hands and finger nails looked almost bluish at the end of his fingers. His nose looked too small with a noticeable up-lifting of at the tip. His eyes were large, abnormal large compared to the rest of his face.

I watched him as he lifted a wood chair and put it beside my bed. I couldn't help but notice he had a difficult time to carry the chair, as if it was too heavy and too large for him. When he sat down on the chair he looked like out of place, as if the chair was way too big for him.

Then, he scooted to the edge of the chair and leaned close to my face, and to my shock every time he leaned closer towards me, his eyes grew larger! At first, I thought it was due to his vantage point, and his eyes actually looked bigger because he was closer to me. Finally, I knew it wasn't an optical illusion – this man's eyes grew over two inches bigger, and a slight bulging out too. I was horrified and wanted to cry, but I couldn't. To make it worse, I couldn't seem to utter a sound.

I grabbed my blanket and pulled it up to cover my face, but slowly time he would slowly pull the blanket back down forcing me to gaze into his huge eyes!

It didn't take me very long for me to figure out that I couldn't move except to pull my blanket up. I knew every time I pulled my blanket over my head, he would slowly pull them back down and lean closer to my face, maybe one inch away, with a sneer or a smile; he kept up the "game" all night. I could smell his breath, and it smelled like the ripe earth in a forest. I didn't like that smell.

The little man wore a jump suit that resembled a business suit, and it covered him from his head to the bottom of his feet, only exposing his face and his hands. I couldn't say if he was bald or had hair at all, simply because the one piece outfit tightly covered his head.

Just before dawn, I was exhausted and tired of his relented game. I was too tired to care, and I fell asleep, with him still sitting in the wood chair.

Later that morning I woke up, afraid to open my eyes, thinking he was still beside me. I dared to take a stolen glance, but the humanoid was gone. I raced to my mother's side, and told her about the encounter, and she refused to believe it. I took her to my bed, showed the wood chair, told her again about his 'game' - but again she denied it, and said it was just a dream.

I cried and begged her to believe me, and did my best to convince her it was real, and that small man taunted me all night. My mother refused to believe it all. She insisted it was just a bad dream.

I know the difference between a dream, and reality. I also know the difference between a lucid dream and a real small man standing beside me. This man was very real.

If your child comes to you and tells you a small strange man stands inside their bedroom, believe them, and listen to them. I know that humanoid was not a dream, perhaps he was is an alternative reality, or a man from a different dimension, maybe he was just an alien. The Greys are real. Millions of people have talked about their alien experiences.

3

BIGFOOT ENCOUNTER IN THE CALIFORNIA FOREST

I must admit I did experience a Bigfoot in the forest in northern California back in 1977, but I rarely want to talk about it because I was not supposed to be there anyway. I had been driving all day and had traveled by any side roads that were not highways. That made the trip from Lake Tahoe, Nevada to a California point that was in the northern part of the state. I was in the northern rugged mountains of that state, and deep inside a vast forest and beside a beautiful mountain river. There was nothing to see but mature trees and shrubs from all directions. Imagine a forest so vast it reminds me of huge waves of deep green trees – or like an Ocean of trees, nothing to see but endless tree covered mountains.

It must have been nearly late evening, but since it was summer, there was still a lingering hint of light in the sky. There was no way to hide my fatigue if someone found me, and I knew I was too tired to drive on to the next town because I was in need of a few hours of sleep - at least that my mood at exact at that time, too tired to explore, and too tired to open my cooler and eat a piece of fruit. I could only think of rest and how good the sleeping bag would feel right now.

I am usually careful and always abide by the laws of the land and do not knowingly break any laws or rules posted by the roads. I guess that night I didn't care that I ignored the sign that said 'no overnight camping,' instead that evening I just pulled into the very wide area. I was so tired all I could think about was a few hours of sleep.

There must have been enough space to park 50 or 60 cars in that area, but I was alone when I pulled the car close to the river. It was a beautiful area, trees, smooth dirt roads, lots of beach-like sand beside the cold water in the wide river. Some of the beautiful trees grew so close to the water they provided a lot of shade that part of the river. The parking area if clear of debris, there were mostly tall Ponderosa trees with a few conifers near the river's edge. In one glance I saw a few sparse large boulders here and there near the river. If wanted to, I could have parked much closer to the river and I suspect I could have open the driver's door and cool my feet in the cold water of the brisk water. But I parked about 10 to 12 feet from the water edge. I just wanted to rest, not swim or cool my feet.

I had a vague plan in mind that night I'd just sleep for a three or four hours and then head up into Oregon, it couldn't be more than an hour's drive at the time, with me being so tired, that idea sounded great.

I think it would be a good idea that I tell you about my car at this point. Back in the late 1970s my car was a station wagon and this car had the back seat folded down flat and had deep a foam pad under my sleeping bag and pillows. No one could be more comfortable that me than the cozy roomy area I fashioned for this planned long road trip. I even had hanging lantern type lights so I could read a little if I wanted to – but I used the lantern mostly to read the local maps to find the back roads and avoid the highways and freeways, it is a wonderful way to enjoy a leisure trip.

Before I left home that summer, I had designed my own blackout curtains for the back of my car. Plus I added a lots of pillows, and plenty of extra blankets to give me a cozy spot to sleep, safe inside the locked car. The crisp night air would drift under and over the curtains and it sure made sleeping a pleasure. Too, I had curtains on both sides and the back window, and between the front seat and the back the area was very private, so at night no one could look into my sleeping area. I felt comfortable and very safe back there.

On the night I encountered the gargantuan creature known as Bigfoot, I had a few items I needed to do before decided to sleep. I settled in the sleeping bag, plumped up my pillows, turned on the lantern for a few minutes to check the map. I looked for the next town on the map, making sure the route I'd follow in the wee hours of the morning was clear in my mind.

I had both the back side windows open about an inch or so, and the smell of the cool night breeze hinted of aged pine and maybe the scent of brisk cold water babbling along the river, I could hear the water splashing on the rocks a few feet from my car. It was so tranquil and peaceful to be there in the mountains, enjoying the fresh mountain air, so cool, so fresh - it was wonderful - until the sickening smell of skunk-like odor hit me.

It was also about that time I became aware of the well-defined sound of heavy footsteps slowly approaching. The steps sounded overly heavy and about 60 feet away. Judging from the sound, the steps were in front of my car, and near the river. The heard the distinct sound of brittle leaves crushed and the sounds of branches snapping under his feet as he approached my car. The clear and vivid sounds became closer and my heart started to pound in my ears. It sounded like a really big man was on his way towards my car. I listened carefully – holding my breath - when I realized he was sneaking up on me, very slowly, several seconds between each step. There is no way I could be mistaken on this; I could clearly hear his approach getting closer and closer! I sure didn't like that idea one bit and I knew I might be in serious trouble. I felt my mouth getting dry and longed to drink deep from my canteen, but resisted that urge. I quickly turned off the lantern and fumbled around for a weapon I could use if I needed it, I found my car jack on right side of the car. Meanwhile the stench of the powerful odor got stronger with each step he got closer.

The smell was repulsive, and it is nothing you want to smell twice in your lifetime. This odor was overpoweringly strong and unpleasant, similar to a skunk, but it clearly not a skunk. Not only the stench was very unpleasant, I kept thinking that the smell it's self created a wave of fear. All these notions were in my mind as I lay there getting thirsty and afraid in the cool night air. I tried to allow reasoning take over and consider the idea but the thought refuses to believe this is not happening, because I love being outside, love the dark, the forest up in these mountains is dense and so beautiful I never fear the wonder of the forest at night. But this night, I felt a clear sense of sharp fear and an unreasoning fear that goes against everything I believe and felt all my life. I was never afraid at night in the forest and the sound of steps outside my window - they never bother me in the past, so I thought "this bad odor is creating the fear I feel."

My normal methods to overcome fear refused or ignored and that night my apprehensive tactics did not win the battle. I knew had to escape and avoid the sound of the determined humanoid that was approaching my car! I pulled my keys out my jeans pocket, my fingers found the ignition key in the dark car and grabbed the curtains between the front the seat and ripped the curtains open fast, I quickly slid into the driver's wheel position and started the car. My hands froze on the steering wheel, locked in position and ready to take off in a cloud of dust – but I couldn't move. My eyes witnessed the spectacle of a huge Bigfoot standing beside the right front fender. My eyes too, felt frozen in place, taking in the sight of too big non-human humanoid standing only inches from my car.

When I say he was huge you can really trust me on this one - he must have been 8 to 9 feet tall, and his body was covered with thick long fur on his very broad shoulders and face, I could see his wide chest, be was built like a powerful gorilla. With one hand he put his left hand on his chest and he looked like he was about to put his right hand on the fender of the car. In the light of the moon above I could see him clearly. I turned on the headlights, and I could see the auburn fur in the reflection of the headlights. He was so tall I couldn't see all of his face, just his angular jaw and part of his wide dark lips.

All of this I saw it clear as a bell in the clear night. It takes a long time to describe all of it, but at the time it happened, it took only seconds, and I turned and looked once again at the smelly creature standing beside my car fender - and the overpowering fear hit the pit of my stomach. Meanwhile, I kept thinking this fear is not real, I am never afraid with animals, people, aliens - why do I fear this time? But the fear won, and I pulled the transmission gears into drive, stomped on the gas, and left the side if the river and the amazing Bigfoot still standing in place.

Sometimes I contemplate that amazing night, wondering why the fear was so unstoppable. Other times I wonder what might have happened if I conquered my fear and stayed beside that river. Would I be now one of the few humans that communicated with a Bigfoot? Or would I just be just another missing woman, another lady that the authorities assume I got lost in the forest? I'll never know for sure because that night I didn't stop my car until I found a town with street lights. I sat filled with fear, and I parked under the street light, and stayed in that position for another hour until the sun came up.

4

REPTILIAN ENCOUNTER IN THE NEVADA DESERT

The city of Las Vegas and well-known Las Vegas Strip with is their glittering casinos, as well as the communities of North Las Vegas and Henderson, fills this crowded desert Nevada valley.

Black Mountain looms over the desert community of Henderson, situated on the east slopes of the valley. That dark mountain is the home of many television towers and other towers on the top. It is the home of mines and caves that pock the sides of Black Mountain.

Today, there are businesses and homes, and a freeway that cut into the lower slopes of that mountain, but in the middle of the 1970's there was just open desert from the middle Henderson to the mountain. More open undisturbed miles of desert until sparkling Las Vegas. With the building boom, homes and businesses crowd the once open desert.

In 1977, every kid in town knew the rules - do not climb or play on that mountain. All parents understood of the constant danger of the abandoned deep open mines and caves, but danger lures the younger set, and several deaths occurred on the slopes of Black Mountain.

It was on a pleasant day, and my thirteen-year-old son Marc and his friend Harry, roamed in the empty desert between my house, and the forbidden Black Mountain. Being adventurous boys, the chance to explore a cave and carry back a rock or two, and a lifetime of memories is enough to break the rules.

The boys hiked the scant one mile or so across the desert and climbed the little hills in front of Black Mountain. On the backside of one of the little hills, Marc and Harry located a cave. They had to squirm into the narrow opening, and belly crawl through the cave to the larger room and turned on their small pocket flashlights. They saw a circular room roughly nine feet across. Near the back wall, they spotted a large deeper hole. They found limbs and branches that someone had dragged through the cave's entrance. Those large branches were about a mile from closest tree, but someone tossed those branches into the hole creating a makeshift ladder to climb down into the lower pit.

The pit was roomy, with a short annex. Occasional debris littered the rocky floor, like a tin can or two, a battered teen magazine perched on a small outcrop of rock that served as shelf. The boys explored to main cave, then turned their attention to the short tunnel or annex.

Sounds carry in a cave, and the walls slightly vibrate if a loud voice reverberates throughout the small room. It was then, that the boys heard the sounds of a voices and maybe the distance humming of machines. Intrigued by the thought of they were mining nearby, the boys went a deeper into the tunnel. On the far end, they found a rusty metal door, and near the door a strange metal rod. The one-foot rod was lightweight and resembled aluminum, with a cap on one end and a few strange engravings on one side.

Marc weaved the rod in the belt loops of his jeans, focused the beam of his flashlight on the door, and tried the doorknob. He discovered a strong bolt secured the door from the reverse side. Harry shook the doorknob and pounded on it a few times. Startled, the boys heard the sound or guttural harsh voices talking, and the certain sound of approaching footsteps. They suddenly felt a wave of fear, knowing they were inside a forbidden cave, weaponless, and an angry animalistic growling voice attempted to open to the door any second.

Marc, the taller of the two, pushed Harry up the makeshift ladder and scrambled up the wood branch to the upper level of the cave. They heard the metal door clank and squeak loudly as the door it opened. The boys crawled as quickly through the narrow tunnel, and outside, the stood up and ran about the distance of a city block away from the cave entrance. They laughed at their dirty hands and faces, relieved the escaped from and the unknown man with harsh voices in the cave. They looked at the strangely engraved rod, trying to figure out what language might include circles, ovals, swirls and triangles.

Without a warning, they heard a loud threatening growl. Harry and Marc looked back at the cave entrance and to their horrified eyes; they watched as a very large greenish humanoid struggled to force his big body out of narrow cave. The boys screamed and started running down the slope of the hill, running top speed! They didn't look back until they were near my back yard. They slowed down, breathing hard and glanced back to the mountain.

To their shock and fear, the huge humanoid was trotting towards them! They started screaming again put on a burst of speed and ran into the house; Marc locked the door screaming "MOM! MOM! Help us Mom!

He's going to get us!" Alarmed, I ran into family room, and both boys threw their arms around me, crying. They both were shaking, not just their hands, but also their entire body shook! Wet tears left muddy tracks across their cheeks. Marc begged, "Don't open the door Mom, he going to get us!"

Meanwhile, Harry added, "He is big, and looks mean! Don't open that door – please, please, don't open that door!" Instantly I was furious with the man that generated such terror these young boys! At thirteen, boys are usually trying to impress everyone how brave they can be, so I know it took a lot of nerve to admit that much fear.

"Boys, you go get a drink of water and let me go talk to this man," I suggested, but they tightened their grip on me, screaming "NO, NO, NO! That guy will kill you! He is not a man! Don't go out there Mom!"

I managed to coax one arm free from each boy. I looked into their worried eyes. "Boys - nobody is going to kill anybody, and you know I won't allow anyone hurt you! Now - what do you mean he is not a man? It's a woman that is threatening you?"

"No Mom, it's a man, sort of, he looks like a man, but his face looks like a snake or YEAH, he's like a lizardman! He's ugly and he doesn't wear anything. He's naked Mom, except a wide belt with stuff on it."

I stared at my son, imagining some teenager wearing a Halloween costume. I laughed a little, and said, "Boys, it was just someone playing a joke on you!" Both boys started protesting again, both talking at the same time. I could hear the panic in their voices rising again, and finally Harry said,

"That guy couldn't be wear a costume, he could barely squeeze himself out of the cave, he would have ripped he costume into pieces!"

"What cave? Did you go boys up on Black Mountain even when you knew the danger?" I asked.

"Mom – really listen to me, he was a lizardman and he was naked. I've never seen a costume that shows EVERYTHING, he was naked Mom, and it was NOT a costume! You know what I mean Mom?"

With difficulty, I untangled myself from the tight grip boys, and looked out the window. I peered carefully out the widow expecting the spectacle of a lizardman, but nothing moved, not a child, not a man and no lizardman. I reassured the boys the danger is in the past and the man was long gone.

It was at that point, I noticed Marc was holding a strange metal rod. "What do you have in your hand son?" Marc glanced at the rod and threw it on the floor as if it would burn his hand. I leaned to pick it up but Harry grabbed my arm, warning it was dangerous, maybe a weapon. I picked it up reminding them they carried it from the mountain safely all that time, so it couldn't be too dangerous.

The rod was approximate one and a half inch across, maybe a foot long with a slight indentation at one end and a plain gray cap on the other. I looked at the bizarre symbols engraved in a three-inch section of the rod. It was just symbols, from spirals, circles of different sizes, a few triangles, and a few unknown symbols. There were no levers or buttons, and the cap at the end didn't seem to move. The rod, with its professionally created symbols and smooth to the touch, I knew it was not a toy, but nothing I recognized.

It was late afternoon, and the long shadows cast ominous shapes in the yard, I knew Harry was still too nervous to walk home alone. Marc and I walked the distance of two houses and made sure he was safe inside with his father before we walked home.

That night, Marc was still nervous, peeking out the curtains often, expecting the worse. Marc played Scrabble with his sisters, anything to keep his mind busy. Near midnight, we went to bed.

It must have been around two in the morning when Marc shook me whispering harshly that someone is trying to get into his bedroom window. I hoped it was just a nightmare, or his nerves were still on edge. Quietly we slipped into his bedroom and listened to the sounds of scraping at the window edge! He was not mistaken – in the light of the moon I could make out the silhouette head and shoulders of a man.

I was alone with my four kids, no husband to protect us, so I grabbed my flashlight; suddenly tossed the curtains open to face the man. There was a glare from the flashlight on the window, but past glare that I could clearly see a large head with ridges on the top, other ridges on his cheekbones, and the glow of golden eyes. Marc and I stood still, unmoving, both fear and shock kept us frozen. The lizardman didn't move either, his hand still poised in his attempt pry the window open. He hand was large, with webbed rough, gnarly looking fingers, with powerful claws.

After a couple minutes, not seconds, but long agonized minutes with our hearts pounding I knew I had to do something. One hand still holding the flashlight beam on his face and my eyes still locked into those golden eyes, I fumbled around in the dark with my other hand, hoping to find something to use as a weapon, is needed. He glanced at my hand, looked back into my eyes. He turned his head a little, as if he was asking a questioning, he slightly opened his lipless mouth, displaying four of his pointed teeth, and suddenly he turned and ran off into the desert.

Marc suddenly closed the curtains, grabbed my hand and led my shaking legs to the edge of his bed. We sat there for a few silent minutes. We just sat there, trying to comprehend the incredible event, with little success. We started talking at the same time, and started checking the doors and windows repeatedly. His sisters were completely awake by then, and we all talked all night, going from windows to doors until full sunlight.

Later in the morning, we decided the reason the lizardman was breaking in the house was to reclaim that metal rod. Marc and I hiked back to the cave and placed the strange rod beside the cave entrance, and quickly returned home.

The lizardman never again attempted to enter this house, and for that, I am relieved.

After a few days, I went outside and looked at that window. It was then that I found that that bottom edge of that window is close to six feet high from the ground. It was a shock to realize the lizardman must have been very tall, over seven feet tall! Inside the windows are high, but about five feet high from the floor to the bottom of that window, from outside there is no way no one could look through this window – unless they were extremely tall.

This event is real. "Harry" is not the real name, but since I have been unable to locate him and ask permission, I used a pseudo name. Marc's name is real, and he was my only son. Marc died in 1999.

I still live in sight of Black Mountain. People living close to that mountain sometimes report underground rumbling at night when it is quiet. UFOs are often seen and photographed over Black Mountain, that shouldn't be too surprising; we live not far from Area 51 in Nevada.

5

THE MEN-IN-BLACK ABDUCTED ME FROM MY HOSPITAL ROOM

To understand the "why and where" I offer this pre-information regarding what happened in this case. *Thanks.*) {In 1972 I was in a car accident that torn the muscles in my back, it left me in a rigid back brace back and rigid neck brace, (I wore the back brace for over 12 years) and I suffered headaches from that car wreck. I moved from Las Vegas Nevada to Colorado in September 1979. In December 1979, Tom Castello visited me in Colorado and talked to me about the infamous Dulce Base. In January 1980 my doctor suggested I should have an angiogram to find out why I had these headaches. Meanwhile, the CIA, FBI and other groups visited my home, many times, looking for Tom Castello. I agreed to take this medical test, but the small Colorado town I lived in didn't have a medical facility, he suggested to a different town in a different state, roughly 80 miles away. In early February 1980 I scheduled an appointment for that medical test. And now you can understand the following events.

Abducted from my hospital room? I would have laughed if someone suggested it might happen… the thought is ludicrous, things like that never happen in federally owned hospitals, right? But don't laugh yet – because sometimes Fate gives you a big shock, a wake-up call. Looking back wondering could I have prevented the horrid experience of three men abducting me from my hospital room in the middle of the night. Let me go back and attempt to explain what happened.

My Colorado doctor promised it would be no big deal, a simple angiogram of the brain to determine why I had severe headaches; it was hardly more than a Cat-Scan or X-Ray of my brain, a simple one hour medical procedure. My doctor suggested it would be best if I would agree to an overnight stay in the hospital because they want the medical test at 6am, and I lived over 80 miles away, in a different state.

I checked into the hospital at 9pm. At bedtime, put on my nightgown, I took the little white pill the nurse gave me after she assured me it would allow me to sleep well, and the doctor wanted me rested for the angiogram in the morning.

I don't how long I'd been sleeping when I felt the palm of man's hand firmly over my mouth. I struggled to clear the sleep from my mind and to see the thin face of the man leaning over my face. I grabbed his hand, trying to pull his hand off my mouth, but he was strong and determined to keep me from crying out. "If I remove my hand off your mouth will remain silent?" the man asked. Looking into his dark sunglasses I silently nodded my yes. I was a small trim five foot woman, so it was easy for the two other men to lift me off my bed and strapped me firmly on a gurney, and draped me with sheets. The third warned me to remain silent, if I wanted to survive. The man dressed in black had a large dark wool scarf wrapped over his other hand, and I suspected a weapon was wrapped in that scarf. I saw no one in the halls; it was if the entire hospital was sleeping, except us.

I didn't say a word to the men, just stared up at the other two men dressed in hospital scrubs, trying to use will power my mind to remember their faces, and the third - tall gaunt man wearing a black suit, dark sunglasses, black necktie and matching hat. He looked like character from a bad 1940s detective movie. But this was the wrong era, today it was the second month of 1980 – and this man looks out of place. The three men rolled my gurney down the hall to the elevator. Inside the large hospital elevator I felt the surge as we dropped several floors.

We entered a cavernous room that looked like a storage area for mixture of medical equipment; I saw three X-ray tables, and what looked like four MRI machines and other medical equipment I didn't recognize. I watched nervously as we approached the last MRI machine, it was a little wider and higher than the others, and I noticed someone had moved the table to the left, allowing the gurney – and me – to be push through the round entrance of MRI machine. The men ducked to enter the MRI machine. To my bewilderment, the wall opened and the three men pushed me through the door into a well lighted hall, and the wall silently closed again.

It was then I felt the sting of an injection needle in my left arm and my heart started racing. My mind struggled to remain awake, and rejected the concept of forced to sleep. I tried to fight off the injection's solution, it was a powerful drug, almost instantly I felt a little confused and dazed, and in a few seconds more I felt as if I was floating, in my mind I thought the hospital walls were melting around me. My last conscious thought was the Men-In-Black were abducting me from this hospital! God help me, what did I do to deserve being this abduction? And then - the nothingness of drugged sleep.

I remember waking up slowly, keeping my eyes closed, calmly listening to the rhythmic clicking of the wheels as it rolled down the very long underground passage. I opened my eyes and watched as dim overhead lights clicked in and out of view in the narrow corridor ceiling. "What a strange dream," I thought "I am dreaming of a tunnel, how odd."

"She's awaking up Doc, want me to put her back under?" one of men in hospital garb asked.

"No, we are almost there," the MIB agent mumbled.

In the few seconds it took to utter those few words, I was fully awake and frightened - and I knew this was no dream! I felt the coldness of fear in my chest, and I turned my head to my right, to see the MIB agent tautly sitting beside me. I noticed his sallow skin, the prominent boniness of his face, the hollowed wide cheeks, and the jet-black hair jutting from under his hat. I knew he wore a bad toupee. The two men in hospital scrubs looked average in size; the both wore cropped brown hair, and were muscular in build. One man had small brown eyes that were too close to his nose; the others had blue eyes, and had a small surgical scar at the base of his throat. Now that I remember the abduction, I wanted to escape the three men sitting only inches away, but I remained strapped down on a gurney, going underground in a tunnel and only God knows where I'd end up. I didn't know how long I slept from that injection; it could have been minutes or hours. I turned my head and looked at the 1940s man, "Please, where am I? Where are you taking me?"

I looked at the MIB expecting a response, but said nothing in return; he never even indicated he heard my question; he just totally ignored me, as if I didn't exist.

I took a deep breath and struggled with the braided canvas-like restraint, hoping I could wiggle my hands free, but the straps were sturdy, I had no chance I could escape. I felt the wheels of the electric cart start slowing down, and to my horror I watched a huge grotesque humanoid approach the cart. He wore a copper colored uniform, but just past his wide shoulders I noticed what looked like tan wet leather wings, with thick veins in sight. In shock I couldn't speak, but just stared at the reptilian face with ridges on his cheekbones, forehead and skull.

"Is this one you told me about Doc? Isn't she the one from Nevada - the female that have seen our race before?" the reptilian man asked. His voice was raspy and rumbling, with accent was heavy from an unknown language. I couldn't believe he was so large, it is just a guess but I think he must have been nearly eight feet tall with a barrel chest. He was correct, three years ago; in 1977 my son and his friend and I witnessed a reptilian in Nevada.

"She's the one. I knew you'd want to see this one, she's been a major headache for us for weeks," 1940s man replied. He took off his dark glasses, unfolded his white handkerchief and cleaned his sunglasses. He looked up at me and I looked directly into his eyes, suddenly I felt a wave of fear because his entire eyes were black, with no white parts of his eyes, not one section of his large eyes that didn't gleam a jet black. I don't know what frightened me more – the reptilian giant or those solid black eyes. The MIB called 'Doc' helped me off the gurney and escorted me into a roomy but Spartan room. The furniture was plain, two maple wood library tables, one large elongated but nondescript wood box and a half dozen of padded brown office chairs. Not one picture or documents to add interest to the plain drab rock walls. I did notice the clean beige tiles on the floor shined from a recent coat of wax. I considered that floor was the most decorative part of the room.

During the long dreary hours I spent in that underground facility, a man in a copper uniform kept placing photographs and sketched images and objects on the table in front of me, they never explained why they wanted me to see these items, and they didn't request comments regarding the images. The photographs seems to be a lot of eight by ten photos of animals, a lot of those photos were young animals, like kittens, puppies and ponies but even photos of little fish. The never explained why they wanted me to look at those animals photos. To the best my knowledge, all the scores of photographs seemed to be plain photos in natural poses, like a photo of a puppy with his front paws in a mud puddle, and I didn't notice anything unique in any of them.

Later, they asked me a lot of questions about Tom Castello. Plus they questions about my family, my children, my sibling and my parents, they even asked about my distant family, like cousins I've never met, but they expected me to know all about them. I didn't know my cousins, I just never met them. They never asked for any specific family, they just asked about cousins, like "did you ever meet your aunt Mable's children?" I was surprised that he knew the names of my aunts and uncles. I never really answered those questions about my family, I just kept telling them I never met them. They seemed to already know all about all my family. Maybe they just wanted me to know *they* about my family. But that was just a guess.

They seemed more interested in intimidating me with comments like rather or not I wanted to survive these questions. To this day, I am not allowed discuss the details regarding the threats they used or *how* they threatened me, but I can confirm I was in fear for my life. They warned me to never reveal the details of these questions, or discuss the other bizarre events I witnessed inside that facility. I will also mention that I am not at liberty to confirm or deny the name of the underground facility. They warned me that I must sign a specific document they had already prepared for me, or I will never again see the blue skies of the surface of Earth.

I noticed the paper alleged to witnessed by "my personal physician" – at least that is what the document stated, but I do not know that "doctor," and never met him in my life; he wasn't even one of the three men that abducted me.

The reptilian humanoid stayed in the room the entire session, but he did not question me. Once or twice men wearing the same copper colored uniforms glanced into the room or hesitated a few seconds at the door, but didn't enter the room.

I was thirsty, hungry and tired, but the three men, the 1940's man called Doc and two other MIB in suits questioned me. There was only three men in business suits, everyone else I saw wore the same copper colored uniforms.

After two or three of hours I was cold from the cool underground room, a female took me to a ladies room and I was supplied a warmer copper colored uniform rather than my thin nightgown, for that, I was grateful. The uniform was too big for me, but I was able to roll up the legs of the uniform and fold up the arms of the uniform.

The two men in scrubs from the hospital may or may not be workers in that hospital, after they took me from the hospital room and transported me to this underground facility in a western state, I never saw them again.

These three MIB questioned me about Tom Castello, and demanded answers, sometimes they threatened to kill me, or even worse, to silence me - medically. Being maimed or tortured is enough to strike fear in your heart, I didn't know exactly how they meant to silence me, but before that 24 hour session ended, and I fully understood what he meant.

Being at least slightly intelligent, I offered to trade my information for their information, I didn't really wanted any information they might have, I just said it in an effort to buy time, to find a way to get out of this abduction alive because they were getting angry with me. I kept telling them I didn't know anything – and they seemed knew that fact was not completely the truth. They partially agreed to trade information with me. However, I mostly wanted to trade whatever I needed to survive this abduction. Doc asked what I wanted, and without hesitation I asked for the ultimate truth - the Secret of Secrets - who are the ancient gods, and who these beings that float through Earth's sky.

It took them about 15 minutes for them to clear the information I demanded – the UFO truth. When the information arrived, a man brought it in a thick Manila envelope. I freely admit I was curious, wondering if this mysterious envelope contains the same dangerous material that so many people have died trying to share it with the world.

The MIB said "OK, I've got the information in my hands, now you tell me what I want - where is Tom Castello and how do you contact him?" I looked at him, and laughed – you can be very certain he didn't my laughter one bit.

Without hesitation I admit I was frightened, and it may sound obvious a faked laughter, but I didn't want them to have the satisfaction of knowing I was terrified, so I said "Oh get serious please, I promise you I was not born yesterday, and that is a very weak and pitiful trick. I told you I would trade for information, I didn't say 'you lie to me, and I'll believe anything.' You better get serious gentlemen, because I am not going to fall for that worn out trick." I folded my arms against my chest and then added, "You know all about me – so you know I am natural psychic, when you tell me the truth, I will know it, and if you know try to trick me, I'll never tell you a thing."

The three men mumbled together quietly for a few minutes near the door of the room, but they knew I was dead serious, they already knew I was born psychic and can see the colors of human aura. I proved it with a strange photograph that shows the bright colors of the aura. I described the correct colors of three men in the room, so they know I was accurate and know when they lie to me. They knew I would know if they lie, because their aura turns the color a muddy reddish brown and the outer edges of the aura gets tinged with a sickening pea green when someone lies.

They decided to tell me – all of it, and looking back on that event, I truly wish they didn't tell me anything. But you can't "unheard" things you heard, and you can't "unlearn" things you learn. Once you know something, there is no way you can pretend you didn't know. For the rest of your life you must be responsible for that knowledge.

In my case, the MIB agent just opened up and told me the ultimate horrid truth. For the next hour they talked about the horrifying truth and I felt sick to my stomach. I felt spiritually betrayed; I couldn't prevent the bitterness I felt in my heart, any more than I could feel the hot felt anger when I heard the ultimate truth about the UFOs. The more I learned, the more upset I felt. I didn't want to hear any more, I wished I never heard of UFOs – but it is too late, know I do know.

Everybody claims they want to know it all – but when you DO learn all of it, all you can do is you wish you could go back in time and erase that information from your brain.

I always thought I was concerned with truthful facts, I always said I always wanted to know all the facts, all of it – but in reality was I guess I was dead wrong, because that was before I knew the horrible real truth. That day I found out that our so called "real" is "wrong" too. I wish I never heard about of aliens or flying saucers You may say I found out evil was good, and good was evil, and in that way every aspect of this life is a joke. Life is NOT what we think. There is no way I could explain anything that would help you understand how I felt, but in that room when I heard the truth. Instead of glad I finally found the ultimate truth - I felt disgusted, horrified and felt an empty feeling in my soul.

The MIB agent placed a holy bible on the table and opened one or two references in the spiritual book, offering to prove his words. I closed the book. I didn't want to hear the verses he was reading loud it that way. I still needed my faith, and I wanted my faith needed to be unchanged.

I wanted to escape the bitter truth – now that I learned the truth, I didn't want to hear it. I turned on the MIB agent, lashed out like a wild animal. I slapping him, the other men grabbed me and I pushed them away, and took off running down a long hallway. I knew they'd catch me, because there is no way out, but still I felt the need to calm my mind a little. I needed to digest the disturbing information they told me. I know I asked for the ultimate truth, but like everybody else, no one could prepare me for the shock of the Secret of Secrets, and no one could prepare me so I could understand exactly what the horrid truth meant. I thought it was strictly information about aliens – the secret of the aliens - now I knew I was wrong. I ran as fast as my legs would move, but after just a few minutes two men caught me from a side door, and they escorted me back to back to the first room.

I was surprised when they gave me a glass of cool water and allowed me to rest for a few minutes, thinking silently. When I rested a few minutes, the man they called 'Doc' told me they knew how I felt, and that everybody feels that way when they learn the truth. They almost seemed sympathetic towards me. They refilled my glass of water, and let me just sit there for a few more minutes, and then they wanted Tom's information. I looked at the MIB agent and I sipped the water, and then replied - "Look, I'm sorry but I don't have any information about Tom. I kept telling you over and over, but you don't want that answer." That was a fact, they didn't like it one bit.

Once again, they tried to warn me, to threaten me again, and as they again threatened to kill me, or worse, to maim me and other frightening tactics. Hearing those words and knowing these men are dead serious, I knew the wanted me to tell them everything I knew about Tom. I stayed firm and repeating the same thing - Tom left, I haven't seen him since early December 1979. They tried getting loud and when the more they yelled, the quieter I got, after a heated hour or so, I refused to talk at all. I told them I had a headache, and wish they would stop yelling at me. I knew Doc was upset because I wouldn't tell him anything. He injected something into my arm to force me to talk - but instead of making me talk, it made me vomit, and I still didn't talk. They gave me "one more chance" (as they called it) I was exhausted, had nothing in my stomach except that a one glass of water and a few swallows of a second of more water. My stomach felt raw and empty, not to mention a little nauseated, because they removed me from the hospital almost 23 hours ago. I felt the urgent need for food and sleep.

"Cherry, I can keep you here in this base, or release you – if you at least try to cooperate with me," Doc said.

"I've never said these words to anyone Doc, but you go straight to hell."

"Woman, I gave you a chance – I rarely do that – but you had to be unreasonable. For the rest of your life you will regret your lost chance. You will remember this for the rest of your life Cherry, but you will never be able to tell anyone about it."

He sat in his chair staring at the floor for a few more seconds and then nodded his head, he gestured to a table nearby and three men again strapped me down on a gurney again. I stayed quiet, and just watched them as they injected an amber liquid into my left arm. Once again I saw the walls melting - and then just blackness.

I heard the sound of crisp steps walking near my bed and with an effort, I opened my eyes, I knew they returned me the hospital, and judging from the large room with filled several beds, this must be a recovery room. I heard the steps get closer, and then stopped beside my bed, I looked up to see was talking to me.

The nurse stood beside me and it was obvious she ask a question. I looked up at her and I knew she was she was speaking to me, but I couldn't understand her words. I glanced around wondering if they MIB placed me in a foreign hospital, but nurse's words were more than just a different language – it appeared she were uttering total gibberish. I attempted to reply to her, but I seemed to have forgotten how to speak, I was astonished. I tried a few more times, but each time all I managed to so be moan or groan, not one clear word. I could think clearly, but I failed to uttered clear words. I couldn't understand why I couldn't speak. The nurse walked away.

Using my left hand I searched around in the sheets trying to find my right hand, it was numb, and couldn't feel it at all. I thought it had fallen asleep and was numb, but when I finally managed to pull my right hand and arm onto my chest, it felt like a heavy log. I rubbed my arm trying to coax feeling into my arm and hand, but after a few more minutes I felt a sinking fear in my heart and I knew my right arm didn't work. The fear magnified when I attempted to move my right leg, and it didn't respond at my efforts to turn and sit up. Quietly, desperation took over and I cried like a baby for the first time in many years. By then, I knew I had suffered a major stroke, and I know it was from the hand of the MIB.

A few hours later, they put me in a very quiet private room, it was away from any other patients, I could only hear a few sounds once in a while. After a day or so I noticed I had liquids being injected in my arm, and I have no idea what they liquid contained. Too, I was aware that no one entered my room except they brought fresh water and food.

I managed to pull my right leg to the edge of the bed, and I attempted to stand up and walk to the sink, it was in sight, only about seven or eight feet away. I needed to wash my face, in hope it might clear my thoughts and the hope the little walk might do wonders, and restore my worthless right limbs. I stood up carefully, standing on my left foot and tried to take one step and felt my body collapse to the floor, it was a hard fall, and my head ached from hitting the wall and the floor. I felt like a limp ragdoll, and another wave of fear hit me when I discovered I was on the floor and had no way to get up. I inched slowly towards the bed, grabbing the metal edge of the bed frame, hoping I could use the bed to help pull myself up and get back in bed. I tried to get up, but I couldn't get up. I tried several times, then gave up, but just rested not trying to get up.

I don't know how long I stayed laid on the floor, it felt like a long time, hoping someone would come and help me. When I fell, the needle in my left arm was pulled out from and that bled a little, but not much. I tried to reach a blanket, but the bed was too high, so I could only touch the edge of one sheet, but couldn't pull it down to warm me. I dozed a few times on the cold hard floor, I tried to call out for help, but no one heard me. I could only lay flat on my back, or try move to my left side but I couldn't sit up, or get back onto the bed. I was weak, and dizzy and starting to shake from the cold floor. Finally I heard someone enter the room to bring my evening meal. He placed the tray on the table and left, in another minute or so, he and another attendant and together helped me get off the floor and into bed, quickly and covered me with a warm blanket.

I was aware, fully aware, but couldn't speak, and couldn't understand anyone's words. I found out I wouldn't read or write either. I remember Doc's warning that I would regret my chance to give him the information. I knew I was in grave danger, but I couldn't speak, couldn't walk, and I suspected Doc was still watching me.

The next few days were just a blur, and they kept me drugged, and what was worse, I found out they placed me in a very strange room, a room hidden off a broom closet. I have no idea why. I don't expect everyone to believe this; looking back it still horrifies me remembering that bizarre room, I can only testify that everything is 100% just as I claim it.

That hospital room looked like something from a science fiction movie, with two way cameras in the room, but seemingly few nurses bother looked at my room. There was with a small monitor screen beside my bed. Once two men they added overhead rods over my bed with hand grasp levers to help me move myself in position. Still, I rarely saw anyone, I never saw a doctor, and a few times a nurse came to adjust the required tubes. One attendant arrived once a day at the at evening when my dinner meal arrived. It was very odd.

Almost two years later, when I was able to speak a little I ask questions, I found out I was missing from that hospital for 23 hours, and they claimed I left during the night, without telling anyone. The nurses claimed they searched for me in the hospital, and after not finding me, they assumed I left. What is worse, the nurses decided I must left on my own, and the nurses were baffled when they found me in the recovery room. No one knew I had been kidnapped for twenty four hours, and returned to the hospital. I was not capable to explain what happened.

When the nurses found me in the recovery room that night, I couldn't say a word, and I couldn't understand the words of the medical team. I wanted to explain I had been abducted, but I no way to communicate what happened. I suspect someone knew, and they kept me in that bizarre room off a janitor's room. I stayed there nine more days, I would have been longer because the medical facility told my family I had checked out, and no one knew when or what exactly what happened to me. My teenage son, Marc, refused to give up and kept looking for me. Even after the hospital claimed I left, Marc searched for me in every room, and finally noticed a broom closet, through the glass door window if the janitors broom supply room, Marc saw another door and on the door it claimed "private" – he entered that room and found me. Quickly, he got my things together, helped me dressed and sneaked me out of the hospital. I am alive today because my 15 year old son refused to believe I left the hospital.

6

JAHEL – THE UNPLANNED VISITOR – THE ALIEN

It had been a rough day, the kind of day that no matter what I tried to do - it was wrong. I had been packing all day, and in the process, two of my favorite blue glasses from my set of 12 had been shattered. I was too tired to cry over broken glasses. I was tired and it was time to take a break and escape the rest of bad day and visit with my sister.

I hadn't told my sister Phyllis yet that I was moving to the same town, and would be just a few blocks away from her house. I just found out a few days ago a few days ago. My first husband Aaron, accepted a position in a town nearby, and didn't mention it until he found a two bedroom house. That was his way; he rarely discussed anything with anyone. I don't know if you understand what I mean, but in the early 1960's, Southern men consider packing household items in the home to relocate to another town is strictly "women's work." Men pack manly items, such as lawn motors, fishing poles, tool chests, even the inside the utility room in the garage. However, no self respecting Southern man would be caught doing woman's work. He would lift the heavy boxes for me, and the furniture, but not household items, such as clothing dishes, books, no matter the size or weight, nothing inside the house. It made life a little difficult sometimes since I am a small woman, a scant five feet tall and almost weighs 100 pounds. However, like most other ladies, I managed to do whatever I must with a lot of determination.

I always tried to accept my husband's ways and joined into his hobbies. He enjoyed fishing in the many rivers and lakes in central Florida. I learned to fish and learned to handle a fishing boat with no problem. In no time, I could bring a big catfish almost as big as me. It isn't easy, but I managed to get that fish into the boat. Aaron always expected me to handle the fish I caught, by myself, no matter the size. Only once did I cut the line and let that big fish return to the river, I had to let him go, because that catfish was bigger than me.

On other week-ends, he wanted to be driving his race stock cars. I learned to enjoy the roar of the engines, and on the days they had Powder-Puff Derbies, I would put on a helmet, strap on the restraining belts and race around the half mile track with the other driver wives. It was a good way to learn to handle a car in a wreck and I admit I liked the few trophies I won. I liked looking up at those shiny five trophies, and I kept them on the top of my kitchen shelves. Looking up at the five golden trophies, I made a mental note not to forget them, I need to borrow a ladder from a neighbor and get them packed too. So much to do, but I desperately needed a break.

By 7pm, my two little young daughters, Monica and Sabrina, were two and three years old were asleep for the night, and my husband was watching TV in the living room. I told him was going to visit my sister, twenty miles south of here, and that I would be home by midnight. Surprised, he glanced up at me, but with my jacket on and a 'don't push me' look on my face he didn't say a word. After five years of marriage, he knew better than to challenge me when I tell him I'm going somewhere and I had 'that look' on my face.

If I ask him if he minded if I go, there wouldn't be any problem. This time I really needed to get away, and so I didn't ask him – I simply told him.

I drove south on the Orange Blossom Drive, headed to Kissimmee. Back then, 1963, that drive was just a straight drive, not much to see, just miles of orange groves. It is not like now, with Disney World with the freeway, the traffic, the motels and countless other businesses.

I saw the flashing lights ahead on the dark road and slowed the car, police cars and an ambulance blocked the travel lane, and like all other traffic, I went carefully around the wrecked cars aware of the danger of night travel, if you are not paying attention to the road. The police stopped my car, and two others behind me, beside one of the bandaged driver, he leaned on the left front fender of his wrecked car. He was telling the officer he hadn't been drinking that he really saw a flying saucer in the sky and that explained why his attention was distracted and didn't see the stopped car ahead. Maybe the car in front of the saucer too, and why he stopped in the middle of the road?

"You've got to be kidding me," I thought. Wondering if the police officer believed him? I hope so.

When the officer waved me to continue, I saw that I was just a just a few blocks to my sister's house. I felt a twinge of excitement, and could barely contain the bubble of laughter, imagining my sister's surprise when I tell her we will be neighbors!

Phyllis and Jimmy (my brother-in-law) turned on the porch light and opened the front door when they saw my car lights pull into their driveway. After our usual initial family hugs and kisses, and a couple minutes of chit-chat,

I hit them with my big news – next week we would be neighbors! We spent the next couple hours talking about the best stores in the area, and the fun of us four will have playing cards and planning pick-nicks on the river.

I was about to leave when I remembered the wreck and told Jimmy about the flying saucer remark I overheard. He told me he and Phyllis had seen a lot of strange lights in the sky towards Orlando, and I better be careful driving home. Phyllis suggested that Jimmy follow me home to make home safely, and he grabbed his keys, ready to drop everything and make sure I made it home safely. I reassured I'd be home in no time in just a few minutes, not to worry. They both are sweet and willing to help out no matter what the situation. I gave Jimmy an extra hug, and teased him by telling him instead of following me home; he could help me unpack everything next week. I should have known better, he instantly said he and Phyllis would be at the new house Saturday morning ready to get to work.

On the way home I heard a few odd harsh whispering voices, fearing a child might have sneaked into the car back seat of my car, I pulled into the next commercial building I saw, and parked under the lights. I opened the rear door left back seat, but no child was crouching in the seat. I opened the trunk, expecting to see one of my nieces, or maybe one of their friends, but the trunk was empty. I felt an odd uncomfortable sensation, not different when you feel when something is staring at you. I looked around carefully, but saw no one, not even other cars. It was then I felt a creepy feeling and thought of the wrecked cars and the flying saucer remarked. Without thinking my eyes glanced up at the sky, but just saw stars. Finally convinced I was alone in the car, I pulled back into the light traffic, headed home.

On Saturday morning, as they promised, Phyllis and Jimmy were waiting when I pulled into the driveway in the new house. My car was loaded with clothing, and pillows and a few toys, leaving a cozy spot in the back seat for my daughters to play on the way to their new home. We were barely finished unpacking the car when Aaron arrived with the furniture and boxes of household items.

When the unpacking work was finished, Phyllis and I made a quick salad and a stack of thick meatloaf sandwiches, and thinner sandwiches for the younger children, as well as small servings of vanilla pudding for their dessert. I added chipped ice and a few sprigs of fresh cut mint to the fresh made sun tea, it made a pleasant and fast meal.

By the end of a couple weeks time, a kept hearing strange and odd whispering harsh voice that often interrupted my thoughts, my work, and even my sleep. I did my best to ignore the strange whispering dialog, but I was beginning to worry if my mind was slipping. I thought I'd ask my sister what she thought it may be I am hearing. Phyllis has been a different person, and her conversation is usually different too. Phyllis is the only person I ever knew that used antiquated terms. Phyllis often used "shall" and "eventide" in her normal conversation.

"Let me ask a hypothetical question Phyllis, can a person hear a voice that no other people can hear, and still be sane?"

"I can't see why not. I mean if one of the people has acute hearing, and the other has normal hearing, then that would be totally possible." Phyllis said.

"OK, now just remember that fact that we are talking about acute hearing, so let's just ignore any wise remarks you have in mind - do you just hear that harsh whisper?" I asked.

"I will clarify my remark, no, I didn't hear any whispers or singing or shouting either. As a matter of fact you have been quiet this morning. I didn't hear you whisper to any one anything, is that's what you wanted to hear? Or did you mean another voice here in this room? If somebody whispered, I certainly didn't hear it," Phyllis said, and added two teaspoons sugar to the fresh brewed coffee. "Who did it sound like Cherry?"

"I really don't know Phyllis; I can't make out the words. The whisper is either so loud I can't understand the words, or so quiet no words can be hear the words, just 'shh' sounds."

Phyllis smiled and quipped "well doesn't this sound great? My little sister is hearing voices that aren't there. Shall I call the white coats now, or do you want to finish your coffee first? But I mean this seriously girl, if you are hearing voices that I can't hear, something is wrong here. How long has this been going on?" Phyllis asked, but she looked concerned.

"It started a couple months ago. I started hearing whispering voices but I can't understand what the words say. I can rarely understand any of the words, and I admit it is starting to get to me. Good grief Phyllis; and I going crazy?" I didn't like this perplexing problem. I've always had a lot of exciting things going on in my life, but in the past, everything makes sense. I admit these voices seemed to be a never ending mystery.

A month later, it was December and it was time to do shopping for Christmas gifts for my daughters. I left my young daughters with their daddy, and left the small town of Kissimmee, and headed toward the city of Orlando for a few hours of shopping in my favorite shops. My mind was on educational toys, colorful blocks, maybe a few of the painted wood jigsaw puzzles I saw in the catalogs. I know the stacking fabric blocks would be great, and maybe a rocking horse, both of my girls love horses.

I was driving north toward my favorite shopping center, and my thoughts were on the Christmas gifts. It may have been about five or six miles north of Kissimmee, when I noticed a bluish white round disk in the sky. I kept my eyes on both the crowded traffic and the milky disk in the sky, I noticed the flying disk got larger - and much closer. I could feel my heart beating faster, and the hair on the back of my neck raised as the round object got closer, it looked like it might be about thirty or thirty five feet diameter. When the bluish saucer got closer to my car, the engine in my car failed. It was strange, one second I could hear the engine, and the next second I couldn't hear anything except the pounding of my heart. I looked at the other cars, they all were slowing down, so it wasn't just my car; I witnessed three other cars coaxing their cars off the side of the road. To my horror, I couldn't was no longer in control of my car, and it continued to drive forward, silently. The UFO darted out of sight into a vast grove of citrus trees.

I slammed on the brakes, but the car kept moving silently forward and I couldn't control it! My heart started racing like crazy when the car made a right turn towards the citrus grove, and my car seemed to be driving by its self. I didn't like that one bit. Slowly the car drove over a little bump on the dirt road and continued over the railroad tracks. It was at that time knew my car was not on the road, but floating slightly over the road into the citrus grove. I was fascinated by the floating car, but at the same time, I wanted to cry, I wanted to jump out of the car, I tried to scream, but my body wouldn't move! I seemed to be frozen in position inside the car. In a few minutes, the car rolled and stopped into a clearing. In the middle of that large clearing sat a real life bluish shiny flying saucer! Again, I tried to get out and run, but my body sat frozen in position. Try as I could, I couldn't move. I kept looking at the amazing sight of a real flying saucer right in front of my eyes.

To my utter fear and shock I watch three humanoid men wearing black jumpsuits walked out of the wide door of the alien craft and approached my car. I was terrorized when I saw their gray skin, their very long fingers and their elongated golden eyes! They were small, and about as tall as me, in other words, they were about five feet tall, I noticed their bodies were thin, and the color of their hands and heads were gray.

I could feel tears welling up into my eyes, as the two humanoids opened my car door, and gently pulled me out of the car. A fourth humanoid wearing black robes, touched my left shoulder gently, in a comfortingly manner. He placed a bluish disk about the size of a silver dollar in the middle of my forehead and at once, I felt peaceful and calm. I was no longer afraid or terrorized, I didn't want to run away, and I only felt curious as they men floated me into the craft. Calmly, I asked "Would you please turn off my car, turn off the lights and get my keys?" I heard the words, and I know I said it, but the words sounded foolish and out of place. The man in robes simply said "As you request."

As I entered the craft, brilliant light stunned my vision. Outside, it was night, and although I could see a dim light at the door, I wasn't ready for the lights inside the craft. I must tell you that it is very difficult to explain the odd lightings inside that strange craft. Outside the craft, I noticed a dim light barely visible, but once we cross the threshold and was inside the craft there is brilliant light everywhere. That brilliant light is only inside the craft, and that light does not shine through the door to outside.

I was amazed at the time, and I am still amazed by the strange lighting that is barely visible outside that saucer at that strange door. It is as if an unseen veil of darkness covered the door. The brilliant lighting made my eyes water, so I had to keep my head down looking down to the floor.

When I could see again, I noticed I was in a curved hall; it seemed to curve to the left or spiraled left. I was ushered into a room that resembled a doctor's examination room. The aliens gently placed me on a table and I watched the silent humanoids placed narrow shelves beside me. Those shelves floated freely beside the table.

In a few seconds, a robed humanoid approached the table and slightly smiled. He opened his small lipless mouth and I heard a humming and strange sounds. He looked questioningly, as if he was asking me a question. I shook my head no, and he touched a few buttons on a box near his waist. Clearly I heard his ask "Can you understand me?" I said 'Yes.' "Are my words too loud?" I said 'no,' and it was then that I knew that the words I heard were inside my brain, not inside my ears. I tried to get up, because that bothered me more than anything else had so far. He said "Recline Cherry, and listen to my words." I wondered how he knew my name, but I did exactly what he wanted.

The next thing I was aware of was the pounding of a headache. I felt strange, confused - and why was I sitting in the car? Nothing made sense; I couldn't remember where I was going and why I parked on the side of a dirt road. I heard two ping sounds and suddenly I was awake, clear headed and remembered everything. I looked around for the saucer, but it was gone. A car crossed in front of me and I knew I was at the edge of a citrus grove near the highway and I was going to Christmas shopping. I looked at my watch, to my shock it was almost midnight. I went home.

This was the first introduction of Jahel, and the beings that visited me many years over the years. He still visits me sometimes. Over the years a lot of people have seen Jahel, some of my family, and once a pair of visiting Mormon Missionaries. Those poor men were very startled when

Jahel suddenly appear in my living room. I tried to explain, but it was very difficult to try to explain it to them, I just allowed them leave. (or should I have said 'escape?' They were really afraid of Jahel.)

I wanted to mention that after the actually face-to-face meeting with these pleasant aliens, I never again heard the odd whispering voice. However, to this day, I get very uncomfortable when I hear anyone whispering near me.

7

SHADOW MAN - SHADOW CRAFT

Many years ago - a long time ago, (I admit I don't remember the exact date) but I believe it was around 1975 but I remember it was in the early spring. I was delighted to enjoy one of those rare days alone. As the mother of four active children, days alone as very rare, and I believe any parent can relate to that rare days.

On the date I want to tell you about, was the time my son spent the weekend with his grandparents, and my mom and dad were pleased when I agreed to let Marc spend time with them. My dad was already cleaning a small tool chest as well as a few tools he planned to give to Marc. When mark Marc and I arrived at their house, it was only 8 in the morning but my mom was already at the stove, stirring the sauce for the meal she wanted to cook that evening. She planned to cook her special meal she named "Marco's Taco Macaroni Mountain." That dish is a dish she created strictly for Marc. He loved tacos, he loved macaroni and he loved cheese. The name of that dish was named because the family called him "Marco."

Meanwhile, when my teenage daughters Monica and Sabrina were visiting friends, those fun days include a two day trip to Panguitch, Utah. It is always exciting when friends have cabin up in the mountains, with horses to ride. The same day - strictly by coincidence, my youngest daughter Mystique, spent the night with her daddy, enjoying a long motorcycle ride to Blythe, California. Mystique always enjoyed those motorcycle rides.

With the day alone I decided to spend a few hours out alone in the desert. I headed north, and drove a two or three hours out of Vegas, and found the rustic ghost town known as Delamar, Nevada. I had been alone in this ghost town, exploring the old ruins of a mining town for about 40 minutes when I noticed a classic flying saucer in the sky. At first, I was delighted to witness a classic disk standard oval shape craft. It appeared to be flying high, then, I realized it was not that far up, maybe only three miles up. (Roughly 15,800 feet, commercial jets fly at 50,000 feet, so it was sort of low, as planes fly.)

Suddenly the disk dropped elevation until it was maybe half mile above me. It made me feel slightly uncomfortable; you might say it made me feel aware that they knew I was here. As I watched the disk, it changed from solid craft with the classic saucer shape to a vague difficult to find shape; it became toilsome to identify the edges of the disk shape.

In front of my eyes, the once firm metallic disk became an appearance of a gray shadow. I realized it was getting closer, and I became uncomfortable with its impending approach. I stood still, watching the shadow because part of me wanted me to run away, but the other part of me wanted to see what happens next. My curiosity won, and I stood still. The shadow was so close I could feel the hair on my head starting to rise, and it reminded me of the sensation of high electricity when it starts 'itching my skin' when I walk under any high tension power lines.

The shadow changed, and I was fascinated when the disk took the shape of several of trees. But once again, it resembled like a shadow of rounded trees, about three of them, and obviously the 'trees' were not solid. I know they didn't look solid like real solid trees; there was nothing solid in that craft. I know I could look through that shadow, as if it was a veil. My thoughts were on the odd shadow shaped craft, and I kept thinking about the many shapes they could copy, and I why they took maintaining the shape of trees when there are so few trees in the desert? I wondered if they didn't notice the lack of trees in this area.

That was about the time I became aware there is a new sound - an odd sound of rhythmic unusual clicking, I looked towards the sounds and witnessed the shadow shape of a thin and svelte tall man approached me. I wanted to flee, to take off running away, but by now, I couldn't run. I was powerless and it frightened me to know I couldn't move. I felt that tingling in my chest I recognized it as strong fear, but couldn't move anything except my eyes. I tried to find his eyes in his face, but that face was just a gray shadow, I noticed a second shadow man, and my fear was enhanced. I could feel tears welling into my eyes, blurring my vision.

I looked back to the first shadow man and saw him take aim something, I know it aimed towards me, but I couldn't identify the shape in his hands. I suddenly felt the sensation of heat hitting my face and chest.

Then.... nothing............

I woke up a few hours later inside my car, the sun was setting and for a few minutes I couldn't remember why I was out in the desert. Then my thoughts cleared, and I remember the shadow man. I looked around for him but I was alone. I started the car and went home.

To this day I do not know what happened in those few hours.

8

TWO LITTLE MEN AND ONE DOG NAMED CHICKEN

In 1969 I lived out in the country, but still had close-by neighbors. I considered it in the country, the neighbors had a cow, two horses and a few turkeys, but those turkeys were considered more like pets, not food. Our house was at the east edge of Nashville, Tennessee, those many years and worked as a song writer and singer in Nashville.

My four kids had been asleep about an hour and a half when I finally put the last load of laundry in the dryer. That load was just a few fluffy white towels, and it would take less than 45 minutes to dry since I put the towels on "High Heat Cycle" on the dryer. It was the last chore I planned to complete that day, and because I was tired, I wish the dryer would hurry and dry those towels because I was tired and felt out of sorts. It appears I may have caught a slight sore throat that day. I had worked all day trying to finish a few remaining lines of an unfinished song. I was tired, and longed to relax and forget the sore throat feels like a little fever is moving in too. It seems every time I move into an area with a lot of humidity I end up catching something.

With a sigh I eased my aching back into my recliner, but my back pain was too much to relax, so I stood up, stretched my back, taking giant steps I walked the end of the hall. I stood in the middle of the hall, a little leaned over from the pain, but leaned over and placed the palms of my hands against the back wall. I used the exercise I know always ease back pain, I allowed let my hands "walk" down the wall until my fingers almost touched the floor. I had to stretch hard to reach the last few feet, but that exercise does make my back feel much better.

I walked slowly to my recliner, concentrating on the rhythmic soft sound of the towels tossing around is the dryer. I've always found to that sound pleasant and comforting, although I can't explain why.

I sat slowly rocking in my recliner, allowing the hypnotic soft clicks of the dryer ease pain away, when I began noticing a new sound. I focused on the sound, it sounded like a series of dull hums, with a few measured clicks. The sounds reminded me of a conversation, with two distinct voices exchanging words. The sounds made me think about machines - if machines could talk. I was sure this was not human voices, there were no sounds that I would recognize as speaking, at least nothing human - in any language. I didn't know what I was listening to, but I know it made me feel uncomfortable, as if I was eavesdropping, and on purpose. It seems I have heard that sound before – but where?

I got up and went to the window looking for the source of the clicking and humming, but saw nothing, nothing unusual, only the neighbor's dog standing on his back paws peering over the fence. It first I thought the dog was looking at me, growling, and that is certainly different, that dog is a cream-puff, just an elderly mutt that rarely barks and never growls at anything. He wasn't looking at me, he was looking at something under my window, something I couldn't see because the window box with flowers, blocked my view of whatever the dog was seeing.

Determined to finding the source of the clicks and humming, and to find is causing that passive old dog to baring his teeth, growling and having his hackles up. That old dog hasn't shown any aggressive behavior as long as I've lived here, and that change makes me very curious. The name of the dog backs up my claim that this dog is the most passive dog I've ever known. Perhaps that is why the neighbor gave him the name "Chicken." The poor dog ended up with the nickname "Chickee."

I slipped a light jacket over my shoulders, and slipped out the side sliding door, staying as quiet as possible I peeked over the corner of the house and pushed the rose bush out of my way. It was dark, but there is a soft dim light glowing from the window and from that light, I could clearly see two small men, in metallic coveralls. They appeared to be grown men but very small, maybe three feet tall, they had slim bodies, skinny limbs and bald over grown heads. I remained frozen in position, and I freely admit I stared at these humanoids standing under the window box, pressed against the house. They appeared to be conversing and the hums and clicks were the sound of their talking. These small size 'men' seemed to very worried by the noise of neighbor's dog, and it was visible these men were becoming even more frightened by each threatening growl from my neighbor's dog. I can understand that, that dog is a lot bigger than those child size humanoids.

Without hesitation, I stepped up around the rose bush and walked straight to Chickee, soothing him, telling it is ok. I pet his head, and he licked my hand and sat down put for a second, but seemed to remember he was upset about the humanoids, he put his paws back on the fence, and growled again. Finally, I had the nerve to look straight into the faces of the alien faces. Their eyes were quite round, not oval like a human. In the semi-dark I could see the rough details of the face. I noticed they had small up-lifted noses; their faces were round too, with small pointed chins. They were bald and had no eyebrows and no eyelashes. As for their size, let me just say I am almost five feet tall, and these men were no taller than chin high on me.

Their eyes kept switching from my eyes to the growling dog. I turn around and faced them and looked down into the terrified faces of these creatures.

I don't know if they were more afraid of dog or me, but I said nothing, I assumed they wouldn't understand my words anyway. But maybe they would understand, if I could give them a chance to run away.

I glanced towards the open gate, and their eyes too followed, just the past gate I could see the flickering lights of something out of my vision due to the tall wood fence. I gestured towards the fence, but they again were staring at the snarling dog.

I finally I spoke up and said, "Its alright, you can go. It is OK. I won't get the dog bite you." The humanoid men started inching towards the fence, and the minute they started to move Chickee started barking. I could tell they were terrified, and literally too afraid to move. I leaned over the fence and grabbed Chickee's collar, and using my other arm to indicate they should run, again, I said, "GO! RUN! Hurry!" They ran without looking back. I remember that it took all my strength to hold Chickee so they wouldn't go after the little men. He barked and snarled, and struggled to get out of his collar. It was not easy to hold that big old dog against the wood fence. The Chickee was on the other on the other side of the fence and it wasn't an easy to keep that determined dog against the fence. He was surprisingly strong and he struggled to ran after the two small men. It took all my strength to keep Chickee against the wood fence.

I'll never know what would have happened if I hadn't held Chickee back, but I suspect he would have managed to jumped the fence and attack the little men if I hadn't held him back. I don't know if the little men and his craft flew away or if they merely disappeared in a beam of light, because I was too busy fighting to keeping Chickee so he couldn't chase the little men.

When I think back of that night, it bothers me, because I have no idea why these little men were outside my window, but I have never found a logical reason. Too, I never figured out why that passive old dog didn't like those small men.

I am glad I went outside and checked on those sounds that night. Or why these small men were generating the strange noises in the dark night. No telling what strange events may have happened if the dog didn't growl that night. It is one of the nights that I am happy to say nothing drastic happened that night, and for that, I have always thanked my lucky stars!

9

MY LETTERS RETURNED IN THE HANDS OF THE MIB

For over sixty five years I have been trying to enlighten the world about the E.T./UFOs that fly across the skies of Earth and it has become obvious that the military forces of Earth are helpless against these beings. These alien beings can fly circles around in our military craft. The military Air Force of this world are limited to fly in linear paths - the UFOs are not limited that way they can make right angles in mid-air, they can instantly stop in the air, or take off in any direction faster than you can blink your eye.

The higher ranking men and women of military of Earth know the truth of the beings, and a few of the more mundane citizens of this planet sometimes stumble across the truth while doing UFO studies, when we do find the truth, we just stop and wonder why the rest of the world haven't found it too?

I believe it is because no one can believe anything so basic can be so obvious, so real and easy to figure it out. The truth is fantastic, and beyond belief ---- but real. If I tried to tell you how it works, no one would believe me.

The problem is, every time a citizen accidentally finds the truth; "they" stop you from telling anyone. I am one of the citizens that stumbled across the truth, and I thought "can this be the big secret? This silly idea is the Secrets of Secrets?" Basically yes, but there is other things that are horrid and unspeakable about the UFO community, but I won't discuss that aspect this time.

Quite a few years ago, I decided to send three copies of my idea to three well known UFO researchers, I sent the copies through the normal U.S. Postal service - the next day three men showed up at my door - I had barely had them inside my home and invite them to sit down and the produced the three letters I mailed the day before.

I was shocked, of course, but the important thing is I want to point out is that my letters to the researchers was still sealed - they didn't open my letters - in other words, the letters hadn't been opened and resealed, it was a fact my letters never reached the researchers. However, I know I sent those to letters to three friends, but they never reached them. One of the men told me exactly what my letters said - even stranger was the fact he also knew I kept my original letter and demanded my original letter too. I bulked on that one, and told them I wanted to keep my original letter and told them my letter belonged to me, and they have no right to claim my own letter and I refused to give it to them. (No one knew I hid my original letter inside a certain book.) But one of these three men walked straight to my stack of books opened the third book, took produced my original letter. I have no idea how they knew that is how they hid the location of that letter. But I assure you, but after that day I became afraid because I knew they knew you can't keep a secret from the MIB.

That day - and all days since then, I found I can't share the special secret knowledge. I found that secret strictly by accident. But it doesn't matter that I found it by accident, it wouldn't matter if I found it by plan - the only fact counts to them is I DO know - and that fact seems to be detrimental to their lives. I am pressing my luck by writing this much - but the world needs to stop looking for a wild complex theory and think that will lead them for the truth - instead they just need to look for the basic simple most logical thought - and then will find the simple truth.

They – (the "MIB") refuse to allow the basic truth be told - so all I can do is give you a few clues - but before you start looking for the truth, please be aware that if you do guess the truth, I assure you your life will never been the same.

If you try to warn your friends – even if it is just one person, and tell them what you suspect, it is too late and "they" will show up before you can tell your friends. I found that from personal experience.

When you guess the truth - "they" will show up and block you, they will give you a choice to live or die - I chose to live.

But if you think you can out smart them, and find a way to sneak the truth out - think again, that day your life will be end, like several of my friends they had sudden heart attacks, or the sudden urge to commit "suicide" - or be "suicided" by the hand of the MIB.

My friends, if you guess the Ultimate Game - keep your mouth shut and you will live on. I am speaking from experience.

10

UFO CRASH IN NASHVILLE TENNESSEE

You never know when you will suddenly witness something historic. In the same way, a person can't pick and choose when suddenly you are called to see a bizarre event you witnessed by chance. Sometimes a person remembers certain events in your life because you witnessed something shocking, and when that happens, you tend to recall the day with crystal clarity. You remember the event, and the strange objects you saw that day.

Over the years I managed to collect a few strange objects I witnessed. This is one of my mystery objects I witnessed on one of those clear days.

I'll tell you about one of the mystery objects, because I have shown photos to a few of it, but only a few handful of people actually saw this device, or handled the heavy weight, or feel the amazing welding of the pieces. I rarely allow anyone to see it or touch it. I keep it under lock and key.

This particular object resembles part of an old milking machine. At least that is the opinion of a few farmers with automatic milking machines in their barns. The farmers are convinced because it looks similar to their devices. However, when asked about their equipment, the confidently state their machines are made of stainless steel or other known metal. My object is NOT made of steel or metal, because no magnets will stick to it, and metal detectors do not consider the object a metal. So - I still say it is NOT part of a standard milking machine. It just resembles part of a milking machine. A piece of an old milking machine wouldn't be made of such strange metal that a White's Metal Detector does not react to it. To me, it looks like stainless steel, it is shiny and too heavy for its size, although it looks like stainless steel, it doesn't seem to be a 'regular' metal. I can tell you that magnets will not stick to the side of this strange object and three brands of metal detector do not consider this object as metal.

I know where I found it. I witnessed a UFO crash in Tennessee years ago. I was the second person at the crash. I looked for survivors, so did the other person. We rushed to the main part of craft, and at the side of the broken craft, we looking for a door, or a window to get inside and help anyone inside.

When the military arrived, they yelled at us and told us to get away from the craft. They told us they would take care of the "situation" and we were physically abruptly ushered out of the area.

The military demanded our identification, and the other witness, a man around in his late forties, produced his ID, and I too provided my driver license. They asked us if we were together, we both agreed we didn't know each other, and be were strangers to each other.

We both stated we just witnessed the sudden problem the UFO had, and we were looking for anyone that may be hurt. We both stated we didn't see anyone outside the craft. The military were more interested what we witnessed on the ground, than the visible explosion we witnessed in the sky. The military asked us if we saw the pilot or any other people inside the crashed craft.

I know I didn't see anyone, I didn't see very far inside the craft and didn't see any person, dead or alive and clearly stated that fact. The stranger stated he didn't see anyone alive. I don't know if that meant he saw a dead person, or that he didn't see any one at all. Finally the military decided we were simply innocent witnesses and they military took us to our cars and told us to leave, but cautioned us not to discuss the craft with anyone, especially not to notify the media. We agreed not to discuss the crash with anyone. I never saw the other witness again, and I wish I knew his name or tried to find him. I wonder if he too, picked up something from that day.

I know we were one of the first people there, and I know I witnessed a UFO crash in Tennessee. The debris was spread everywhere the entire area. I know I picked up part of a piece that UFO that sort of shattered when slammed into the earth. I noticed the damaged craft had broken parts all over the ground. When it hit the ground, it gouged a big hole where it hit. I admit I have to guess the size but I guess that elongated gouge might have been about a long as generous city block, or more. The gouged area was a lot bigger than I would have expected I saw many little parts all over the area, without thinking, I picked up one of the strange pieces of metal and put it in my purse, without thinking about of it. I just happened, I didn't plan it, it was the first thing I saw that wasn't buried into the ground. Maybe that is why I picked it up and zipped it into my purse. When the military questioned me, for unknown reasons they didn't search my purse. I have always thought it was because they were just seconds behind me and the other stranger that witnessed the crash. I assume the military I didn't have time to pick up a piece of broken UFO and put it my purse. But I did. Like I said, I didn't plan to pick it up, it just happened.

Then the military arrived, I was questioned and told to leave the area. (They didn't allow us to see anything else, because we were TOLD to get out and do not return to this area. I guess they didn't want anyone to see anything.) As I approached the small craft, I could feel the hair on my body rising, as if there is a lot of electricity in the air. I was not there long enough to enter the craft. This event happened around 1971 in out in the country of Nashville, Tennessee. This strange heavy piece of metal(?) is very bizarre, it LOOKS like stainless steel, but it does not react like other metals. No magnets will stick to it. It weighs over two pounds, it never rusts.

Yes, I agree it LOOKS like a part milking machine – but let me point out that the land (where the UFO crashed) since has been used as a sausage company since the late 1880s. It is NOT part of a dairy company, and never was part of a dairy company. (The land is STILL owned by a sausage company, and that company was owned by a country music star, and it remains to be owned country music star.)

When you think about exactly what a milking machine does - it uses a suction device to removes liquid - (milk) from a cow, goat or other animal - and then think about the aliens that remove the blood of an animal – I would assume it MAY use a similar device. Think about it.

My comment: whatever this device is I intend to keep it, because I KNOW where I found, I know how the ground looked like after that UFO crashed, and know there was a LOT of odd other parts of broken items - when I say "broken" I mean metal that was torn the way a glass shatters when it breaks. There was a gouge in the Earth, it was deep and the grass and weeds were sort of pressed past the far side of the crashed craft. There were broken parts of the crashed saucer and other items along the path of the gouged earth. The crashed UFO looked as if hit the ground hard, and it broke the edges of the craft as it landed. As a writer, I also noticed the lack of paper in the debris. I would expect a lot of paper work was an airplane type crash laying around. It is sort of something you don't think about it at the time, but later, when you think about what you saw, you realize there was no paper debris, just solid broken parts of the flying object. Also, after thinking about it, I saw in one section of that gouged area and I noticed it looked 'wet' looking, and the wet looking area was sort of 'shiny' with a yellowish green.

The item I picked up and put it in my purse it certainly looked like stainless steel - even my cookware is stainless steel and looks just like it - BUT - this device is NOT steel, it is not recognized as metal by four different metal detectors. The milking devices DO look like the device I picked up, but whatever it was; it was checked by a local (Las Vegas NV) authority on metals. He confirmed it is NOT any well known metal. He doesn't know it is metal or other substance. He stated is does not match any metal he recognises. Too - is it is NOT magnetic.

I did a history of the area to see if the area was once part of a daily farm. Come to find out the same area us used to house pigs, they are kept there for a year or so before they fatten them previous their slaughter. The pigs are made to make sausage all those years ago, they still do to this current day. The same area has been used for pigs since the early 1800s. That land has always been used for pigs, and although the same sausage has been sold a few times, the company is currently is now owned by a well-known a top sausage maker. The company was closed for a few months immediately after the UFO crash and was sold to a popular entertainer. The entertainer sold sausage.

To me, this strange object remains a mystery to a few local experts on metals, and to me.

11

WHAT HAPPENED LAST NIGHT?

Early one morning at 3:16am, I awoke hearing a pulsing hum outside my window. I didn't move knowing what the sound meant. I've heard it before – many times. Usually the pulsing hum is brief, and I know "they" are inside my house. But this time they stayed outside, getting closer and then pulling away.

My heart started pounding a little, knowing something slightly different is going on. After over 15 minutes of the pulling away, getting closer, and repeating that action countless time, the hum get very close to the glass of my northern view window.

That window is in front of bed, meaning, the sound was very close. No doubting at all this was a man-made drone and was trying to listen to any sounds inside that room. The problem – for the maker of the drone – is that I happen to possess hearing that exceeds the average person, a pleasant blessing I've enjoyed since birth. I always laugh and say I can hear ant hiccup fifty yards away.

That's why I can hear the synthetic drones; it is even easier for me in the quiet of the pre dawn morning. This morning after always a half hour of the drone humming, I heard it pull away and didn't return.

A few minutes after 4am, I started to doze back to sleep, when the air in the room changed to bitter cold, and I sensed a little Grey was standing at the side of my bed. I opened my eyes and witness three little Greys standing beside my bed, and behind them, sort of hunched over in the doorway of the closet stood one of those cross between Mantis and a long tall pilots many folded legs that rarely leave their ship. They are never far more away then maybe 20 feet from their ship not more than a short period of time, or both the pilot and the ship will die. I guessed the UFO must be directly over top my house.

I looked at the gentle eyes of the pilot, wondering why he was here, he is not supposed to be here, and I know that. I started to ask him "why are you here?" But before I could form the words, he reached out his hand and touched my forehead, and I fell into a dreamless slumber. When I woke up, it was 9am, and I quickly opened my eyes, looking for the little Greys, or the pilot – but I was alone in the room.

Normally I am an early riser, and usually wake up around 5 in the morning. I rarely sleep past 7am, on days that I am in need of extra sleep, I might sleep to eight – but unless I am ill, I never sleep that heavy until nine in the morning. My normal sleep pattern is bed around 10-11 pm, get up 5 to 6am.

I don't know what happened or why the alien pilot was in my bedroom, these tall pilots do not make "house calls" – that is the job of the little Greys, the saucer pilots are so private and shy that makes me look like a real social butterfly. The never leave their craft, because they are made of the same biological materials – one the disk, the other the pilot. Both the pilot and the saucer are biologically created together. I wish they explained why they were in my house, but the aliens are not good at explaining anything... at least not to a human.

I spent my entire day looking for something missing from my house. Trust me, that is no minor chore, I am a pack rat, the collector of countless odd unusual items, even more files, photographs, sketches. I have thousands of files, items or letters, so trying to find out if one file may be missing is just about impossible. There MUST have been a reason they had a man-made drone stay beside my window until they arrived. I haven't found anything missing, of course I searched Tom Castello's files – searched my personal files – searched my kids files - - - - nothing.

Four days before Christmas and here is a mini-mystery. I have to wonder what may have been important enough to request a man-made drone and have it stay beside my window a half hour – and important enough to stop my thoughts before I could say any words – What did they look for? Or did they leave something? Did they remove my implant? Add a new implant to my body?

I searched all day – with no answers. The mystery remain.

12

A LOVE STORY – BILL & CHERRY

I want to tell you a love story - the story of Bill & Cherry - The beginning – over 40 years ago.

Bill and I beat the odds – we were married for 30 years we are still like honeymooners! I knew Bill was "the man" for me that first time I looked into his eyes - my friend Theresa, thought I was joking when I said "I'm going to marry this man." - but I was 100% being honest - I knew it was love at first glance! (You should be aware that at the time, I didn't believe love at first glance. I thought it was a silly myth to sell books and movies - until I looked into his chocolate brown eyes - at that moment, the doubt was all over for me!) But let me start at the beginning...

You never know what the future hold.

That day started when I met Bill – the year was 1982 - I was a 40 year old dental assistant student, learning a new trade after a traumatic stroke, I could barely speak enough to make myself understood, so was my friend Theresa, she was a dental assistant student too – and she wanted to go to bar that just reopened, and wanted me to go with her. She liked to bars – but not me, I NEVER go to bars, I never drink alcohol - but she begged to go with her to a bar, in the day time!! I was horrified at the thought of me going to a bar - and even MORE horrified going in the day time - where people might I know see me going to a bar! But she wore me down, and convinced me to just once, so she could see the new remodeling they did at that bar. The bar was called "Baldies" – so that afternoon I went with her. I admit I was shocked and afraid to go, but I went. I stood near the inside the front door, waiting for the brilliant sunlight outside my vision adjusted to easier to see in the dark and smoky bar. To make it worse for me, I wanted to go hide in a dark corner booth where no one could see me - but no - Theresa wanted to sit at the bar! Geeze!! Sitting at a bar? Not very ladylike, I thought.

I was speechless on that one, trying to imagine me sitting at a bar! I finally got the nerve to go sit at the bar beside Theresa and after a few seconds the bartender turned around, placed his hands on the bar and he said "Hello ladies - what would you like?" That bartender turned and looked into my eyes - and I was in love - right now and forever with that handsome bartender.

Theresa ordered a drink, I think I mumbled something about a Coke, I have no idea what I was about to drink, I didn't care - and when he went to fix the drinks I turned to her and said "I'm going to married that man!" She laughed - but I KNEW this was it – I fell in love with Bill the minute I looked into his chocolate brown eyes. I knew Bill was the love of my life.

Suddenly bold and brave - I returned to that bar again, alone, several times just to see Bill. I admit I stared at this bearded man – just wanted to look at him, wondering how could I attract a man like him? I didn't have much to offer to a handsome man. I didn't talk much with him, because talking was a major problem for me, due to the major stroke I suffered in 1980. After about a month of me just ogling at this handsome man whenever I could get the nerve to visit the bar, one night he walked around the bar and approached me and said - "Do you want to go somewhere?" without hesitation I said "Yes!" After that first night - we have never been apart - except when he is at work, or later, when he needs to go to the hospital.

That first night I didn't care where we went - as long as it was with him. Within two hours of that first date - he said "Marry me Cherry!" - No pretending, just the truth - come to find out he felt the same about me that I felt about him - instantly. I didn't pretend either - I was crazy over him, and didn't try to hide it. We both discovered there was an age difference, I was a 40 year divorced mother of four, and Bill was a divorced man of 28 with no children of his own. We didn't care about these differences.

We both knew I was still trying to recover from a major stroke, and I was trying to regain my life, struggling to learn to walk with the help of a cane again, (I walked with a heavy limp.) I was learning to speak clearly again. I struggled to make my speech be clearly understood. I could think clearly, but speaking clearly was still a major a problem. Due to that major stroke, I had a serious speech impediment, as well as a soft lisp, and I struggled to express myself.

At the beginning Bill assumed my lisp was cute, but for me, I was searching for the correct word. At first Bill didn't know I had speech impediment, instead he thought I was a foreign lady and learning to speak English. I had too many trouble to try to explain my problems very well. My difficulty to speak was my biggest problem. To Bill, my different speech language made me sound French to him. Bill didn't care that I had a strong limp, nor did he care I didn't speak well. By the time I could explain it was a medical problem, he loved me he loved me anyway.

Bill didn't rush me, he was very patient, and I agreed to live with him, that first night - he and my 14 year old youngest daughter - I was brazen, but in love with this man and didn't want to live without him. I wanted Bill to understand that I would not stay the same - I needed to become everything I was before that MIB induced stroke. But Bill refused to give up, he kept asking me to marry him, he asked every day - several times every day. "Marry me Cherry!" he asked over and over! - He kept telling me he didn't care if I stay the same, or if I changed - he loved me the way I was - and he was sure he didn't care if I changed and improved myself.

After a few months (it was late January of 1983) of Bill asking me every day to marry him - one day he asked and I said "OK Bill, I'll marry you." He was so happy - so was I, in minutes he called his mother, and Bill & his mom - Alta, the wonderful lady she is - they made the arrangements in a hurry, I suspect he was afraid I'd weenie out and change my mind. We were married in the afternoon on Valentine's Day at a Chapel in Las Vegas. Thirty years later - I still adore this man the same way - I am crazy over Bill - and I'll love him like that for the rest of my life. There is no two ways about it, Bill is my soul-mate.

Side Note: After a four year pain filled illness, death claimed Bill. He died in 6 June 2013 from hepatitis after 30 years of a wonderful marriage. As I write these words it has been over ten years, and after all the years, I still feel the same thing about Bill.

13

ANGEL TO THE RESCUE

"Those tonsils must be removed Cherry." That wasn't what I wanted to hear, but I kept having the dreaded strep throat, with a high fever, I had it five times in less than two years. I looked at Dr. T. and managed a weak "OK, let's take them out."

The surgery plans were made and I had the required tonsillectomy, but there were complications, not unexpected when a woman in her forties. Normally preteen kids have their tonsils removed years before the problems pops up, but here I was, in the same hospital ward that children were recovering.

Immediately after the surgery, Dr. T. warned me not only my tonsils had been infected when he removed, but he noticed and also took an odd growth he found lodged beside my vocal chords. That strange growth he found beside my 'voice box', was abnormal and roughly twice the size of a large grain of rice. The doctor hushed my efforts to ask questions about that growth and warning me not to even attempt to speak, or I'll do severe damage to my throat. The doctor smiled and said "Cherry, the only way I can explain what it looked like is to say it appeared you tried to swallow an electronic transistor a few years ago, and the item ended up being housed beside your vocal chords. It was bizarre, and we had a hard time removing it without risking permanent damage to your vocal chords. You must not try to speak Cherry, at least for a week. I made an appointment for you, come back and see in four days. Do not even whisper, and no matter what - do not use the phone because it stressed the throat."

Only Dr. T and the nurses actually saw the metallic/glass item during he removed that day, and he explained my tonsils and the bizarre item immediately destroyed after the surgery. According to the doctor, it looked like I swallowed a little half glass/half metal item and it got caught beside my voice box. I suspect it might have been an implant, but that is only a guess.

Three days after my surgery and I was still weak and in need of bed rest, so rest and sleep was an easy chore, as well as avoiding the phone, and I had no problem with attempting to talk to anyone. That was no problem at all; I could just sleep, read or watch TV. Bill worked and used a car pool to and from home every day, and his parents were out of town and most our friends else also worked the same hours as Bills.

All was fine – until the phone rang. I remembered the doctor told me not to speak on the telephone. I looked at the ringing phone wonder who would be calling me. They all know better to call, so I assumed it must be salesmen and they'd give up after a few rings – but it kept ringing. I picked up the phone without saying the usual "hello?" I heard Bill's voice warn "don't speak, honey, but I'm sick and I hate to ask this, but can you come get me? If you think you can handle it, can tap on the phone twice." I tapped twice my wedding ring on the phone handset, listening and heard his reply, "OK honey, thanks darling, I'll wait for you over at the guard shack, if the front of the plants, OK?" I tapped twice again.

Quickly I dressed, grabbed the keys, locked the house and in a minute I managed to ease the white Buick into the light traffic. It wasn't that far, maybe a scant five miles to the aging complex of businesses. Those dark buildings had a beginning in Henderson, Nevada as a war effort back in the early 1940s, but now the buildings house Timet Titanium and State Industries water heater companies and a few others.

I stopped at the red light a little more than a mile to State Industries and the guard shack where a sick Bill waited. The light changed green and I stepped on the gas pedal and barely got half way off the intersection and car engine died. I tried to restart the engine but nothing happened, just a quiet few clicks of the ignition. I slowly coaxed the Buick to the curb, out of the flow of traffic.

This is not good, and a bad timing for the car to breakdown. Poor Bill was ill and I couldn't get to him, couldn't call him and tell him I was on the way, parked on the curb, worried about him but having with car trouble. I quietly closed my eyes and offered a prayer – "Lord in Heaven, please help me because I'm in trouble, please hear my prayer me Lord, Bill is sick, I am too weak to walk that far to tell him why I am not there. I need help Lord; help me get the car started again, please hear this prayer."

I barely ended this prayer and opened my eyes when a brown car pull to the curb in front of my car and stop. A young man, looked like he might be in his early 30s, smiled and leaned down and asked "Are you having car trouble?" I nodded a yes, and gestured to my throat and shook my head and hoped he would understand that I can't utter many words. "I saw you ease your car to the curb and figured you had car trouble, so I want past you, drove a couple blocks and turn and came back to make sure you were OK."

My hand still at my throat I whispered "throat surgery, can't talk much."

He replied, "I understand, do you alright? Do you need a ride home?"

"My husband is sick at work, need to get him, just down at the end of the plants," I pointed to the business plants in clear sight of my car.

"You want me to go get him for you? I'll do it, where is he?" He looked at straight into my eyes, and his large eyes looked so serious, and yet gentle looking.

"State Industries, the guard shack, his name is Bill. Please, I'm so worried," I could feel the tears welling into my eyes.

"You just sit here and rest and I'll go get Bill for you. Don't worry, we will get the car started again for you," he touched my hand and felt a warm wave of worry melt away.

I sat there amazed watching that this remarkable young man drive away, why would he drop everything to rescue a stranger and go pick up a sick man and try to reassure a worried stranded woman?

It wasn't even ten minutes and I saw that car brown car circle around and parked again in front of my car again. I was so relieved to see Bill step out of that car and look at me and give me a little nod and I knew he was pale, sick with a little flu, but he was OK.

A few minutes under the hood and Bill and the young man had the car started again. He closed the hood of the Buick for Bill and I watched him shake hands with this wonderful man – it was then I noticed he wore a cap with the stitching at the front, the emblem of the outline of a fish, the earliest symbol of Christian faith. The stranger smiled at me through the windshield, and still shaking hands with Bill I hear him say "Bill – God loves you, don't ever forget that." He returned to his car and waved at me and drove away. It was then when I knew beyond any doubt that young man was angel send to answer my prayers.

I never again saw that angel here in the Las Vegas area, but every time I see a brown car I think of him and remember his large eyes, his gentle outstanding kindness.

Angels are everywhere, and you never know when one will come to help you when you are in trouble.

14

IS THERE A TIME WARP OUT SIDE LAS VEGAS NEVADA?

Bill and I were on the dry lake west of Boulder City, Nevada, but we were still in sight of Railroad Pass Casino. There was no specific reason we chose that location, we just thought we'd drive across the dry lake near the mountains so see if we could find any crystals on the back side of those dark mountains. Bill and I were happy he had another pleasant day off, one of the benefits he earn by working for the City of Las Vegas. I can't remember the reason he had the day off, I was glad enough to know that both of us would be together.

It was early, maybe 7:30am when we drove the pick up off the highway and drove into the raw desert, not even a rough trail for a while, but after about fifteen or twenty minutes we noticed there was a break through the mountains, and a way to turn west toward Las Vegas again. We stopped for a couple minutes when we noticed an old abandoned car – well - I assume it once was a car, all I saw was only the rusted metal 'skeleton' of the old car. There was nothing left to indicate the year that I could guess its age, but looking at the metallic wreckage I'd be willing to bet the car was from the early 1940s, or who know - maybe the 1930s. Bill and I looked around poking around the shrubs wondering if there might be a clue to indicate the brand of car, and we were about to give up and travel further across the bare desert, when Bill notices an old gutted wagon trail.

Not far from that old car, we could see the marks on the ground to indicate covered wagons crossed this area a long time ago. You could see that covered wagons left clear-marks on the ground. You could clearly see that the dried mud left a history of a rainy day when a wagon slid sideways because to mud slid sideways making the wagons loose traction, it must have been difficult to continue travel in such a difficult area.

Bill and I looked stood down at the trail, silently just lost in thought. Suddenly I felt Bill's hand slip into mine and I looked at his face. I could see the surprise and I glanced in the direction he was looking. At first, I saw nothing, but then I heard the sound of three or four male voices, and then the rattling of a couple teams of horses in their harnesses pulling their canvas covered wagons. It first I thought it was similar to looking at a heat wave, but that quickly cleared. Through the odd image I could see four or five men, a few children, preteen age, and in the covered wagon seats, I saw two women in the first wagon and three in the second. Every one appeared over heated and tired. One of the faded sunbonnet one woman wore was mostly off her head. I could clearly see the only thing that held the bonnet on place was the thick bun of on back of her head.

The wagons stopped and Bill and I stood looking at a group of these people, and there was no two ways about it, I could tell these travelers could see us. I could see the wonder on their faces.

Bill's hand was tight against mine and I could tell him too, saw exactly what I saw. Bill and I stood eye to eye with these people, just looking at each other, saying nothing. However, I developed a strong feeling of fear when I witnessed a man pull an old long rifle out the end of the wagon. As he raised his weapon, the vision or mirage wavered and faded into nothingness.

We just stood still too shocked to speak or run around. I was about to ask what Bill saw, wanting to make sure I was not losing my sanity – when suddenly the heat wave image again appeared.

It was not the same image, it was only a couple, maybe in their mid 40s and the clothing and the car appeared to be from the mid 1930s era. They were not a wealthy couple, they looked like a tired hungry, they too, appeared over heated and tired as they sat on the fender of the car eating saltines and what I think was sardines.

It took me a few seconds or so for me to figure it what I was looking but on the car's hood I could see the edge of a canvas 'canteen' or water bag. They didn't see us at first because of their position, they too, were headed west, like the other travelers in the wagon, and we could only see the best view of back and side of the car.

Bill stepped forward a step or two and I joined him. Bill said: "Hey – what are you doing?" The couple turned and looked at us, we could see the surprise, and obviously they clearly heard us too. The man slid off the fender and stood in front of the woman, and I know he said something to her, but at the exact she turned and looked at Bill, to answer, the entire scene or mirage disappeared.

Bill uttered a curse word I can't relay here, but we both started talking at the same time, he hugged me – hard – and said, "Let's get the hell out of here!" We ran to the pickup and quickly turned back the same way we arrived, not the rough desert trek to home we planned. That day will remain forever as a mysterious event as we parked at the side of the McCullough Range Mountains. It is the kind of thing no one can explain, unless we consider some sort of a time warp that floated in and out of time phases. On that remarkable day, Bill and I stood shocked, speechless looking into more than a hundred years of the past, and then we witnessed a couple eating crackers in the era the Hoover Dam was being built.

The area we stood looking into history is scant five miles from Black Mountain, Henderson, Nevada, the site of many UFO sightings and home of reptilian humanoid creatures.

15

I WITNESSED A DIMENSIONAL PORTAL OPEN

There are times when you clearly recall every detail of an incident with startling clarity, and other times there is only a vague memory of a haunting event – but once in a while the memory of a brief occasion is so the strange, that no matter what, you will remember it all your life.

The first time I consciously remember seeing a portal opening in the sky, I was in central Florida, and I was a young woman of 21 years old. At the time of the event, I didn't think about of my age. Actually, that was the last thing on my mind. As a youthful mother of two active toddlers - my young daughters - laundry was important chore. I had a washer, but not many mothers I knew had driers inside their home in 1962. Everybody I knew used a clothesline like mine, usually in the back yard.

It felt as if there was an endless need of clean diapers. Monica, my first-born, was just starting to be trained, when my second daughter Sabrina was born. Sabrina had just reached the stage in her life that the need for constant fresh diapers. Sabrina was 18 months old, but since Monica's birth, there was a daily wash of diapers, plus the usual loads of household clothing, towels, sheets, like I said – laundry was a next to endless chore.

I was looking forward to that stage after having less laundry to do, but that day, like every other day since I was 18, there was another load to diapers to hand on the clothesline. Back in 1962 there were very few mothers had disposable diapers. Instead, all mothers washed and dried fresh diapers, and folded then too. They had just created pre-shaped diapers, and they were popular because it saved a lot of time from folding diapers and a lot of hard work. I had a mixture of both, the original square diapers and the modern pre-shaped.

As Fate would have it, it was that endless laundry caused me to find the portal in the sky. On that day, my daughters, Monica and Sabrina were napping, and as always, I used that time I took time to hang the wet clothing on the clothesline. The events that day are etched in my memory, I picked up the fourth diaper pinned it on the line – and I heard a deep tone, rather like a hollow sound, plus an echoing 'ping.' As if life itself became slow motion, and with it, the sound of the near-by birds chirping sounded slow and distorted. I moved slowly, like a film on too slow mode, but this was not a film, this was real, and very confusing. I slowly turned my head to the left, because that 'hollow' sound came from that direction, and to my surprise, I saw an elongated tunnel in the sky, but it was near the clothesline posts. I believe the portal was in a circular 8 feet wide, and close to the entrance of the tunnel, I could see wispy clouds moving in a clock-wise direction.

The big shock came when I looked deeper into the portal – there was a woman inside, and like me, she was hanging clothes on a line too. In a split second, I wondered if I was looking at a strange mirror. Her clothing was odd, her hair was different from mine, and the clothing she was hanging did not match the four diapers on my own line. At the same time she was different, but doing the exact same thing I was doing. Was it something that mundane that created that time portal? Just two women hanging clothing in a line, but did that connection opened that distant portal to a different time, different space? I can't imagine what possible importance could be found in two women hanging clothes on a line – but that portal DID open and both of us witnessed it.

I started to move and walk towards the portal and her hand reach up and waved to me, but as soon as she waved her hand the portal began closing. I tried to hold into the image of the woman in the portal and see more – to talk to her, to find out did she speak my language, but suddenly the hollow sound was gone, and the slow motion effects were gone too.

I noticed the birds seemed to chirp louder, their chirping seemed more fresh-sounding. I never heard the birds chirp so clearly. Too, the colors of the forest about fifty feet away were more vivid that I have ever seen, and the powerful thunderhead clouds in the distant looked more white, more fluffy than I remember. Even the air felt fresh and cooler than ever.

After experiencing that strange event, life was never quite the same. Something happened that day – I am not sure what changed – but I am positive on that day I became aware of the other dimensions, and the closeness of these dimensions.

I still wonder about that strange friendly woman on the other side of that portal – is she still there? If I could reopen that portal, would that same woman be waiting looking to find me again?

I know I still keep hope that someday I'll open that portal again and wave back to her, and have a conversation with her. Somehow, I just know she is waiting and searching too.

16

WINGED TERROR UNDER LAKE TAHOE IN NEVADA

There is no doubt regarding the rumor of a cryptic animal that hides in any deep water, and I am sure that reminds many folks of the lovable monster, Tessie, at Loch Ness, Scotland. We all know there are many different creatures in many lakes, some friendly others are deadly. Lake Tahoe in Nevada claims a deadly lake monster that has been there for many centuries. Rather or not the creature is an isolated ancient creature or an entire horde of monsters, no one knows.

Lake Tahoe is in north Nevada, and it is a beautiful alpine lake, with its 72 miles of shoreline is fed by the Truckee River a few other minor streams. This lake is the highest alpine lake in the USA, and it stands 6,225 feet above the sea level. The average depth at Lake Tahoe is about 1000 feet deep, although the actual deepest depth of that lake has never been actually proven. In the year 2017 the estimated depth was a deep 1645 feet, no one was ever been able to find the actual depth. Some people say Lake Tahoe is bottomless, and since there is no proven depth, maybe those people could be correct. It has been said that if someone managed to remove all the water on Lake Tahoe, it would take almost 700 years to refill it again. It is one of the deepest lake in the USA. Lake Tahoe is very clear, and very large and very deep.

The problem of finding the bottom of this alpine lake is due to the unbearable crushing force the submersible power requires to withstand the over 1,600 feet of water, as well as the over 750 pounds-per-square-inch to reach the bottom if that lake. So far, no one has been able to achieve that incredible crushing power of that alpine water. This beautiful alpine lake is very deep, and at an elevated location. That high location adds to the problem, because it also adds to the pressure when anyone to tries to reach the bottom.

As long as there have been humans at the Lake Tahoe area, there have also been stories of unknown mysterious creatures in or near that lake. The first Native American, an American Indian can claim the first humans found Lake Tahoe and stayed around 9000 years ago.

For at least a couple centuries there is a legend about a strange monstrous creature that lives deep inside Lake Tahoe, Nevada. This chimera has both bird and amphibian traits. He swims like a fish, has the appetite of a crocodile and yet he can fly like an eagle. Both the historic Washoe and the Paiute Indians once lived near or at the shores of Lake Tahoe. The fresh water of that high mountain lake held enough fish to feed both friendly tribes.

The only dilemma for the Indians living there was the strange beast the local Indians called the Ong. This frightening monster can swim faster than the fish, can move faster than mankind on the ground, and can fly faster than any known bird. Aside from that little problem, the huge beast has a healthy appetite and a desire for meat, it prefers to eat any form of animal flesh, and this beast does not feast on fish or vegetables.

A creature like that would always create serious problems, but for the Paiute or the Washoe Indians the biggest worry is the Ong also has a strong desire of human flesh. A few stories say the Ong can carry off a half dozen people in one swift grab with his powerful claws, taking the victims to the his underwater lair. Other stories indicate the Ong is not quite that large, but it could be large enough to grab one human in each claw as he dives into the deep water of Lake Tahoe.

That creature sometimes first comes to the surface of the water, and then, dripping huge amounts of water from its body as it leaves the water, beating the air with his enormous wings. They say each wing is so strong that the air from the down-swing of one wing is enough to knock down a full grown elk to the ground. According to the Indians, that monster was gigantic is size, with huge feathered wings and matching long tail. The powerful feet of this creature are supposed to have long claws with strong webbing between each toe. The muscular body of this creature is protected by wide impassable scales and none of the arrows of the Paiutes or Washoe can pierce those scales. The face of the Ong is humanoid, with a sharp hooked nose, with brilliant large jet-black eyes. They say the cry of the Ong is enough to generate terror because the cry of that terrifying creature sounds like the screech of a humongous demented eagle.

The legend of the monster at Lake Tahoe was not enough to keep humans away - the deep and mysterious lake is now circled by communities, such as Incline Village, and many other attractive little towns grew up around Lake Tahoe. The deep alpine lake is a two state lake, one half is in Nevada the other half is in California - both states have had many people disappear from the shores of this lake.

They say the Ong was killed many years ago, other say the monster lives on. The question is, did the Ong have an entire family of other Ong under Lake Tahoe? Does any of the Ong family still show up in the skies or water around Lake Tahoe?

17

DO YOU OWN YOUR BODY?

Exactly who owns your body?

Think it is YOU? You better think again.

According to the U.S. Patent & Trademark office, U.S. corporations and universities already own 20% of your genetic code.

You may possess your own body, (right now) but according to the corporations they may be able to claim your body because it is partially the property of someone else. (The corporations and universities currently own all the genetic codes, worldwide.) They will be able to claim your body, sell or trade the genetic materials in your body and you won't be allowed say no. Right now they own 20% of your genetic material - when they reach the 100% ownership, you become a piece of property - in other words - you will be a slave with zero rights.

Folks - you better think twice and start waking up - there is a LOT of things you do not know about. More than likely you will ignore this warning and go back to your football game, go back to your TV shows - until it is too late. If you do not wake up and demand the stop ownership of human genetic code, in the near future you will discover it is too late. The human will be sold on the market as slaves. I am NOT making this up, it is as real and soon it will be too late to stop them. Don't take my word on that, do some research yourself and I assure you will quickly discover this is a fact. In the very near future your body will be sold on the market just like a bag of potatoes and just as common as those potatoes too.

The owners will be the elect - the Elite, the Illuminati, the Religious Group (you know who I mean) and the Hidden Civilization Underground.

They are working hard and fast to own all the genetic code – when they are finished with their work, and they own the genetic code - - it will be too late, and who will be try to warn you then?

18

WHO OWNS THE MOON?

If someone asked you the question "who owns the Moon?" How would you answer?

That is a heavy question. Would you know how to answer that question? Have you thought about that question?

Here is a deeper question - does the human race own the Moon just because we see it in the sky? Probably not; seeing something does not mean you own it.

So - think about it for a minute, who actually owns the Moon? Is the human race? When did the human race buy it? Or did the just claim it? Or perhaps the Moon may be owned by God? Perhaps the Moon owned by unknown aliens? Or maybe it is owned by angels? Does anyone really know that answer?

The Moon rings like a bell when a meteorite hits the Lunar surface. To ring like a bell - a sphere must be hollow - so the Moon must be hollow too. If the Moon is solid an object when landing would sound with a flat 'thud' when it landed. With that in mind, you have to wonder if it is possible that an alien race could live inside the hollow Moon?

What if the Moon is owned by another alien race and when human men walked on the Moon they found themselves in trouble of trespassing? Is that why no human has been allowed to step on the Moon since 1972? That is a serious thought.

American humans physically first visited the Moon in 1969, and those plans promptly ended in 1972. For over 50 years not one human stepped on the surface of the Lunar surface.

Why? Why did the human race abandon their efforts to return to the Moon?

What happened to all the plans to colonize the Moon? What happened to all the other plans NASA talked about, like the plans to mine the minerals on the Moon? What happened to those plans? It is a fact that NASA's astronauts did plan go to the Moon, and in the late 1960s NASA had lots of other plans. NASA talked about colonizing the Moon and talked about those Lunar plans often.

However, after the 1969- 1972 trips to the Moon all those plans suddenly changed after men walked on the Moon. The first man to step on the surface of the Moon was Neil Armstrong, and he became the first human to step onto the surface of the Moon, at 02:56 UCT (Universal Coordinated Time) on 21 July 1969, with over 500 million viewers watched that historic event. The human race has always been very interested in the Moon. On 14 December 1972, Gene Cernan became the last man to step on surface of the Moon. Why did the human race abort the Moon plans?

It has been over 50 years and aside of a few planned crashing on the Moon by various countries, not one human thought about walking on the Moon. It leaves me wonder why. Could it be that a few of the strange rumors I have heard are true? I heard that the human race are not welcome on the Moon, and humans were told to go away and don't return. It is an interesting rumor, and I'm not alone in wanting to know what happened.

I think everyone would like to know who told the humans to go away? Who stopped all those plans to visit the Moon? Who stopped all those plans? Was it the original owners of the Moon? Is the original owner still living on the Moon? Aliens? Could that rumor true?

NASA stopped talking about the Moon.

Why?

It is still a fact that not one human attempted to visited the Moon in the last 50 years. That is a long time, and it makes everyone wonder who changed NASA's plans for the Moon?

So the same question still needs to be answered - exactly who owns the Moon?

19

WHERE ON EARTH DO THE ANGELS HIDE?

Did you ever meet an angel? Or did you ever wonder if you met and angel and you didn't know for sure he or she was an angel? Did you ever wonder where do the angels stay when they are not needed? I have. I've met them several times in my life, and that question has been one big question with no answers - where do they live or hide?

I mean if they live on Earth - how come we never see signs like: "Gated Residents, Angels Only." Maybe the angels live in exclusive major resorts near a lofty mountain top. But there are no resorts, and no gated complexes. We all know that fact. No human has ever seen the inside an angels home.

- If the angels are on our beck and call, why don't we see them reclining on a cloud or see them at the beach?
- Here is another strange question - do angels sleep? So they need rest too? Do they also eat? How can an immortal being require food? It seems angels do eat. There are stories in the holy bible tell us that sometimes the angels do share a meal with humans. The holy bible mentions the angel's food is called manna. (KJV Psalms 78:23-25)

Too, we also know the angels can be attracted to human, and maybe fall in love.

- Where are the angels when they are not busy rescuing foolish humans that get them self in trouble?
- Where do the angels live on this planet if there are active and available to our call?
- To me, that is a big question and I would like to know the answer. Where do the angels hide and live on planet earth? Do they live in another dimension?
- While you are questioning angels, you might as well ask a few other questions – like are the angels actually the aliens that every fear?
- Another question to consider are the flying saucers that fly around the Earth in the blink of an eye, are piloted by angels?

Have you ever thought about that? (I have.

The so called Tall White aliens look like the statues of angels that have been depicted for centuries on Earth. They look human enough that they could walk on the streets of any town and not one alarm bell would start ringing. They look pleasant and attractive, but they do have a few physical differences, for example the nose is not exactly like the average human, but nobody would freak-out just because they noticed they saw a different nose. There is no indentation between the eyes, so their nose start in the middle of the forehead, but it doesn't look bizarre, and many humans have that same type of nose. {Look at the twin angels seen at the top of Hoover Dam in South Nevada and you will see the nose I am talking about.}

Their ears are slightly different, and the teeth of angels are different - if you know what you know what to look for, you can notice the difference.

There are a few different visible differences but you wouldn't know what to look for unless you did the same study I did for over 60 years.

Aliens and angels - I have reasons to assume they are very similar, if not identical. I am not saying all ETs are angels; any more that I would be safe to assume all aliens are kind and considerate. You have to think, VERY deeply, to contemplate the reasons the aliens are here at this time. Yes, they have always been here, the human history is filled with the "Other-ians" (aliens/angels) that co-exist on this planet.

The question you need to ask yourself is why have the aliens been more active since the late 1940s? If you really think about that question, maybe you will be on the way to solving that question.

So – Where do the angels the hide? Do they go underground? Do they phase into another dimension?

Did you ever read Richard Shaver's books? Mr. Shaver mentions the Dero and the Tero - (the bad guys and the good guys of the underground.) When you think about it, don't they sound like the fallen angels and also a little like the redeemed angels of Earth?

So what do you have on planet Earth? Humans and animals (including fish and birds, all types of life form, etc.) live and co-exist on this world; they are native to this planet. That is all the human race sees, and that is all the scientists willingly acknowledge.

If a living "something" is on Earth, the general public noticed that sure would have seen it. Too, that "something" would have been noticed by the scientists and the military of this world - especially if that "something" happened to be an alien race.

The military of Earth have captured aliens and they have talked to them. The military also held several aliens. (Or did the military actually capture an angel?) The military captured the unidentified race and after they were shot down from the sky, they even autopsied the dead bodies of the unidentified race. When they were first shot down, some of them lived, others died. But how could an immortal angel or alien die? What happens if a human decides to do an autopsy on a damaged immortal angel or alien? How can an immortal being die? I don't think an immortal being can die, that is what makes them "immortal" - the word means "without death." Think about that for a few minutes – if you take an immortal body apart (an autopsy) wouldn't the rest of the immortal beings get more than a little upset? Or would the immortal being just automatically be restored? (An interesting thought.)

Here is another interesting question – was it the angels or was it the aliens created the semi-living Greys? Or was there a different race involved? (Perhaps the reptilian race called the Reptons.)

The archangels are one step aside from the gods, and the intelligence of archangels is staggering, they are capable to create a life form any time they choose to. They are demi-gods, what mere human could dare to say the "can't" create anything? What human would dare to say they "can't" do anything?

Archangels they are in charge of life and death, who would argue with them? Not me. I know what they are, and what they are capable to do and I give the highest respect for their position on Earth and Heaven. It doesn't matter if they are redeemed or still fallen, their power is awesome and not one human should ever attempt to disrespect these advanced beings.

If you really want to think about it, what ARE the angels? They are not human. They are not an animal. So if they are here on planet Earth, they resemble the human race. (They say some of the angels have wings and can fly if they want to, very much like the reptons.) If they are not human, and they are not animal, they must be alien life form.

In reality, that is only category option that remaining. So my question remains, if we can't find them, where on Earth do the angels hide?

20

FLYING METALLIC DISKS UNDER THE CARIBBEAN SEA?

I do not mind telling people I enjoyed my years in the community known as LaCeiba, Honduras, in Central America. One of my favorite memories from that era includes witnessing the lifting of three large glowing disks from the deep water of the Caribbean Sea.

Those years I lived in LaCeiba, was different and mostly pleasant. Honduras is not very far miles to North America and the United States. If you look at a map of the USA, it is just south of Mexico, to Central America continue looking south to past a couple small countries to Honduras.

In 1954 I was a young teenager and only thirteen, and like most teenagers, I tried to spend most of my spare time at the beach collecting colorful seashells, or searching from odd shaped of driftwood that floated onto the beach. I loved being on the beach, especially the section of the beach when a small river joins the waters of the Caribbean Sea. Most of the teenagers loved that section, we could swim in the very deep of the sea, then walk a few steps and rinse the salt water off our hair and body in the cool deep fresh river water.

It was a different life back then, and one of my friends at that time was Esther Owens. She lived at the dairy ranch just outside the city limits of LaCeiba, but still considered part of the so called White Settlement, the designated fenced special area for the Americans that worked for Standard Fruit companies in Honduras. That fruit company grew the thousands of banana trees that grew there.

My friend Esther and I enjoyed riding the horses found at the large ranch, and often as time allowed us, we would be riding. There would usually be a small group of us kids, all young teenagers, maybe 8 or 10 of us and we would risk the danger of riding out to the experimental fruit groves, where they ranchers attempted to create hybrid fruits, before they tried to market them. Being kids, we loved to try the strange mixtures of fruits we found at the experimental groves. We knew the rules – they include never eat those bizarre fruits – but forbidden fruit is the sweetest, so we ate them anyway, well, just one or two fruits. The reason the farmers said never eat them, is because it was a small grove, and if the kids ate the fruit, they wouldn't have a lot of sample fruit. The fruit was not dangerous anyway – they were just fruits that they were trying to mix the fruits together, such as apricot and peach, or a plum and an apricot blended so both fruits grew on the same trees. Some of the fruits were pleasant; a few were a slightly bitter aftertaste, none of us liked the bitter fruits. I liked the fruit that tasted like half peach, half apricot. It was my favorite.

In Honduras we used to create our own amusement, we didn't have a lot of things to do back then, so riding the horses through the groves and trying to act out movies such as Robin Hood, with using our own homemade archery skills was always fun. Our archery skills were far from accurate enough to create anything dangerous, our 'weapons' were crude bows and arrows we made in a few minutes by a fresh branch and a piece of string.

Our arrows were always too crooked to hit anyone, so it was just fun and it was pure innocent amusement. No one was ever harmed.

It was one day, the most of the kids decided to ride out to the groves, but Esther and I decided we wanted to ride up the beach, so it was just the two of us, we packed a lunch just a couple sandwiches, but we didn't really need it, we knew we could always grabbed a wild few fruits that grew everywhere. Fruit like guava, bananas, pineapple, berries, and mangos grew wildly there. Honduras was a wonderful tropical paradise. Esther and I loved the huge mango trees near the beach.

Before 10 in the morning Esther and I were on our horses and riding north on the beach, and we traveled much further than we ever tried to ride. It was a wonderful morning, and before the sun was high in the sky, we had already played in the deep water in the teal colored Caribbean sea, and coaxed the horses into the knee-deep edge of the gentle waves. We knew better go more to ride the horses than a couple feet into the water because the Caribbean Sea suddenly drops from a couple feet of gentle waves to a shocking very deep water, without warning.

As we rode along the beach, we found out we were a few miles from the town of LaCeiba, and we found a small fresh water stream where the stream ended into the sea, and the horses drank deeply from the cool fresh water.

Exactly as we suspected, Esther and I found a lunch of mangoes and guavas plucked from the trees not far from the sea, and Esther even managed to scramble up a coconut tree that grew at an angle over the fresh water. She scrambled up a palm tree picked a few of the coconuts. We carried a few of the large green triangle shaped fruit and tried to packed them in our saddle bags, but they bulged out the top of the saddle bags precariously.

We knew it was time to turn the horses south and return to LeCeiba, or we would be riding down the beach when the sun crossed the mountains and left us in the semi-dark, and in the jungle, they is not safe.

We started the ride back but remembered Esther she left her canteen hanging on the side of the coconut tree. We doubled back and returned to the angled tree over the fresh water, retrieved the canteen and it was then we turned and spotted the first large dome lifted off from the water. It just floated there, silently, just above the surface of Caribbean Sea. We were amazed to watch a huge amount of water dripping off the sides of it of the big round craft. We stopped and just watched the amazing scene, then, as we watched them, a second disk lifted off the water of the sea. That second silent saucer appeared to cause the water of the sea sort of 'round out' just before the second saucer lifted above sea. Suddenly and without the sound of engines of any type, a third silent disk slowly lifted out of the water and it too, made look the sea look as if it had a big rounded bump on the water just before that saucer left the sea. The three of them lifted straight up, it didn't leave at an angle, just floated straight up, and for a few seconds all three disks floated above water, dripping water about 25 feet above the Sea.

Each disk looked roughly 35 to 40 feet across, certainly metallic and has the appearance of polished aluminum. The disks appeared to glow with a soft light greenish light. The disks had looked huge pie pans, and the top appeared equally matched or mirrored on the bottom half. Between the equal halves what appeared to resembled large louvers between them. The louvers turned slowly round anti-clock direction, and the soft green light emitted a brighter light between the louvers. It was then I realized there were sections where I would see windows clearly seen behind the louvers. Esther and I stood there fascinated with the spectacle of three huge flying saucers leaving the Caribbean Sea!

Then, suddenly it crossed my mind that if there were windows on that craft, there must be people inside those crafts – and I was afraid the people inside the saucers could see me. The disks were close by– maybe a scant half a mile or so, and they could cross that short distance and beside me in a few heartbeats! But before I could suggest that we leave and hurry and ride home, all disks slightly dipped the north edge of the crafts and flew in a straight direction, headed towards the United States. We watched them leave towards North, until they quickly were out of our view, but they appeared to remain low over the water.

To this day I still can't remember if Esther and I talked about the disks on the hard ride home. We rode hard, fast and silent because we had nothing we could explain to each other.

I know when we took the horses back to the corral, we didn't speak. I know we never again talked about that day, and we never wanted to discuss the strange oval metallic disks we both know we witnessed take off from the Sea. What could we say? We were just young teenagers and we knew could not explain what we witnessed. I know didn't tell anyone, and to the best of my knowledge, neither did Esther.

That day, we just looked at each other, and we both felt the same fear, the same questions – what were those strange round disks? Who were inside those windows? What were they doing under the deep water of Caribbean Sea? How did they float over the sea without of a sound?

That were they doing and how did they survive inside the deep water off the coast of Honduras? I know I'll never know those answers.

Many years later, I finally talked to my parents about the saucer we saw that day, and asked if they knew anything about the saucers under the deep waters off the coast off Honduras. They asked a few questions, but even after all those years my parents were more concerned as to why did Esther and I drove so far north up the beach, they knew I was not supposed to go beyond visible the city limits of LaCeiba, but we just lost track of the distance and time that day.

I am glad I did, because that day I witnessed something that remains a mystery to me after all these many years.

21

FACE TO FACE WITH THE ALIENS – WHAT TO DO

(Plus What *Not* To Do!)

Did it ever cross your mind that someday you may need any suggestion on "how-to-meet-aliens-and-not-fall-apart"? Most people have no idea what they would do if that fated day ever arrived.

Think about it, shouldn't you get ready before you need that information? The first time you meet an alien face to face could be the most exciting encounter you will ever experience in your life! Nothing is your life has prepared you to meet an unearthly visitor.

Do you remember they day your parents, your parents taught you that it is not polite to stare at people? Do you remember that advice? I'm sure they warned you that it is not acceptable behavior to stare at people that are a little different from the average. I'll bet they didn't say one word about staring at aliens. Now this is the day - you stand faced with the "what if…" situation, what do you do when you are looking straight into those large black alien eyes. What do you do when you know when they are peering straight looking into your eyes and you have no idea what they want from you. Do you have any idea what to do when that happens?

What do you do when you suddenly find yourself standing in front of an alien being that leaves you breathless in wonder? You are both afraid and curious as your eyes take in the spectacle of a humanoid creature, and instantly you know this being is not human. In the first few seconds, your heart pounds, your mouth is dry, your knees feel weak and your hands tremble uncontrollably.

Meanwhile, your brain searches its memory banks for anything that matches the being in front of your eyes. Finally, the brain-scan stops, and your memory cells screams back one word *alien!* you want to run and escape the alien invader, but you just stand there, frozen is position.

Let me offer a few suggestions that you may find helpful when and if an alien visits you.

If the alien being is a small Grey:

Do not attempt to run away.

Do not start screaming at them.

Do not throw anything towards the aliens.

Do nothing, just stand still and look straight into their eyes and do not look away.

This shows them you are not afraid, and willing to allow them to complete their work. There are usually three Greys. Each Grey has a specific chore they must complete before they leave you. No matter what you do or say, the Grey will complete the chore they were supposed to finish.

Most of the Greys were created without emotion and will fulfill their job no matter what happens, and I assure you it is easier for you if you do not attempt to attack them. They strength is amazing and you cannot win in a physical struggle against them.

When the Greys are standing in front you, slowly lower your arms and open your hands, your palms forward. Holding your arms in this position indicates you are not hostile and will not attempt to harm the alien. In addition - the Greys recognize a human smile, and a smile means the human is passive and will be cooperative. Greys have instructions and those instruction include instantly stun any human holding a weapon of any type in their hands. If you do not want to be hurt, I suggest you do not carry anything because the aliens know the human race will use anything in their hands as a weapon. It is best you stand still and say nothing, because your attempts to communicate will mean nothing to them.

Do not cry or attempt to fight with an alien, because crying or fighting will only upset you, and the grey is not impressed. Greys do not feel emotions of any type, and since they do not experience empathy, and it is physically impossible for them to understand how you feel. Greys can't feel pity, anger, or love. Greys do not feel emotion of any type. They were created without emotions of any type. It is like expecting your car to understand how you feel. Being humanoid in shape does not mean they mean they share your emotion. They do not.

If you are in your home when aliens arrive, allow them investigate different items, remain silent and do not attempt to tell them what the item means to you. They do understand your words, but your emotion when talking about an item, means nothing to them. The Greys cannot understand the *meaning* of your words.

They do not understand the memory and your emotional connection with those words. The Greys are well trained will not damage your fragile items in your home. They are trained to examine certain items more closely. For example they may spend a little extra time looking at a display of collection of alien photos on a wall, or spend more time looking at large map complete with pins marking the location of alien abductions. They are just as interested in those maps as you everyone else, and will be fascinated by the time and care you spent made to create this display.

Do not attempt to touch the black-eyed Greys and do not reach out to shake their hands, and do not attempt to push away the alien. They consider the human race an assignment, and do not understand that humans are living entities with emotions. The Greys would not be impressed if a person cried and produced tears. They have seen tears before, and they mean nothing to them.

Do not try to be friendly to a Grey. It is like trying to be friendly with your car. Your car does only the acts you order, but your car does not understand why you do it. Your car "understand" nothing, it is a machine. Greys are like your car, most of the Greys are intelligent living machines, but they are not emotional. Most Greys with large black eyes have a computer driven brain and are not living creatures.

They are more robotic than humanoid. Greys have instructions and those instruction include instantly stun any human holding any item in their hands. They are aware the human may use any item in their hands as a weapon. If you do not want to be hurt, I suggest you do not pick up or carry anything may even suggest a weapon.

If the Being is Reptilian: If the alien is reptilian, they are living creatures with emotions and empathy. Like the Greys, they have a chore to complete and pleasant or not, they will finish their job. Their assignment will finish their job regardless the chore. If a repton enters your home, you have a chance to enter a conversation. No matter what, they will fulfill their designated chore, but again they understand all languages and are capable to ask questions and answer your questions. Again, use the arms down, palm of your hands exposed towards them. Hands in that position indicates the human is cooperative and will not attack.

The repton race (reptilian) is curious about the human race, and as long as you stand still and try to look straight into their eyes they will tolerate your nervousness. Don't move around and don't attempt to touch them, even if they have been there and have talked you for a few minutes. They consider the human race as 'smelly being' and they do not appreciate perfumes and other products the human regularly use. Their sense of smell is much stronger, and they get irritated if you perspire profusely. They find it threatening when a human body emits liquids from your face. Reptons do not perspire.

They do have a sense of humor, but they do not express humor with a smiling face. When a repton shows they enjoy humor, their eyes get larger, and laughter comes from deep in their chest, sounding a little similar of growling as their mouth will open wider. They just don't smile like the human race.

A few reptons would enjoy a candid conversation with a human, but the average repton would reject any suggest of talking. The reptons will simply arrive, complete their designated chore, and finish the job and leave without any conversation.

I hope these few suggestions will help prepare for the first time you meet an alien. I have already had the experience to meet an alien face-to-face in 1961 in Florida, and I assure you, it is an awesome event!

It is important that you realize that these aliens are doing a job, and their job includes meet the humans, sometimes give you an implant and then leave. It may scare you, but in reality, they just do their best not to scare you, and after they complete they must do, they leave you in peace. They do not hurt you, but sometimes you hurt yourself by trying to escape the face-to-face meeting. People should realize the aliens do not permanently harm anyone.

22

WHAT TO BRING - IF YOU PLAN TO LEAVE EARTH

Let's pretend an alien race found Earth, and the aliens what to know more about the human race. The alien race decided they didn't want to talk to the leaders of this world, instead the aliens wanted to talk to average man or female on planet Earth. While we are pretending, let's think these aliens chose a few people at random, and *you* are one of the people in your area. The aliens say you have one week to choose select ten items that could explain the human race planet Earth. What ten items would you choose?

My ten items that explains the human race:

1. One complete set of illustrated Britannica Encyclopedia

2. An Oxford Dictionary of the English language

3. A copy of the History of the World

4. A copy of the history of mankind's literature

5. A good book on comparative religion

6. The history of wars on Earth

7. The history of food and cooking

8. The history of mankind's art and music

9. A computer/monitor/printer filled with everything inside my computer, including my UFO studies.

10. A book about platonic love, romantic love, family love and the love of spiritual love

Think about it, what ten items would you choose to explain the human race?

23

WHAT HAPPENED TO THE MOON AND MARDUK?

There are many theories of the Moon, but one of my favorite quotation is in a book called "Worlds In Collision" by Immanuel Velikovsky While discussing his statements regarding the gigantic craters on the Moon, they may the result of volcanic activity on the once active life little planet, or perhaps the end result a meteor storm hit the little planet. Velikovsky said, and I quote: "The Moon is a great unmarked cemetery flying around our earth, a reminder of what can happen to a planet." I like that statement, so clear, so overwhelming to contemplate. (Velikovsky was a Jewish Russian-American, a known psychoanalyst writer as well as one of the top catastrophists. Velikovsky is the author of quite a few books that offer pseudo-historical interpretations ancient history.)

It could be accurate, but I like to think the Moon is much more a small dead planet orbiting Earth. It is a known fact that the Moon rings like a bell each time something hits its surface. That is a strong indication of a hollow sphere. I don't think the Moon is 'dead.'

I really wish more people think about the Moon, it's ancient history, the visible "scars" on its surface, rather or not is it the results of the most incredible meteorite storm that bombarded that little planet, or the result of an internal volcanic action in the early prehistoric era of the formation of the Moon, the result is shocking and terrifying when you look at that countless craters that litters that surface. Can you guess what it would be like to be an eye witness to that much destructive power? Can you guess what it would be like to be on that planet when it all those craters were made? That thought it makes a person really think and think HARD.

If all the meteorites hit the Moon, it must have happened BEFORE it ever arrived around Earth - because look at it - it sits still, showing the same face, facing Earth, so how come we see all MANY those craters, but the Earth has only a couple craters? How - if the Moon never revolves - the Moon ended up with so many craters on the sheltered side? It is worth contemplating the idea that those craters happens some other place, and the battle scarred Moon finally came to rest around planet Earth.

Perhaps the craters on the Moon are not natural at all. Maybe it shows a struggle with a previous civilizations - millions years ago - on Earth - a civilization battled with a visiting alien race that tried to conquer planet Earth, but the aliens were defeated when the Earth-based civilization bombed the Moon - but the invaders all died in the battle, leaving a scar pocked dead little planet in orbit. At least that is another one of theory about the Moon.

No one really knows what happened to the destroyed planet - Marduk - we know about the asteroid belt, and we know it is the residue of the destroyed planet Marduk. But no one can say for sure what happened. It could be a natural disaster, perhaps a huge meteor slammed into Marduk and that planet shattered like a broken glass tree ornament. What actually happened to that planet is unknown. We only know it was certainly totally destroyed.

It is possible all the craters on all the planets and moons in this solar system were hit by the exploding Marduk, and the craters all bear witness of the force of that exploding planet. All the planets near that destroyed planet are marked by craters, perhaps these craters are the scars of that destruction. Why or how that planet was destroyed remains a mystery, but there are many theories. Was the Moon in orbit around Marduk when that planet exploded? Does that explain the countless craters the sides of the Moon? Was the Moon hit by debris and tossed and bounced of parts of a destroyed planet?

It could be the planet Marduk was destroyed by war, and perhaps that war was known as the War in Heaven. There is no large written history on Earth that talks suggest the War in Heaven was really an intergalactic war. The ancient scriptures tell us that the Living God once lived on planet Earth, but he left for unknown reasons. Maybe Earth and Marduk were involved with an intergalactic war. No living human knows for sure, but it is known that Marduk was totally destroyed in that war. Is the destruction of Marduk as part of the War in Heaven? It is assumed all the inhabitants of Marduk were destroyed. Some say maybe they left the planet before it was destroyed. No one knows the truth about that planet. All we know about that event is there may have been an amazing war, and that information from a few isolated ancient written comments.

The population of Earth knows the Creator of Earth was once involved with an amazing war and one third of all the inhabitants of a planet known as Heaven lost the battle. The losers were banned from their native planet, and sent to a distant planet at the edge of this galaxy, and that planet had the name as Earth. The losers of the War in Heaven – the losing survivors of that ancient war – were placed on Earth, and they are forbidden to leave Earth. These advanced beings were survivors were not the type to stopped struggling to living, so they to create biological creatures to carry out their work for them. Some say the biological creatures are known as the human race. According to the ancient scrolls, the name of the loser in that war had the name of Satan.

24

THE ALIENS ARE COMING - WHAT DO YOU HAVE TO OFFER?

Here is something to think about...

The enlightened elite have a big surprise coming. The end of the world we know is going to end, and with it, their life too, will end. They think they are the "chosen few" and will survive the war, but the reptilian brothers have already decided that this time, no human will survive the cleansing this time.

The human life is too weak, with built-in diseases that weaken their bodies. Humans have short lives, and by the time they are mature, theirs life has been weakened by life and they become too old and feeble to use the intelligence they gained.

It is a sad fact, but each human must waste many years learning the simple basics of required intelligence on planet Earth. By the time many of the humans learn the basic rules of life, they are too old and feeble to use the intelligence. The coming race already have their new stronger superior race standing by, ready to take over the beautiful planet Earth, and erase the hostile short living humans.

Sure there is a lot of humans, millions of them, and there is always someone better, more wise, someone 'newer and stronger' ready to fill in the popular fallen human. The arriving "new race" lives longer, is smarter, the younger-set won't have to be taught anything, they will be born with the knowledge they need to survive, and in minutes of birth they will be ready to fit in to their society. There will have no need to schools, saving years of time, and like the animals in the wilds, in minutes after birth, the new humans can run. The next race will live for hundreds of years.

The foolish elite - but still very human - believe the reptilian lies and really believe the chosen few humans will be important enough that will survive. But so what? How long will they live after the war?

The most of the chosen elite are already mature, so they might live another 30 years before they die - and that what? They die, that is it. Nothing special.

They will not be given some 'magic pill' that will make them immune to death, they will live die just like the other humans. The elite do not care if the rest of the human race die as long as they survive and gain wealthy before they die. Literally - they do not care about any one as long as they get what they want.

The elite plan to sell the other humans to the highest bid, because it is their hope and plan they can live in a life of luxury the rest of their life. The average human will die, but the elite can handle that, and they don't mind the hatred of the other humans as long as they remain wealthy and isolated from the dying humans around them. As long as there have been humans, there have always people like that mind set.

What kind of a race would exterminate complete species without a second thought? You know the answer don't you? Just look at the history of the human race and you know it is a known fact - a race just similar the human race, only the "better race" that lives longer and is more a little more violent than the human race.

Try to look at the human race from an alien point of view - the human race has nothing exceptional to offer to an advanced race. The human race have nothing of value, no real cures anywhere, no exceptional high technology that would amaze an advance race, no incredible powerful humans with outstanding abilities, nothing an advanced race to want to join and welcome into the galactic family. All the humans are just about the same, no one that stand as above average, and even the best and smartest humans are just a step or two above everyone else.

The only difference is some humans have all the material gains of the world, and the rest of the humans struggle through their existence. The richest people on this planet are not better or smarter, no healthier than the other humans, they are just have own more wealth.

Think about that for a minute, what would that look like to a visiting alien race? It looks like the average wealthy human is ego-based and do not care about their fellow race.

Why don't you try to think like an alien - and visualize the human race, in reality, what does the human have to offer? - - - Not much....

*The average human race spends roughly 30 year to learn to be a responsible adult.

*The next 30 years in creating 'self-replacement.' In other words, the male and female humans give birth and raise their young. Those years are the most productive and healthiest years in their life, and the strongest years in each human. The human race teaches the youngest child the art of violence. As a child they are taught how to fight, how to practice for war, how to be stronger, more selfish and meaner than the other humans. The children of Earth are taught to play sports games that teach them to be competitive and to try to win at any cost.

*The final 30 years are the closing years for the human race. By the human has completed their second stage of their life and reached the age of 60, their mental peak has reached and the human body becomes weaker, and medical problems plagues the body, but if a human tries hard, they may be lucky enough to survive to golden age in 100.

So – think about it, what does the human race have to offer to the long living advanced race? The alien lives forms enjoy their lives and survive well over 1000 years, what in the world would an advanced race have to offer to any other race? What does any human have offer? Nothing worthwhile.

25

WHAT CAN BE WORSE THAN EATEN BY AN ALIEN CREATURE?

What if the human race is food to race of aliens? You must agree almost nothing generates terror more than the concept of a human being eaten by an alien creature.

In nature big animals eat small creatures. A good sized animal being eaten by a tiger or a human eaten by alligator or a lion is far from shocking news - it happens in nature. What happens if the creature is much smaller than the average victim? Don't laugh, it happens all the time – like the tiny army ants can swarm over cow and kill them in minutes.

Maybe it's just me, but I'd never choose a Grey alien as the man-eating creature to do the job. Perhaps the reptilian aliens maybe looks threatening enough to eat a human.

What if there is something far worse than being the dinner course on an alien menu? Did you just say 'nothing could be worse than that', is that what you say? Don't bet your last taco on that statement being true, because you would lose your taco and perhaps your lunch if you find the truth.

Inside the alien section of Dulce Base in New Mexico USA, there is a cathedral that few human eyes have seen. It is ornate and looks imposing, with thousands of small round disks stacked to create a façade for the cavernous building. Inside, filled shelves or small alcoves pack the thousands of well-rounded spindle copper 'spheres.' They resemble rounded ended copper footballs.

According to one of the co-workers of Tom Castello each copper spheres contain the soul of one human, the living essence of an alert living man, woman or child, trapped inside a copper spindle inside Dulce Base.

Imagine, if you can, the everlasting horror of being aware - fully aware of your life, as a powerful alien slowly steals the atomic parts of your body, one atom at a time, while you get weaker and weaker, until your body becomes so unstable that your atomic body begs for the release known as death? But death is denied to these hapless souls – the atomic body is too fragile, with not enough atoms to maintain the shape of a human, and the lost human's body can no longer become host of disease and too ethereal to age. It is then - and only then - the alien coaxes the soul into a copper vial and becomes an imprisoned soul.

When you are alive and your soul is aware and alert, but your body now exists only as a mere transparent vapor - and your soul wants to die, but your body no longer has enough atoms to house disease or death? You are aware while your soul in trapped into a copper football-shaped sphere held in an alien cathedral inside Dulce Base for thousands of years. That concept is far worse than merely eaten by an alien creature!

26

WANT TO WRESTLE
WITH AN ANGEL?

At least at one human had an experience like that, his name was Jacob, he wrestled with an angel all night, and the story is still recorded in the books of Genesis. (Gen 32:24-30)

But that is not why I mentioned wrestling with angels, it is another biblical reference.

Perhaps you heard these words before:

"For we wrestle not against human flesh and blood, but against the fallen angels called Principalities, also against the fallen angels called Powers, and against the Rulers of the Darkness of this world, against spiritual wickedness in high places..." (Ephesians 6:12)

"The Rulers of the Darkness of this world" - wow, that is one heavy title. Did you notice they specified "THIS world"? (in other words, planet Earth)

The "Ruler of Darkness" is also known as the "Prince of the air." This Prince lives on this world, (planet Earth,) but his original home was on a different planet. Any way you look at it, if this Prince is from another world he is an extraterrestrial being that moved to Earth a long ago. I assume you know those titles belongs to the owner of Earth, and his name is called Satan.

Powers and Principalities are orders or titles of angels, and since you may remember that the angels are not human either. Some of the angels live on Earth, but they too, had previous home on a different planet. I want you think about this - if the angels are not human and they are from a different world - what else can you call them? Aliens? Friends? Or...? Think about it.

Please do not be confused by the vintage terminology in those few lines, just be aware the words "... against spiritual wickedness in high places ..." is just another way of saying "evil world leaders."

I believe you should pay attention when they point out that they do not "wrestle not against flesh and blood" (flesh and blood means humans) - they are also pointing out that the Principalities and the Powers are NOT human.

There are nine orders or titles of angels available, Seraphim, Cherubim, Thrones, Dominions, Virtues, Powers, Principalities, Archangels and Angels. Each order of angels is in charge specific 'departments' on Earth. If you think about it, it is the job of the Powers and Principalities to "wrestle" with the complex thoughts each human.

If they are not human and yet they are wrestling with 3rd dimensional beings (humans), what are they?

Who are these Powers and Principalities? Where do they live? Do they live underground? Or do you think they live in a different dimension? The ancient scrolls clearly state they live *in* the Earth. In caverns? In the hollow Earth?

27

VAMPIRES, ROYALTY & ALIENS

The blue blood of Royalty, the thirst of Vampires and the Aliens that search for a certain blood type seem to have one connection and that connection is to be their need for the right blood for their need.

The men and women with their need to keep their Royal blue blood untainted by the common human blood of the average man or woman. Royal blue blood - but still human – with its so-called blue blood must have crossed bred or with the more blue blood of the reptilian race. These privileged humans received the "gift" of an infusion of reptilian DNA, not for themselves, but for their following children born after that infusion.

It is the same in today's society, maybe I am a descendant of that blood blue too, (I am a descendant of world leaders through presidents John Adams and John Quincy Adams) and at the time of my birth, it meant my generation were born more intelligent than my parents were. If I too, received an additional DNA infusion, my children would be more intelligent than I would. Each time 'common human blood' mixed into the pure DNA of the pure blue blood, that blue blood is diluted. If a human female produces a half human/half reptilian child, the child of the woman is more intelligent. The woman that had a sexual encounter with a reptilian is no smarter than she was before, but her child will be much smarter than his mother.

In ages past the so-called "vampires' with their thirst for blood was simply a misunderstood thought. What if the uneducated people of that era knew "advanced and intelligent people from somewhere else" knew these advanced beings needed certain blood, and these people from 'somewhere else' took the needed blood.

What if the needed blood was taken through an extreme blood donation taken from the jugular vein? What if the needed blood was taken from a dual needle, and the marks it left was the size of snake bite make on the jugular vein?

Sometimes the so called vampires completely drained all the blood of the victim, leaving the dead body. What are the uneducated people saw the makes on the throat, saw the blood is gone from the body, and they assumed they were bite marks?

The 'somewhere else' visitors stayed for a while, and looked human enough to pass for human. They stayed long enough to produce children and then left. (Could it be possible these "beings from elsewhere" are the tall white Greys?) The crossbred children were pale and weak and knowing the fathers of these children needed blood, they convinced the youngsters to bite and drink the common blood, thinking that might be enough? It is an interesting concept.

28

TWO WORDS TO AVOID - "I AM"

How many times have you heard someone said "I-knew-you-were-going-to-say-that?" Let's face it, those words are very common.

"I knew it....." and you remember that too.

Did you ever hear of the Ten Commandments? They are explained in the holy bible.

They are rules or commandments and the third commandment is a big one, it states: "Thou shalt not take the name of the Lord in vain." (Exodus 20:26)

(The dictionary says to use a word "in vain" means don't use the Lord's name lightly, or don't use his name for common reason.)

It doesn't say don't talk about the Lord - instead it says it seems to state you shouldn't use the *name* of the Lord for trivial reasons.

So what is the Lord's name? The bible clearly states that the Lord's name is "I am." The holy bible clearly states his name is 'I am that I am'. (Exodus 3:14)

The commandment is do not use the term "I am" lightly. Have a valid reason when you use the words "I am" for any reason.

So ~ every time you say "I am broke" or "I am a poor man" you are asking the Powers Above to make sure you remain broke and poor. Don't say those words, instead be positive, and say "I am happy" or "I am wealthy" - every time you say "I am wealthy" you are reminding the Powers Above to send wealth to you, and it WILL happen.

No matter what you do, never say "I am ill" because using the "I am" words it is like a command from Powers Above to be sick. Think I am mistaken? Think again. Go read it yourself and you will quickly see it is written as I stated.

For example, although history the ancient world leaders, such as royalty (kings, queens, etc) knew that rule - they never used the "I am" in vain, instead they used a plural terms. They wouldn't say "I am ill" - instead they always said "we are ill" simply because they knew the God Within of each person commanded they not use the name of the Lord in vain. Remember that Jesus Christ himself reminded his disciples that the Kingdom of God is WITH-IN each person.

Every time you say "I am ...." you are using the words 'in vain' because you are commanding the Power Above to manifest the terms you command. It is a fact, if you want to command power; you better know the correct way to command.

Be careful with the words "I am" - and remember the wise ones throughout history always stated "thoughts are things, and when you think your words, that thought goes out and tried to make it happen."

Think about those words - thoughts are things - ALL words are thoughts, in thought form, written or spoken. Before you utter those words, take time to clearly think about them, rather it is consciously or not, you cause things to happen every time think you speak.

"I-knew-that-was-going-to-happen" - yes, you knew it, but maybe it was because it was the power of thought of those words that you caused it to happen.

Be careful when you say "I am.....", and think carefully before you say something anything. Use positive words like "I am happy" "I am contented" "I am wealthy" (those words are always positive commands, and if you use them often, it will be true) and don't even *think* words about sickness, poverty or sadness.

Your life will be certainly become more smooth and pleasant if you try to use more positive words every day of your life.

29

ARE THERE TOWNS
WITH UFO THEMES?

I often think about how strange it is that some cities offer a wide variety of entertainment, music, arts, sports and more, while some cities are more limited and aside from a cluster of bars, the town are literally boring.... have you ever thought about the town you live in, and what it offers to its population? Have you talked to the mayor of your town? Have you offered suggestions?

To your knowledge, are there any towns or cities that boast or advertises their UFO displays? I have seen a couple statues in a couple towns, for example, I read online there is a science fiction character of a life size statute of Capt. James T. Kirk (actor William Shatner) in Riverside, Iowa. The statue was erected in July 2018. The statue doesn't really looks like actor Bill Shatner of Star Trek fame, but it is easy to recognize the Star Trek uniform.

The television sci-fi series of Star Trek started in September 1966. It starred seven great actors William Shatner as 'Capt. Kirk,' DeForest Kelley as 'Bones,' and Leonard Nimoy as 'Spock', Nichelle Nichols as 'Uhura,' Walter Koenig as 'Chekov,' George Takei as 'Sulu' and James Doohan as 'Scotty.'

Also I found out there is a statue of Mothman is easy to find in Point Pleasant, West Virginia. According to written material, sculptor Robert Roach created the twelve foot statue of the metallic insectoid monster in the year 2000. The statue stands near a Mothman Museum.

Bob Roach lives in New Haven West Virginia.

The true terrifying events began in 1966, and the first author to write about the Mothman was John Keel in his book named "The Mothman Prophecies." That popular book was published in 1975. That frightening true event make into a movie in the year 2002, that film had the same name "The Mothman Prophecies" and starred actors Richard Gere, Will Patton, Laura Linney and Alan Bates.

I heard Roswell, New Mexico has a small Unidentified Flying Object Museum and a few unique items to display. I am surprised that a state that boasts two well-known UFO crashes do not have more information not available to the public. Maybe New Mexico should include the old Datil, N.M. unidentified flying object case, not just Roswell and Aztec. (Fate Magazine wrote about the Datil N.M. UFO and living alien many years ago. I happened in the late 1800s.)

I live in the one of the most exciting city on this planet. I live in Las Vegas, Nevada, and it has the thrilling title of the "Entertainment Center of the Earth!" The most glamorous entertainers have their homes inside our city limits. Too, one of the most important military SAC base is here, with the most vital top secret testing ever know to the human race is in our back yard. In addition, one of the world's largest and most important dam on Earth is here. With helicopters we are minutes to the Grand Canyon, and Death Valley. I suspect everyone knows we have everything here - in the winter, we have snow on the west mountains so we can enjoy snow sports, like snowboarding, sleds, ski, and yet in the summers when it is so very hot, we can enjoy we can enjoy all sorts of activities, we can swim, snorkel, dive, water ski, fish, or even enjoy high-speed boat races. Have no doubt about that hot summers here, because we are a stone's throw to Death Valley, and that area is literally one of the hottest place on earth. It has always thought it was strange that a city that boasts "everything" has next to nothing regarding flying saucers, UFOs, or aliens.

It is true that the "Silver State" of Nevada has everything; we even have the world's only authentic Extraterrestrial Highway, so that boast is not far from their claim. 'If you think about it, you can have it in beautiful Nevada, a western state.' Believe me, I assure you that is not an empty lie.

Within minutes of exciting Las Vegas there are wild horses roaming the untamed desert and mountains. Every man, woman and child felt the awe of Mother Nature's beauty when they witnessed the colorful largest canyon on Earth first time - yes, the Grand Canyon is close by Las Vegas too. Minutes away from this amazing canyon is another type of beauty, the beautiful women found at the legal brothels and Nevada claims the only legal houses of prostitution in the United States.

I am not making up wild stories here, Nevada has everything a person can imagine; we even have a museum for Atomic Testing Power.

How is it that in a state that boasts "we-have-everything" why is there not one flying saucer museum? With the wealth of Las Vegas and obvious know-how why don't we have the world's most authentic exciting UFO exhibits?

We have the world's only Extraterrestrial Highway, and yet not one casino in Las Vegas dares to display an exciting UFO theme? Why? Have the casinos warned not to display UFOs or flying saucers in their decor? That doesn't make sense. Is it because they 'powers that be' fear the truth? There used to be a couple casinos with sort of an outer space theme – the Stratosphere had great images of space, and years ago, the Hilton hosted the Star Trek Experience but not for long. I sure wish we would the casinos bring out more UFO themes. If there was a great place to display Flying Saucers, UFOs, Aliens, Greys, or even perhaps great photos of Outer Space it would UFO fans from all over the world.

Maybe there are other hotels or casinos in the USA or perhaps some in another country that boast the fun and glory of the world's only UFO based casino & hotel, but there none here in Nevada, and to the best of my knowledge, none in the USA too. So - if you hear of a place like that, please write to me and let me know about them, would you please?

Here in Las Vegas, we have a casino the exact size of the great pyramid of Egypt and it is jet black in the light hours, illuminated at night beautiful to see. We have pirate ships fight it out outside the casino every night, and there is no charge to see these exciting exhibits. We also have a replica volcano that explodes several times every night, with the mountain exudes lava every night – and it is free to see every night! But I want to see a big UFO sitting on the as Vegas strip – I would be thrilled to see that building and can you imagine the exhibits the museum could display?

At least, I would like to see a Science Fiction type theme in Las Vegas – think of the unlimited we could see! Try to visualize Star Trek theme, or but what about a Time Travel display or activity?

Just always remember that it is not impossible, as long as we have imagination!

30

TIME STOOD STILL

I have a question about time and I hope someone can offer an opinion. In my opinion nearly everybody has heard the expression "time stood time" - but what do you really think about that saying? In your opinion is it possible that sometimes time actually stops?

Do you think it is possible that there might be a real case of a "slip in time," and like the movie, "Groundhog Day," (a 1993 fantasy comedy starred Bill Murray & Andie MacDowell and Chris Elliott) could someone be doomed to re-live the same day over and over like that funny movie?

Or was it more like the movie, "The Day the Earth Stood Still" (1951 movie, stars Michael Rennie, Patricia Neal, Hugh Marlowe and Lock Martin as Gort the robot) in the movie everything electric stops – all over the world - for a half hour, allowing humans to think about the words of a visitor from a distant planet. Is it possible that at some similar event happened when time stood still? Is there a written or unwritten event when time stood still? According to the spiritual books, at least once the Earth stopped revolving for one day - in the book of the Holy Bible, King James Version, this event mentioned that time did stood time. The event started when time stopped started with large meteors fell and killed the enemies of Joshua, followed with a meteorite shower, then time stood still:

The Book of Joshua, (KJV) 10:13 (chapter 10, verses 12, 13, 14) "...And the sun stood still, and the moon stayed, until the people had avenged themselves upon their enemies. Is not this written in the book of Jasher? So the sun stood still in the midst of heaven, and hasted not to go down about a whole day. And there was no day like that before it or after it, that the Lord hearkened unto the voice of a man: for the Lord fought for Israel."

It seems to me if an event like that happened, the written event would have been recorded all over the entire world would have stories of such a historic day, but there are very few mentions of such a day. But that event was recorded in the spiritual book known the Holy Bible.

In your opinion, do you this time could happen again? Could the Earth stop moving and do not turn around can stop for a day complete? An event like that one would be an amazing event.

Is it possible that if it happened, the people involved would be caught in a time warp? Would the rest of the world feel the 'frozen time' or only the few people that experienced the time warp?

I like to hope nothing drastic would happen in a 'frozen time' event. Do you think if something unusual like the Earth stopped turning for one day, would cause serious side effects? Would the temperatures on the direct sun would suffer severe heat and create fires and the opposite part of the earth, caught in the night hours for 24 hours could be very cold. But then, who knows, would it be just nothing? It is something that has always catches my imagination and wondered if it could actually happen in again.

31

REPTON: THE WEDGE AND THE HOURGLASS

The powerful humanoid body shape of the reptilian male is best described as a living brawny wedge. The male repton are naturally rugged and uncommonly strong. Their barrel shaped chest is muscular, with a few large thick plate-like scales.

The golden face male are drones, the regular reptons are quiet and mostly passive. They are hard workers and do not tire as they work. They have been known to work without rest for over 35 hours without rest to complete a chore. They are not sure what to do on a chore, drones can stand for hours, and without unmoving, while waiting for instructions from a Dracon leader, before doing anything. To their credit, their instructions do nothing until a Dracon Leader tells them to complete their work as instructed. A golden face drone will never get in trouble for stopping their work in doubt. However, after their have the new orders, they will gladly work without rest to complete their chore. The average males stand from five feet to eight feet, and it is not uncommon for the reptons to reach nine feet. It is not unheard of for a drone can reach as tall as 12 feet, and it doesn't happen every day, but it is not uncommon for a drone to be a little taller than the Tall White aliens, and those tall beings are often from nine feet to fifteen feet.

The reptilian warriors usually have an avocado colored face, but many of them have with a face with a strong hint of gold. Most of the reptons have golden eyes, but sometimes their eyes are a soft beige tone. Like all well trained warriors, these reptons are aggressive and unbending in their goals.

The female reptons - and yes - there are females warriors too, are usually more tend to be from four and a half feet to seven feet tall. The females can stand over seven feet, but a female that is over seven feet is considered exceptional. The female repton body is much rounded than her male counterpart; her body is more like the classic hourglass. The female repton can be shapely, and smaller than the male repton. But would be a mistake to assume the female is not as dangerous as the male. Any female repton would be stronger than five humans. Their strength and power is beyond belief. The female repton can pick up a six foot man and throw him over 20 feet and can make sure the man ends in the exact place she planned him to land. The female repton can become a dangerous soldier and one female repton can overcome any five human men with no difficulty.

As a mother, a repton female give birth to her offspring and suckles the child. Like human females, the female repton can be feminine and shapely, and forward in her desires. She is frequently sexually aggressive and much more demanding than the more passive golden face male repton. Inside underground facilities, the repton females often attempt to seduce male humans.

Most of the leaders of the reptons are the beige or tan Dracon, but only a few of the golden face repton were born with wings or a tail. No matter the actual light gold of their face or a darker shade of their golden face, or if their bodies are their tan or green, if they have wings or a long tail it is consider it their destiny to become a leader for their race. They will develop their wings or a tail within the first three to five years of their life. However, having just a tail is not enough, the Dracon cannot lead until they have gone through the complete metamorphosis and develop wings. It doesn't matter if the size of the wings, because the only thing that counts is that they can be seen. Very few of the reptons have working wings, most are more like wings like appendages that in shape they resemble the wings of bats, but surprising large. When a repton possess wings that fly, those wings often reach sixteen to twenty feet wide. When the wings are folded against the body, sometimes those wings can be slightly higher than the reptons head and the wings sometimes touch the ground.

The reptons, warriors or the tan Dracon do not age the same as humans. They are not immortal, but it is not uncommon for the repton race to live over a thousand years. It is thought their long life is due to they spend their lives sheltered inside the caverns of Earth and they avoid the direct detrimental solar rays. (Solar rays are dangerous for humans too. Never-the-less humans spend hours sitting in the sun trying get a tan. The human race - and their shorter life span - live on the surface of the Earth, and often spend a lot of time outside in the Sun. Think about what that means.)

The reptons consider Earth their planet. They consider themselves to be the original owners of planet Earth. They claim they were here on Earth eons before Adam & Eve arrived, and according to Dracons there were hundreds of the Adams and hundreds of Eves, not just a pair of them.

(The bible DOES add credence to that, Genesis 5: 2, "Male and female created them and blessed them and called THEIR name Adam ...")

32

THE LITTLE GREY ALIENS WITH BIG BLACK EYES

This is an information sheet regarding the Grey aliens.

Part One:

1. Size: they stand 40 inches to 65 inches
2. Skin Colors: pale gray or off white; some have a slight beige tinge to their skin, a few Greys have a deeper tan skin tone. (Mostly the newer versions of Greys)
3. Eyes: large black shiny eyes about the size of a large turkey egg, the eyes of the Little Greys do not blink.
4. Fingers: the Greys have three fingers with an opposing thumb, they have two hands; fingers are very long and flexible, with three jointed sections of each digit.
5. Hands: the hands appear to be too narrow and long when compared to the fingers, the palm of their hands deeply cupped.
6. Feet: they have only two wide short toes on their narrow small feet.
7. Arms: quite long and thin with one elbow an each arm, the long arms and fingers reach the mid thigh, and their fingers touch the knee.

8. Legs: their legs are short, thin, and lack of muscular texture in the legs or arms. The legs are flexible at the hip, knee and ankle.

9. Torso: triangle or wedged torso with a rounded abdominal, giving the body the appearance similar of a newborn human infant.

10. The head of the little Grey appears to be too large for the size of the body. Their skull is without hair and the head appears 'lumpy' looking in the frontal area. The Greys do not possess hair on their skull, face, limbs or torso.

Part Two:

1. The little Greys are very different from the human race. The do not possess emotions. Greys do not understand the concepts of fear or sympathy, nor do they understand not understand the human's imagination. The Greys do not possess the ability to imagine.

2. Their brains are not capable to create theoretical scenes. To 'imagine' is beyond their capabilities. The little Greys do not possess fear, anger or any other emotion.

3. The Greys do possess inborn intelligence; the human race should try think of Greys as if they are more like a robot, or perhaps computer's brain.

4. Their computer-like brain recognizes humans' reactions. The Greys understand all the human known languages of this planet, but do not understand what they mean to the human race. The Greys know when if a human is afraid their job would be difficult unless they stun the human before they start their job. The Greys recognize fear as tears on the human face, when the human screams, the human hands shake, and the human will perspire.

They Greys know if any of human reactions are present, they can expect a physical struggle to convince the human to follow them. They have no concept what fear means to a human, any more than your car does not understand where you want unless you guide them.

5. If you can control your fear when the Greys approach you, you can simply stop them by give them a foolish command. They do not understand nonsense, and they do not comprehend when you use a commanding voice but recite children's nursery rhymes. The Greys will leave simply because they do not understand your childish command, and they must return to their masters for new instructions. However, they will return, and the nonsense rhyme will only work once.

6. Do not be deceived by their small stature, they are five times stronger than the average human male. If you struggle with them, you will lose, and you might get hurt, it is not worth the effort. You can't win a struggle with a Grey simply because they will stun you with a device. Usually when they must stun you, the memory of that event will be blocked from your mind.

7. They Greys can walk through solid walls with no trouble. The Greys walk through walls like you can walk through water. It doesn't matter if you don't know how to walk through walls, they do know how, and they will take you through the walls of any material. It is a strange sensation to be taken through a solid wall, and it is highly suggested that when that happens; try to hold your breath until you are through the wall. You will feel the brief sensation of "can't breathe" but it only take a couple seconds, so do not panic.

8. When the Greys abduct a person, the medical tests can be unpleasant and frightening, mostly because you are afraid. Try your best to remain calm and remember that if they wanted to

kill you, they would have killed you a long time ago. They usually return you to your home or car when the tests are complete.

9. Usually, the Greys block the memory of your abduction from your memory. They blocked it from your memory for a reason, usually to protect you and to allow you to continue your normal life without the memory of an alien abduction.

10. Be wise, do not visit a hypnotist and try to remember what happened. It was an unpleasant memory, so forget it. Why would you work hard to remember something unpleasant when the Greys tried to erase it from your memory? It was an unpleasant event simply because you were filled with fear. The Greys went out of their way to block the event from your memory so you wouldn't have to remember it. When you think about it, you will realize it was an act of kindness to block the event from your memory. Why would you spend time and money to remember an unpleasant event?

33

THE LITTLE GREYS AND THE HUMAN RACE

1. The black eyes of the little Greys have actually a protective cover over their natural eyes. The little Greys possess complex eyes, they have 41 separate lens in each eye, although they can see everything within one mile, their distant vision is not well focused clear. They must be within ten feet of a person to clearly identify a person.

2. Most aliens are capable to communicate through a form of mental telepathy. The average human become terrified when they discover an alien is trying to communicate via telepathy. The average human becomes afraid, tries to fight off the physical sensation in their skull. Most humans, male or female, have no idea what to do when an alien touches their mind with telepathy, and refuse to cooperate with the alien. Humans do not like the physical sensation when an alien reaches their mind.

   For that reason, when an alien attempts to touch a human's mind, the alien find total mental chaos, fear, panic and no willingness in the human minds. The human does not understand the alien's efforts to communicate mind-to-mind. The alien usually leaves assuming the human race is not intelligent enough to understand.

3. Although they do have a problem with their vision, the little Greys have other superior senses. They have the ability to "read minds" – that is not an accurate way of explain their ability; it would be more accurate to say they can pick up the human's mental thoughts via a wide broadcast frequency. The human mind is similar to a broken radio, and the radio refuses to stay on the same station, but keeps scanning all the stations.

4. The average person assumes the aliens first arrived in 1947 – but the aliens didn't 'arrive' at all, they have always been here. Some of the aliens on Earth were an ancient civilization thousands of years before they created the human race.

5. There are several unknown civilizations on Earth; however, these civilizations choose to avoid the hostile human race. Who can blame them? The human race kills anything or anyone without thinking about the possible benefits of keeping a person, animal or alien alive. The human race does not feel bad because they are considered the most hostile creatures in this galaxy. Humans would rather kill first, without hesitation, and later they regret their decision.

6. Because the human mind constant changes and never focuses on the same subject more than a split second, any visiting aliens would assumed the human race are not intelligent enough to understand their communications. That is because the human mind thinks in ever changing cycles, and humans never tries to focus or control their thoughts. The human race would benefit if they learned to control their thoughts.

34

TRACKED - FOR 7 GENERATIONS - OR MORE

The aliens track the DNA of families for many generations. You were tracked by aliens, your parents were tracked, and your grandparents were tracked by alien Greys, too, more than likely, your great-grandparents and their great-great-grandparents were tracked too.

Your parents were tracked by alien Greys, and now - your own life is being tracked by aliens Greys. What about your children, are they now being tracked by the aliens? What about your grand-children and great-grand-children? Yep. They are tracked too.

Did all these generations also experience being implanted and maybe terrified during these night alien visitations?

The answer: Yes – they all are being tracked too. Most people feel fear when an alien race visits you in the middle of the night. I know from my personal experience my own parents, my grandparents, my sisters, my children, their children, my great-grand-kids and my great-great-grand-kids I know they were visited my aliens. All tracked, all implanted.

From my own personal knowledge, my own family, I have checked 7 generations that I personally know they went through the experience of being tracked – each generation of us admitted being tracked – Why? Could be for a logical reason?

How many generations in the past were families tracked? My grandmother was visited by "strange small beings with bald heads" - what about HER grandmother? Did she too, experience the same "strange small beings with bald heads"? My maternal grandmother, Phoebe Reamer, was born in 1891, and yet she talked to me about meeting little men with big bald heads when she as a child, and again as an adult.

I've been lucky, and learned a lot, and I have been able to I am share my knowledge on Facebook. I talked about my implants, even posted photos of my implants - you can do the same! At least share your implant experiences here on my Facebook and on your own Facebook wall – post it groups too! The more of people share their information, the more we all benefit. I wish everyone should encourage anyone you know to talk about anything you know about aliens.

35

THOSE LUSTY SONS OF GOD

Let me try to translate a few words from the French language - "…and the daughters of men united with son of the gods." I've read that line countless times, and it always talks about the "…Sons of God…"

God created the Sons and Daughters of God, male and female, on the 6th day of creation. (KJV Genesis 1: 27)

God's male offspring were the lusty Sons of God, and the bible states the Son's of God impregnated the human daughters, the bible and other spiritual writings mention it – but these same spiritual books didn't they mention the "Daughters of God?" Did the Daughters of God give birth to hybrid half human-half gods children too? Maybe they did, however there is nothing written about them. According to the book of Genesis, the Sons of God were lusty males, and took human women as wives. (Genesis 6: 1&2) But there is no written word to indicate the Daughters of God took male humans as husbands.

I'll bet these lusty ladies must have become pregnant and produced half human/half Gods children. There must have been a lot of them - and although there are a few suspected offspring. The bible barely mentions there were Daughters of God - as if it wasn't important. Is it because the human mothers of these offspring become the "mighty men & men of renown," (indications suggest one of them was the biblical Noah, with his Ark) but what about the children of the Daughters of God?

Not a word about them - is it because the Daughters of God didn't stay on Earth?

Where did these cross-bred children live after they grew up? Perhaps these children were the children that were "scattered on the Earth" after the Tower of Babel? (Genesis 11: verse 1-9)

Are the generations of these original half-breed children that left Earth, will they return and expect a welcome home?

36

UFO STUDIES - IN THE
EARLY YEARS – 1950S

In the summer of 1952, a small fleet of controlled strange flying disks flew over Washington D.C. (This fleet of UFOs repeated flew over Washington D.C. on the dates 12 July to 29 July 1952) Photographs of the UFO fleet was published in The Washington Post newspaper.

Not one person decided to panic when the news of unidentified flying objects repeatedly flew over the capital city. However, the average American was only slightly concerned when photographs of the alien fleet hit the newspapers. The U.S. military determined at least one of the oval disks had an estimated speed of at least 7,300 miles per hour.

The next year - 1953 Astronomers discovered a planet size object entered this solar system. Scientists determined the large object is intelligently guided, and the object emitted communication signals. Later in the same year, the U.S. Air Force discovered several over-large alien objects were orbiting Earth at the altitude between 100 to 500 miles.

In the same year, stories of possible fatal alien craft started to be circled, and according to the stories, over 25 dead alien bodies, and at least four surviving aliens. Each injured alien beings were kept isolated, away from their companions. Each alien were kept alone, and not allowed to communicate to other aliens. They were kept hundreds of miles apart, deep inside different underground facilities.

By the end of year 1953 after repeated interviews with each alien, President Eisenhower knew a little more about little Greys, and the President knew the little Greys were not trustworthy. The military determined alien race is here to stay, and according to the interviewed Greys, the Greys are not visiting Earth, they have always been on this planet.

In 1953, there were 10 UFO disk 'crashes', 26 dead and 4 living aliens. Rumors that quickly circulated the entire nation state that the all the UFO crashes happened because the military shot them down.

During the 1950s, there were more alien flying objects that crashed, and each time the alien victims of the crashed objects were kept isolated. A few of the captured Greys decided to cooperate with the U.S. military, and provided advanced technology and advanced weaponry. The Greys also admitted they abduct the general public, and admit they were guilty of gross mutilation of both animal and humans. The studies of the project became known as Project Sigma, and were in the control of the American government groups, the CIA and NSA.

37

THE ALIENS DIDN'T "ARRIVE" - THEY'VE ALWAYS BEEN HERE

1. Ancient civilizations lived on Earth countless thousands of years before the reptilian race created the human race, according to Tom Castello. When the human race heard about the other civilizations hidden deep inside the caverns on Earth, humans named this ancient race "The Elder Race." This hidden race was an advanced civilization thousands of years before the human race was created. Most people today think the aliens arrived in 1947 – but the aliens didn't 'arrive' - they have always been here.

2. The ancient civilizations are smart enough not to let the humans know there was here. There are many unknown civilizations on Earth; however, they choose to avoid the hostile human race. Who can blame them? The human race frequently shoot anything in sight without thinking about the possible benefits of keeping a person, animal or alien alive. The human do not mind that they are called the most hostile creatures in this planet. Humans would rather kill first, without hesitation, and later they regret their decision. The human race assumes all life forms share their violent nature - "kill first, before

they can kill me." Humans assume the worse when they first encounter any life form.

3. The little Greys possess complex eyes, they have 41 separate lens in each eye, although they can see everything within one mile, their distant vision is not well focused or clear. They must be within ten feet of a person to clearly see a person. Although they see the human, their complex eyes see multiple copies of the terrified human. Each alien eye have 41seperate lens that can focus on different sections of the human body. They miss nothing when they look at a human. You might say their brain matches their eyes, and each item they see is stored isolated and separate from the other record.

4. Although they do have a problem with their ocular visual perception, the little Greys have other superior senses. They have the ability to "read minds" – that is not an accurate way of explain their ability; it would be more accurate to say they can pick up the human's mental thoughts via a wide 'broadcast' frequency. The human mind is similar to a broken radio, and the radio refuses to stay on the same station, but keeps scanning all the stations. The Greys do not like to touch minds with a human, simply because the human's chaotic thoughts are not acceptable for them.

5. Because the human mind constant changes and never focuses on the same subject more than a split second, visiting aliens assumed the human race are not intelligent enough to understand their communications. That is because most aliens communicate through a form of mental telepathy. When an alien attempts to touch a human's mental mind, they find total mental chaos.

6. The average human brain is similar to a confusing computer used by hundreds of programmers. Each programmer tossed the information anywhere in the hard drive, the data has no logic and the written information was crammed anywhere in that computer.

    A computer like that would be almost impossible to use, although all the required information is hidden inside in that hard drive. All the knowledge of the ages is listed inside that computer – if - you could find it. That is the way the human brain works. The human brain has no logic, no order, no form, just bits and pieces of information. If an alien attempted to read the mind of a human, the alien would assume the human is not intelligent. The human brain fails any attempt of organization or any form of linear thought. There are very few humans that attempt to control their thoughts. The more the controlled the human brain, the more successful and intelligent the human.

7. The average human allow their thoughts are undecipherable, totally wild and untamed. How could a very controlled telepathic alien understand the tumultuous uncontrolled thoughts of a human?

8. Imagine if you can, the confusion of an alien when the first encounter the human brain. They would first see the human thoughts perhaps a little chaotic, but still mostly calm and still, until the human sees the alien - then uncontrolled fear is present, and the undisciplined human thoughts are more like a wild mental hurricane, or the sudden unleashed water from a broken dam. To their detriment, the human mind thinks in constant changed cycles, and never attempts to focus or control their thoughts.

38

ARE YOU LIKE A FISH?

Albert Einstein once made an interesting comment. He said: "What does a fish know about the water in which he swims all his life?" That is a good question.

Maybe fish is not as smart of Mr. Einstein, but the fish know they have to stay alert most of the time, if they hope to survive. Like humans, fish require a few hours sleep every day, and different types of fish require more sleep. A few types of fish cat-nap a lot, other fish doze for a few hours at a time. Fish look for a safe place to sleep, but even the vast oceans, predators are everywhere. If a fish sleeps too much, a shark or other larger fish will eat him for his dinner.

Now think about your life – to survive you need oxygen, food, sleep and need to stay busy, at most of the time, except the time you require about 6 to 8 hours of sleep, isn't that just like the fish?

What do you use with your life? Do you choose to ignore your life? Do you just work, eat, sleep and do not attempt to investigate what you are, or why you are on planet Earth? What happens when you die? Do you search the answers about life after death? Do you have any idea where you will be in your next life? The average person doesn't bother to investigate anything, and certainly nothing esoteric.

Did it cross your mind that Einstein was trying to tell you something when he asked about that fish?

Or - - - have you tried to find any of these answers, but because it is a complex study, did you give up and forget about those perplexing questions? It is true that life can become complex sometimes, it has the good and the bad - but it all belongs to you.

It is your life to live - or waste it. Please, don't waste your life my friend, life is exciting when you really take time to find it! I love life – all of it - even the bad stuff, because it is the bad stuff that reminds you that you are really alive - and glad you can have a chance to improve your life.

Think my friend – really think - is more to life than a simple existence? Live your life, investigate your life, be something stronger and more an fish. Do something innovative, get out of your normal rut and really live!

39

THE ALIENS ARRIVE - WHAT DO YOU DO?

A few people want to make jokes about what may happen if the aliens visit somebody's house. They stop joking about it when it happens to them. For some reason those same people they stop laughing and they want somebody to explain what happened to them.

I am aware there are people that haven't experienced an alien encounter, they laugh about victims, because they do not believe alien visitation really happen. These types of people like to joke and laugh about UFOs and aliens. It is not funny when it happens to them.

Do you think you can joke your way out of alien invasion? My friend, it won't work my friend, the Greys do not understand human humor, the Greys without a sense of humor. The little Greys were born without any form of emotion. There is no emotion, no love, no hatred, no sympathy, no pity, and no humor in the Greys.

In reality, what would you really do if the aliens came in your home?

Would you try to hide from them?

How in the world can you try to hide from an alien that can hear your thoughts?

Maybe you flatten yourself on a wall and hope you look like a flower on the wall?

That idea never works; they see you and go straight to you.

Or maybe you try to get under the bed?

Or get in the closet and hide in the clothing? Nope. They know where you hid.

Perhaps you are you are the physical type - so you get a weapon and prepare yourself for a physical struggle?

Do you think you can overcome them? Think again, they look weak and spindly, but their strength is amazing! The first time you try to hit them, you might hit them, but faster than a thought more Greys arrive and overcome you with a ray and you can no longer move. Your weapon is worthless when a Grey sees any form of weapon.

Or have you already realized that no matter what you try, it doesn't work? Don't even think about a weapon, because they will make sure you can't move.

You can't hide from a Grey, they will mentally reach inside thoughts and reveal your hiding place in seconds. No matter what you want to do, the Greys will put you exactly where *they* want you to be. The Greys "hear" your thoughts and know exactly where you hide. You can't hide an item from the Greys either, the harder you try not to think about the item you hid, the faster they find it.

The best thing you should do is do nothing, and do not attempt to struggle with them. All you get is a bruise that you caused. Usually the Greys no longer try to convince people, they just render you paralyzed and you can only watch what they are doing and wonder what will happen to you.

So - do nothing - just watch and try to learn something helpful. I know it is difficult not to look at those aliens huge eyes, instead try looking at items in the Greys hands, or try to pay attention and look at the clothing the Grey is wearing. Maybe you can later sketch what you saw. Everyone knows exactly what the Greys look like, so try for to learn something new. Look if you noticed any strange equipment he may carry, or is they wear items on his belt. What does his shoes look like? Did you notice any insignia of any form?

If they transport you to a craft, pay attention and try to remember everything. I know you will be afraid - that is normal - but fight off your fear and look around. You will would be in a position to experience a once in a life time chance to see something no other human experienced. Try being really intelligent, and do something wise, and really pay attention to your surroundings, because with a little luck you may remember and supply helpful information.

I am aware the Greys are very intelligent, but they also seem to be humane. The Greys try hard to make sure you forget your alien experience for a reason - so you don't have to remember the fear you went through.

The last thing I want to mention is a biblical reference that may be helpful. Maybe not - but it may need everything. That reference comes from the Book of Revelations, the last book in the New Testament.

Revelation 7:3 - "Hurt not the earth, neither the sea, nor the trees, till we have sealed the servants of our God in their foreheads."

Is that what the implants are doing? Sealing certain human's fate for future reference? That specific reference continues the exact amount of people will be "sealed." Exactly what are they "sealing" inside?

40

THE STAR CHILD - A MISNOMER

"P.I.E." - The Physical, Intelligence and Emotional Mind Set of the So Called "Star Children": ("Star Children": also known as: "S.C.")

1. The term "Star Child" label is misleading and should be changed. The real "Star Children" are NOT from the stars, and they are not children, they were born on Earth, they have normal human parents just like every person. The individual mind set of each S.C. of unique; however there are certain physical differences too. These individuals are not adults with a child-like mind, they are intelligent people and some of them are highly gifted. To label these people as 'children of the stars' are not only insulting, misleading and erroneous. Certain writers promoted the term Star Child instead of taking time to consider more appropriate terms. Other terms to replace "Star Child" include "Changeling" "Missionary" "Guider" "Psi-Savant."

2. Author Brad Steiger claims 65% of the women are Star Children but only 35% of the men are Star Children. I disagree with those statistics, because in the actual studies, I found out the more females are willing to admit they are Star Children, but the men are not as more likely to

openly discuss these traits. Men tend to listen about the discussions of the Star Children, and they are quite interested, however, they are always comfortable talking about them. From childhood the human males are taught not openly share their emotions, I think if the real statistics were freely exposed, I believe the statistics were far more balanced - 50% female - 50% male.

3. All Star Children (male and female) have compelling eyes and possess a large amount of personal magnetism and almost all the Star Children have inner charisma, and smile more often than people that do not have charisma.

4. Between the decades between puberty to the menopause years, both certain genders tend to find they live with a lot of static electricity, and give off mild static shocks to anyone they touch. Both genders are sensitive to electricity and electromagnetic fields, however, with advancing mature life, the static electricity that cause the sensitivity eases off, and are less a chance to give off static electricity, and life becomes a bit more comfortable.

5. Not all the Star Children experience a lower body temperature than the average body temperatures, but several S.C. members have very lower or higher body temperatures, while maintaining healthy bodies.

6. Most Star Children experiences certain medical problems, including chronic sinusitis, pain in their back, pain their neck - or both, they also find the suffer from painful joints, and are prone to swelling in these painful areas. It is not unusual if the S.C. has an extra or transitional vertebra, the extra vertebra often grow in the lower lumbar area.

7. Sometimes at the end of the spine certain people are born with caudal addition. (short tail.) The S.C. are usually hypersensitive to high pitched sound, they are sensitive to brilliant lights, and uncomfortable around strong pungent odors. They also are adversely affected by high humidity.

41

DO YOU THINK YOU KNOW EVERYTHING ABOUT YOUR HOME?

Do you really know everything about home? I'll bet don't know basic things about you or your house or apartment.

The human race – everyone knows they are creatures of habit, and everyone thinks they know everything about their house and what is inside your walls.

You believe you know everything about yourself, no surprises there, right? Ok, since you know everything about yourself and your house or apartment, would you answer a few questions about your house?

When you stand in front your kitchen sink, what direction are you facing? North? West? South? East? Do you know the answer right away, or did it take it a few minutes to know the answer?

When you lay down to sleep, what direction does your pillow lay? (I hope you know your head should be on the north for the best sleep.)

Do you have any fruit trees in your yard? What is older, your house or the tree in your yard? How tall is your oldest tree? Do you know? Or would you have to offer a guess?

Let's try a different question, in your master bedroom – how many doors is in that the master bedroom? You are in that room every day, you should know the answer instantly, but have you ever counted the actual individual doors in that room?

How many total windows in your house or apartment?

Most houses or apartments have one or more halls, what about your place? Do you have at least one hall in your place, right? You walk through that hall every day, how wide is your hall? How many inches are across that hall? Or is your hall narrow, only three feet wide? What is on the east side of your hall? How long is that hall? When you enter that hall, what direction are you facing? How many total doors are in your main hall? Is there any carpet in your hall? How many rugs are in your house?

Most people know how many bedrooms, and how many bath rooms, but they have no idea how many windows in their house face south. Do you know the answer?

You live here, so how many trees are on your yard? If I knocked at your front door what direction would I be facing?

If I sat on your sofa, would I be facing east? No? What direction would I be facing?

My point in these questions is simple – I want you to think, really think, take time to look at everything in your house, you need to know at in everything about your environment.

Most people do not even know the most basic information about your house or apartment, such if someone asked "Does your front door face south?" The average person struggles to correctly answer that question. In your home do you have an attic or a basement? How many windows in your attic? How many windows face west? How many closets in your basement? Do you still know think you know everything about yourself or your house?

42

THE ORIGINAL ALIENS OF EARTH - POWERFUL ANGELS OF HEAVEN

THE ERELIM, THE VALIANT ONES:

The Erelim, The Valiant Ones, (these angels are sometimes known as Aralim,) are in position of very high power in the celestial hierarchy, and these angels rank third in power, and their title or caste can be identified as Thrones. The Erelim reside in the fourth heaven. However, there is a bit of debate on that fact - a few of the authorities on the angels and not agree on what dimension or heaven the Erelim reside, but at least it they narrow it down to the 3rd, 4th and 5th, a few other authorities suggest the Erelim rule all three heavens.

Erelim are brilliant beings, and according to legend, is composed as white fire, and there are supposed to be over 70,000 of those special angels at work on planet Earth, at all time. It is the Erelim is in charge of the grains, the grass, trees, and fruit trees too. If you are having a problem with your fruit tree or grass, I suggest you at least attempt to communicate with the Erelim and ask what you should do about it. Or you could try to pray to their boss, the archangel Michael.

THE CHALKYDRI:

Chalkydri are amazing creatures, these flying Archangels, they are linked with the Phoenixes and Seraphim; their caste is between the Cherubim and the Seraphim. Each Chalkydri possess 12 wings. Try to image beautiful creatures that grace lovely wings so large and powerful that reach from their head to the ground. Then imagine that each set of wings that they appear to be covered with sets of wings with functional wings that lift them from the ground with silent appendages and allow these humanoids to hover in place. According to the melodious legends, they sing beautiful songs when they approach their home planet or sun. According to ancient Egyptian legends, these beings creatures that look like a mixture of reptilian, humanoid and frightening they are something that cannot be visualized in the 3rd dimension, but still exist in 4th dimension. One or two of the books of Enoch mentions of the Chalkydri, and each time these beings are mention and connected with the Seraphim race. Enoch states the natural habitat of Chalkydri is the fourth heaven or fourth dimension.

These light beings - brilliant and glowing - may be humanoid in basic shape, but unlike humans, these beings are comfortable in the heat and light in the sun. Their home planet or the sun, also known as Sol, but to human race Sol is the Sun.

It is a sad fact but the human ear cannot hear their euphonious voices as they sing their songs, however, according to legend, their songs can be translated into bands of colors in the northern sky and the harmonious songs are seen as visualized and known as the Aurora Borealis.

Enoch states the natural habitat of Chalkydri is the fourth heaven or fourth dimension.

THE OFANIM:

Their name and title Auphanim or Ofanim means "Wheels," and these wheels are identified as the cycles of the Moon. They exercise dominion over the Moon, and it is the Ofanim that is the angel of the Wheel of the Moon, or this angel keeps the cycle of the Moon in motion. If you have a specific problem that includes the cycles of the Moon, I suggest you attempt to contact the Ofanim, because it is their position and they are in charge of the cycles of the Moon.

The author Enoch, states the Ofanim are powerful much more than simple are emissary angels. The Ofanim are known to be the highest caste of the Seraphim, or brilliant fiery beings. The Seraphim are from the caste of Thrones, are one of the highest rank of angelic power. According to the ancient legends, the Ofanim can be recognized as the "many eyed ones," and Enoch describes the Ofanim as a complex angel with 16 faces, 100 pairs of wings, and 8,466 eyes. These beings are the ones that actually carry out the orders of the commands of the Powers. (Powers are caste of angels, and higher in power than the Thrones.) It has been said the Ofanim are very large angels, their foot is too large to ever stand the small Earth. These angels must change their shape and take the shape of an Earthly animal to walk on Earth; he usually chooses to resemble a black and white horse to be on Earth.

You can find the Ofanim mentioned in the Sixth and Seventh Books of Moses, and in the third book of Enoch. Like many angels, their names identify them as a specific being, but at the same time, their names indicate they are more than one being, but a group of a type of beings.

If you study the work of Ezekiel, you read that Ofanim is more than is a specific being, at least in one incarnation the being Ofanim is identified as the archangel Sandalphon - the twin brother of Metatron. They are one of a few authorities identify the Ofanim (sometimes called Auphanim) as a caste of angels higher than the rank of Seraphim, but most authorities rank them as sixth is position in power. The natural habitat of the Ofanim is in the fourth dimension or fourth heaven.

THE MESSIAH:

The Messiah, he is equated as Christ, Metratron, and Savior and also called as Jesus Christ, Son of The Living God. The Messiah is designated as a cherub and guardian angel of Eden. (The famed Garden of Eden.) As a Cherub, the Messiah is always seen with armed with a flaming sword in his hand. In legendary stories, he is similar to Michael, the Warrior of Heaven.

As the title of Head of Days, (aka: End of Days) he sits at the right hand of God, and Resides in the Ultimate First Heaven. He is known as El Soph, (El Soph means The Wise) the wise emanations from the mystical Right Side of Shemhamphorae. The Messiah sits at the head of the Great Council, and is analogous to the Soter, (the Ruling Angels) Angel of the Lord, the Word, or the Logos. He is also known as the King of the Angels. As he all knowing Angel of the Lord, the Messiah also is found in the female aspect of the Ultimate God and is known as the Shekinah, and sometimes known as Metrona, the female manifestation of God in Mankind. She is also known as the only Bride of the Lord, or indwelling manifestation of God.

43

TWISTED ATOMS - ANSWERS FOR QUESTIONS

QUESTION: Cherry, Growing multi-species beings, blood formulas and human parts in vats sounds like a bad plot to a science fiction movie. The doctors and scientists of the world claim you can't mix the species. The concepts mentioned in the Dulce Papers sounds farfetched. Could you provide information that the average surface world reader could understand about similar things?

ANSWER: The doctors and scientists on the surface world may say that, but underground, away from the prying eyes of ethics boards, they do grow trans-genus beings.

There is a lot of written material available at libraries. One of the best sources is an easy to read book published back in 1969, by Prentice-Hall International, with the title of "The Second Genesis, the Coming Control of Life," written by Albert Rosenfelt.

In this book, they discuss "… animals that may be especially bred to supply genetically reliable organs for people." -- and "…the use of fetal or embryonic material from which adult sized organs and tissues may be grown..."

Also he discusses the fact that embryonic tissue has no immunological activity, therefore it cannot provoke the defense mechanism in the recipient. It will join the body not as a foreign antigen, but as a natural protein. He further discusses solitary generation, commonly called virgin birth, but also known as parthenogenesis.

With one virgin birth in 1.6 million births average on the surface of the world, in Dulce that rate is reversed. Occasionally, a normally born human infant is born in the hospital wards on the Seventh Level. Parthenogenesis is the method used to grow type two beings.

The common transsexual surgery that is popular on the surface world began inside the labs of the Dulce Base. Men became women on a whim in the Seventh Level labs, and with the Fourth Level technology, the brain washing the "eager desire to become a woman" and that poor man firmly believes he always wanted to be a woman. No one could convince him to believe the truth.

All things are twisted At Dulce Base.

A quote by Dr. Ralph W. Gerard (in The Second Genesis) put in his now classic statement:

"There can be no twisted thought without a twisted molecule."

That statement most has originated at the labs at Dulce Base.

44

THE TRUTH ABOUT AREA 51
AND THE NEVADA TEST SITE

Area 51. In Nevada Test Site is supposed to be a small square piece of land in Nevada, but it happens to be sitting in a key section of land sitting in of a middle of Nevada. You should know that special piece of land – The Nevada Test Site - covers <u>81 percent</u> if the entire state. The Nevada Test Site much larger than quite a few U.S. states. According to a land summary by the state of Nevada in 2015, the government owns 58,226,015.6 acres of Nevada of the approximately 70,000,000 total acres in Nevada. Meaning that out of 70,000,000 acres of land available in Nevada only 11,773,985 is available to the general public.

Area 51 was also referred to as Groom Lake. (Area 51 is the name of the dry lake in that area.)

I suspect Paradise Ranch was a playful name and a way to consider new employees to accept a job at his very remote place, and to convince the workers to continue working any miles from civilization. Area 51 is a very isolated base, and a lot of it remains underground. The name Watertown the original and official name of the Nevada Test Site back in 1956. The average workers prefer call this facility 'Dreamland'.

Area 51's ended up with the nickname "DREAMLAND" after it became the common name be all the workers. The area Dreamland got that name from an Edgar Allan Poe poem has the same name. The readers of Poe's poem warns the readers to be careful of "the traveler, traveling through it, may not-dare not openly view it; Never its mysteries are exposed, to the weak human eye unclosed." That is about the way it is in Area 51 too.

The first known common use Area 51, it sort of started in that area because way back in was the 1941 they at started with a construction for needed auxiliary airfield for the West Coast Air Corps Training Center, based at Las Vegas Air Field. It became known as the Indian Springs Airfield Auxiliary, No. 1, and it had only two dirt 5000' runways.

Under President Dwight Eisenhower, the Groom Lake facility was put in the hands of the CIA for Project Aquatone, for the development of the Lockheed U-2 reconnaissance aircraft in April 1955.

This very strange fortress-type facility and surrounding grounds are strictly off-limits. A person is based to wonder what secrets they keep hidden inside this well guarded place. There remain countless rumors, but the secrets remain hidden from the public. A lot of photos that have escaped, one way or another, photos of odd craft doing fascinating maneuvers over these secret buildings. Too, pictures and video tapes have been smuggled from inside have become mythic stories. Some of these smuggled photos and papers that show both living or dead aliens, as well as several odd spacecraft of unexplained and futuristic design. Nevertheless the government still denies these claims.

When they first opened in Area 51, the only type of entertainment was one lonesome tennis court made of cement, a little bowling alley. Back then, there was no television because there were no TV relay towers. There were only radio signals that made through the surrounding mountains, and mostly in the late evening.

They claim that the Area 51 mess hall sometimes served oysters and even lobsters specially flew to the facility from California. Also claim that once a week, the meal was potatoes and steak.

Several people believe there must be a thin slice of truth to the conspiracy theory that the moon landing was staged at Area 51. Visitors have seen various space equipment, including more than one land-rovers and their bulky life support systems. It has been said the astronauts themselves tested the Lunar material equipment at the near-by nuclear testing grounds.

Area 51 when the low economy hit the nation, Area 51 was not spared. They say more than 1600 to 2000 employees working at the military facility involved at least a dozen defense contractors, as over of 2000 civilian workers were laid off.

After an increase in UFO sightings in 1952, the CIA agreed that "there is a remote possibility that they may be interplanetary aircraft," and that it was necessary for them to investigate each sighting mentioned.

90% of reported UFO sightings could be easily ignored, but there is another 10% sightings from "a number of incredible reports from credible observers."

#More than half of all UFO reports from the mid to late 1950s and continued throughout the 1960s were considered by manned reconnaissance flights (such as U-2) over the USA skies, and with all these sightings originated from Area 51.

Recently a poll stated that over 73%+ of Americans believe that UFOs are real.

45

THREE TIMES THEY DESTROYED EARTH

I love knowledge, however there is a down side - it hurts when you find the truth and you discover all of your comfortable cozy world of easy to swallow lies that you have been hearing about all your life were not the truth at all.

That tends to make your false images crumble around you, with nothing to lean on, for comfort.

One of the problems is religion beliefs. The first time God got tired when humans tried to get smart and create pitiful hybrid creatures and giants on Earth. (Genesis 6: 4-7) Back then, the hybrid world was still in the making… and God didn't like it one bit. The second time God stopped the men to reach God's craft, to God changed their languages so no one could understand each other. God he 'confounded' their language so people couldn't understand each other at all, and scattered the bad guys them all over the world in one heart beat. (Genesis 11: 1 – 9) That story includes the infamous Tower of Babel, and that was the third time God really get really angry.

I can't blame God - he gave them a clear list of rules - even gave it a catchy name - The Ten Commandments - and what did the human race do? They ignored the list, and tried to find a way to sneak into God's Kingdom. Let's face it, the humans are not exactly known for their intelligence, that's for sure.

Who would be stupid enough to think God wouldn't notice a whoopee-do tower being built right under God's nose? {sigh, humans sometimes are far from intelligent.}

**The First Time God planned to destroy mankind.

The created a world-wide flood. (The story of Noah and his ark. (Genesis 6: 7-22. Chapter 7, Chapter 8, Chapter 9: 1-17. The story of Noah and the Great Flood.)

The First Time God decided to destroy any of his creation was when he decided he didn't like it when Adam and Eve touched the forbidden fruit. God decided to be angry of Adam and Eve, and kicked them out of the Garden of Eden.

The scene is calm, just a male and a female shared some fruit, however this scene was the first time when Eve and the Serpent man ate Forbidden Fruit, and they deep inside the Garden of Eden.

Right from the beginning the human race were weak creatures and couldn't handle temptation. The Serpent in the Garden of Eden was considered evil, because he went out of his way to tempted Adam and Eve, and this innocent couple they were too naïve and weak to follow the rules God warned them about them. But then again, of God wanted Adam and Eve to be perfect, he could have created them that way.

God told Adam and Eve not to touch those trees, and never eat the fruit of those two trees - but right away the first thing they wanted to do was find out they were missing, so the Serpent man found it easy to tempted Eve, and he quickly told her to try the forbidden fruit it wouldn't hurt her. Eve liked the forbidden fruit so she tempted Adam ate the forbidden fruit too, and as history knows, the Serpent Man, Adam and Eve got caught breaking a rule.

Right away Adam whined to God and blamed Eve and Serpent because Adam was not man enough to admit he ate the Forbidden fruit. I guess Adam forgot that God told Adam not to touch the "Two Special Trees" but the first man quickly blamed the Serpent Man and Eve, and Adam complained that Eve tempted him. How soon the the weak humans forgot one little rule, "Don't Eat Any of My Special Trees." Two rules, and it was too much temptation to handle. That little rule was clearly stated as soon as Adam and Eve entered the Garden, so both knew about those Trees. He heard it from Adam. The Serpent Man confirmed the Two Trees were special and made sure Eve know the rules. The Serpent Man told Eve it was OK to eat the Forbidden Fruit, and they wouldn't die for eating from special fruit. It worried her, but she ate the fruit anyway. What a weak female.

So how come the serpent is considered "evil" but Adam and Eve were just "misunderstood innocent babes"? That's not fair that the serpent gets all the blame when Adam and Eve also KNEW the rules and decided to eat the forbidden fruit anyway. Adam and Eve were almost of the guilty as guilty as the Serpent. But the Serpent Man knew about of it for a long time, and knew she wouldn't die from eating the special fruit – at least she stayed in Eden, That was the reason God kicked them out of Eden, and after they ate the fruit, their bodies started to change. They were no longer pure spiritual beings, the broke the rule, and so they had to leave Eden.

They knew the rules, so did the serpent - so all three of them knew they went out of their way to break the rules. They all knew were not supposed to touch those trees. (Genesis 3:1-6) But temptations are strong, and mankind is weak.

I'll bet on that day that God regretted that big mistake and knew he should have never creating the human gardener or his other co-gardeners and wanted to destroy them all. However, who could blame Adam and Eve, knowing what the fruit of those two trees would make anyone intelligent, and the other tree would make a human immortal. That would be one really big temptation.

Any way you read it, the Good Book states that God makes mistakes, and not only he makes mistakes, He freely admits it, and regrets it. He clearly admitted he regrets making the human race. (Genesis 6:6) He decided he didn't want these weak human in his Garden, so he banned them from the Garden of Eden. God put them in a tunnel and told them to leave the area. When they finished the long walk in that tunnel, they found out they were on the outer surface of planet Earth.

[I admit I expect a few harsh notes about that comment, but it is written in the ancient books - all the ancient state God said it, so, who am I to correct a God? He is a God, and I'm just a writer.]

**The Second time God decided to destroy the mankind.

The second time God decided mankind wasn't the worth the bother was when he had to with face flood waters to destroy all mankind from planet Earth. He decided to forget the human race and flood the Earth with water and kill off his created evil creation. But he found one man and his family worth the going through the problems. God talked to Noah, and the Lord created papers that today we would consider a blueprint and with these plans he provided guidance helped Noah understand the need to create the Ark in order to save a few of the human race, at least the few humans happened to be Noah and his family – that family alone, would survive.

God has quite a temper and when he gets angry, everybody on Earth suffers. But being a nice guy sometimes, God decided to spare Noah, his wife and three their adult sons and his son's wives. God taught Noah and his sons how to build a huge ship. The neighbors were fascinated when Noah and his sons started building the Ark. They asked Noah why he is building a ship. Noah explained that he expected it to start raining and the rain would flood the entire world.

The neighbors laughed. The neighbors laughed simply because at that time, no one had ever experienced rain. It had never rained and the people had no idea what it meant to have water fall from the sky. At that time, the entire earth was covered by thick clouds, sort of like the known clouds that cover planet Venus. No sooner had Noah finished the Ark, and the animals were safely inside the Ark, the family moved into the huge ship… and then the rain started. The neighbors were afraid, and they pounded on the side of the ship, begging Noah to let them in - but following Gods orders, no one was allowed to enter the ship after it started to rain. The rest of the story is history......

**Third Time God decided to destroy mankind:

The third time God got tired of the constant trouble from planet Earth. The evil human race tried to build a tower to reach God's Kingdom, and believe me, they, they created an amazing tower! That huge tower would touch the Kingdom of God that was supposed to be in the sky at that time. All the builders and all the brightest men of that era stayed in the same area, they all spoke the same language. Because there was only one language, everywhere, and that language was common all over the world. The busy builders well on the way of reaching God's Kingdom via the Tower of Babel, until God noticed the men were trying to reach his Kingdom God didn't like that one bit.

So, God and his angels decided to physically pick up the key men and relocated them to another place on the Earth. At the same time, he "confounded" the languages, and made sure the people could not understand each other. Instead of having one common language, suddenly every in different area's spoke a different language. The builders could no longer understand the words of the other builders, they were strangers in a different language, and each builder was lost and could no longer attempt to build any tower - certainly not the original Tower.

Because of the loss of communication and they could no longer understand each other, the original Tower became the Tower of Babel, they called that name because it sounded as everyone was babbling and no one knew what the others saying clearly.

God won that battle too. He always does - but the human race keeps trying.

46

I WITNESSED A HUGE TRIANGLE OVER LAS VEGAS, NEVADA

Today I witnessed a very large triangle craft in the skies over Las Vegas/ Henderson, Nevada. It was so large that first I didn't see it at all. I only saw two small white clouds near over Mt. Charleston area. But when I came out of the post office I noticed a bluish white huge triangle shape over Black Mountain but then the lines continue across Las Vegas Valley. It was so large I couldn't believe it. I believe that was my problem - I kept me refusing to believe a craft that large could be flying over a large city and but no one seemed to see it but me.

I am sure a few other people saw it, but who? It was about 1:05pm this afternoon over Henderson, Nevada. (19 May 2016) The triangle was the color of the sky - and high above the Las Vegas Valley. It was higher than the jets that normally fly across Las Vegas every two minutes 24 hours a day. The size is more than I can guess - clearly triangle in shape, it traveled slowly towards north. I can only guess the size as maybe a couple hundred miles wide at each line, and appears almost as half that height. I saw no windows or other features, but near the center there was a darker circular or deeper shadow. That darker shadow in the middle was not a perfect circle - more like a "sort of circular shape." - Bill and I once witnessed a large triangle at night while visiting his cousin in Hiko Nevada. (North of Las Vegas, NV) That dark triangle blocked out our view of the stars that night - we thought was the largest triangle we had ever witnessed, but this triangle in the sky today is clearly larger, and I expected to see it mentioned on the evening news tonight, but no mention of it at all.

… FOLLOWED BY ANOTHER TRIANGLE EVENT …

ONCE UPON A NEVADA NIGHT

One warm night years ago, we visited Bill's cousin Desma and her hubby in tiny desert town of Hiko, Nevada, my husband, Bill, and I witnessed a huge silent black triangle in the star-filled sky.

The totally black triangle shaped craft very moved slowly across the sky. Not a single sound broke the utter silence as the buoyant three-sided vessel moved slowly in the dark sky, until it positioned it's self directly over us.

There is only one word that seems to match the size of this airship - immense - unless you try massive, gigantic or colossal - but no matter what term you use, you need a word to indicate incredible size. Bill called the triangle a "monster size mother-ship."

I believe Bill was correct, that giant triangle was a mother-ship. The size is incredible, totally silent, and outstandingly slow in moving and yet in some way I can't remain above us, that immense craft and did not fall from the sky. There is nothing made by human hands that that can stay in the sky, silent, slowing inching across the sky. This mysterious black triangle was so large it covers the entire valley, from horizon to horizon.

That natural dark night seemed to be just a black sky was filled with countless brilliant twinkling stars, because we were over hundred and fifty miles north from the Las Vegas with its bright city lights. That beautiful night we appreciated the quiet night, the radiant sparkling stars the twinkled above us, and we were enjoying the view of a breathtaking night scene. We were enjoying the beautiful night black sky, and slowly Bill and I noticed the sparkling stars were being blocked by something in the sky. The front of the immense craft had three lights, red in color, and we realized the front of the object was shaped like a triangle, and the front is the leading pointed front.

Hiko, NV is a tiny town many miles north of Las Vegas, with only a few determined ranchers and their hired hands to manage the cattle and horses on the ranches in that area. Too, there might be a little store or two a few miles ago from Bill's cousin's home, but they closed hours ago, so all the night sky was dark and the stars appeared brilliant in the crisp cool air.

That is why it was quite a surprise when we started to notice the star-filled night sky was being blocked by a colossus triangle. It was no challenge to see the three red lights in the front of the craft, and we watched in amazement when this noiseless silent craft blocked our view of the stars.

It was not just a few stars were covered, but the complete view - from one horizon to the other horizon were blotted out until all the stars in the sky were blocked by this floating craft and the entire the only view we could see was the dark giant triangle above us.

Without a sound this silent triangle glided past us until the entire valley, from horizon to horizon, was covered by this immense craft. We watched in awe as it moved slowly northwest. After a few minutes after it started, we started seeing stars again, we clearly see the triangle shape against the background of stars. All this time, this huge dark flying triangle was so low in the sky we could a certain pressure as the craft as it floated over us.

This night is something I'll never forget, Bill and I felt the pressure in the air as it silently floated above us, and that night, in that black silence, if we needed to say something, we felt the urgent need to whisper quietly in hushed tones when they flew above us.

Hiko, Nevada is east of the edge of the Nevada Test Site, and only a few miles away from the famed Area 51 or Dreamland in central Nevada.

*** My additional comment: These black giant triangles are far from the average "regular" flying triangles in the sky, they have been around for many decades. Personally I've seen for decades, at least I saw my flying triangle was decades with I was around ten years old in Nevada, oddly enough about not far from the place I saw this immense triangle. But the gigantic triangles that blocks the sky leaves a person's mind staggered, wondering how can any this huge, this silent, and this slow can remain in the sky. Bill (my late hubby) was convinced the triangle we witnessed was "at least two miles across" and as "barely above the tall cotton trees" (quoted Bill's suggested size, I agree, it may be larger than that. Other witnesses in different locations and different times claimed the huge triangle was over 5 miles.) [One pilot saw a huge triangle from an international super-jet over the Pacific Ocean.]

The triangle Bill and I saw was not just wide, but had a rounded edges, and very high. Bill thought it might be as "tall as a ten story building, or more." Bill was not the type to get carried away with sizes, and was usually accurate is size almost anything. He was an educated man, (college) and was the top crew leader for the City of Las Vegas for 22 years, if he thought it was two miles wide and as tall as a ten story building, you can be sure he was accurate.

47

OCCULTED TRIGGER WORDS

Mysterious, arcane, inexplicable, enigmatic, clandestine, hermetic, secret, sphinxian, cabalistic, impenetrable, occult, unfathomable, and mystical – all your life you have read books and occasionally you stumble across words with similar meanings. Do any of these terms bother you? Or you simply read on and quickly put those terms out of your mind. No one likes to admit certain words triggers a personal reaction, so you read on and ignore the trigger words. A few words generate fear in your mind, and you don't want to read that word because that word triggers an instant reaction in your mind.

Let's think seriously consider those words, everyone is different and my trigger words may not be the same as yours. A few bold folks refuse to admit the mere mention of a word frightens them. They would never admit they fear a word, but the fact is a certain word does generate fear in their mind.

What is your trigger word? It is a term that starts a chain reaction. It can be a common word such as "evil?" Although the word "evil" is a common, some people don't like to think what the word means. Do you shudder at the mere at the term "unholy" and stop reading an article because it is considered "evil" if it is different from the common approach to religious study?

On the other hand, is your trigger word a little more esoteric? Perhaps your trigger word requires a more serious word such as "troglodyte?" (That word summons the thought of a real cave man, or a primitive violent man living in the tunnels underground.)

Common words that generate a personal reaction may be something may be a common term, like "troll" "nightmare" "horror" "murder" – with a few people shudder at the mere thought of being called a "coward."

Or maybe your trigger word is the common term "occult." Although there are many terms people personally fear one of the most common words, is the everyday term of "occult."

Many people fear that word, not only the word 'occult' but also anything hidden, such as the unknown. Remember the brief list I posted a few paragraphs ago? The list started as mysterious, arcane, inexplicable, hermetic, enigmatic, impenetrable, unfathomable, cabalistic, sphinxian and mystical – but in reality, they all have the same basic meaning and that meaning is "occult." Do people fear the actual word occult? Or is it just that the terms occult is something you can't quickly grasp? Would people fear the mere term occult as if the mere thought of that word would cause something unpleasant. Or is it true that there may be well-hidden branch of knowledge and only a few brave souls managed to master that wisdom?

The word "occult" to you does it simply mean "something hidden" or is it possible it have a deeper esoteric meaning to you? When you hear the word "occult" - does your mind cringe from some sinister meaning that leaves you uncomfortable and not willing to discuss the word?

When you hear the discussion of the occult – do you instantly back off? Or do you join the conversation? There are many ways to use the term occult – the word is possible it can be used to discuss forbidden arcane wisdom, but then the term 'occult' could be discussed astronomy and what happens when a planet is hidden from view by a larger planet. It is a common term in astronomy, and there is nothing esoteric about it.

The word it's self is just a word, and no one should fear using any word, unless of course, the term is crude and not acceptable for all family members, such as curse words or crude slang words. No one should use those unpleasant terms. If you must apologize for a word you use, you should never use them in the first place.

The fear of the occult is ancient – the fear of the occult began back in the times when very few people were educated. The people that did have an education, made sure no one knew the facts regarding religion. They wanted the public to depend on them for their religious information. That way, the public must rely on the priests, rabbis, preachers or other educated people to get the basic facts about the esoteric or arcane knowledge found in religions.

The priests made sure the public heard there is a dangerous group that possesses hidden wisdom, and with that hidden wisdom, the evil possessors of ancient hidden knowledge can control the world.

In today's society, no one should hesitate to educate themselves on occulted subjects. We no longer live in the dark ages, and no one person should possess all the knowledge and the public shouldn't depend on educated priests, rabbis and preachers for their religious wisdom. We all are intelligent, we all are educated, knowledge is everywhere, and you can find all the hidden wisdom on a few clicks of a few buttons on a computer keyboard. No one should fear the occult, if you are in doubt, educate yourself and in educating yourself, you find freedom.

48

THE STORY OF THE JINN, DJINN, JINNI OR GENIE

The Genie - the mere thought of the Jinni and the incredible powers they possess are the substance dreams are made of, but those dreams usually turn into nightmares.

Or perhaps you didn't know that Genie was created more than 2000 years before the human race? Could it be that you didn't know that originally the Jinn were a caste of angels more powerful than the archangels? The Genie once ruled the heavens. The powerful Jinn were also called the Djinn, Jinni and Genie. The Jinni or Genie is supernatural beings with powers that are far beyond the grasp of the feeble mind of the human race.

The Genie is also called the Jinn. The Genies (Jinn) are magical beings, and historically have always *appear* to be friendly towards humans, but in reality they are hostile. Legend have it that Genies grant three wishes to any human - but in return they expect one full day of living inside the body of the human.

That sounded great to the human race, all they had to let a generous magical being borrow your body for 24 hours and any three wishes you wanted will come true. What could be better? The humans usually quickly agree, thinking of all the gemstones, and all the stacks of gold, all the land they will soon own.

But the Genies do not play fair.

One of the favorite dirty trick of the Genies is they grant the wishes, but as soon as they are inside the human body, they become hostile and violent and turn the human body into a violent murderer. Since the Genie only have one day, they spend one day doing all the horrible things they wanted to do to a human - they kill and rape freely, knowing the Genie will walk away - free - and the human will pay for the crimes. The human will never enjoy the riches the Genie promised. Yes - the human will own all the riches they wanted, but in prison for life they can't enjoy those riches.

You may wonder why they would do such a horrid dirty trick to unsuspecting but greedy human. There is always a reason when things wrong, and is the same with the Genie.

Are you aware that at one time Jehovah expected the angels and the Genie worship the lowly original human race? (That was 2000 years before they created the current human race and according to the ancient scrolls; the 'original human race' was a very different advanced race of humanoids and the angels & Genie refused to bow to the advanced humans. Maybe that is why the 'original human race' were quickly destroyed that race and created Adamic race?)

It is well known Jehovah has a temper and as soon as the Archangels and the Genie refused to worship God's newest creation, He was very angry.

With Jehovah's tempers flaring there was a conflict in the celestial levels in space. The minute the Genie refused to worship a lower caste of life form, where was instant war in heaven. The Genie lost the battle. Jehovah caste the Genie out of the group, and forced the Genie to live in a violent planet the outer rim of the galaxy.

Not one intelligent race wanted to stay in a prison world that planet was in constant motion from earthquakes, volcanoes and storms, in other words, that planet is very unstable. Nevertheless, Jehovah won the conflict and he sentenced the Genie to exist in this hostile unbalanced planet.

Perhaps you have figured out that the planet the Genie was sent to was Planet Earth.

After thousands of years of living under hostile conditions, the living beings on that planet turned anger and hostile too. I am sure it was not be pleasant to live in a world that is in constant motion with earthquakes, fierce storms, intense hot liquid lava poured out some of the mountains - the human race were created on to this planet too, and to see if a short living life form could survive on a hostile world. They survive, but the once gentle humans too, turned violent.

Try to imagine how difficult it must have been for these high caste angels to be sentenced to such a primitive world. After thousands of centuries of living in a violent hostile world, it shouldn't be a shock to discover some of the Genie became hostile too.

Currently, the human race is barely aware of the Genie, and considers them mere legends or myths. In today's society, if they consider them at all - the human race considers the Genie anything, it would be unpleasant demons.

49

THE BODY OF THE GREYS

Think about the Greys this way - most of the animals on Earth have the same basic type anatomy as the human race; in other words, animals have red blood system of veins, teeth and claws, they have organs - all animals have a heart, liver, a stomach, intestines, kidneys a brain and other vital organs, as well as a skeletal body, and like the human race, the animals have a specific gender, male or female, as well as an excellent muscular system encased in skin and fur or hair, very much like the human race.

However, inside the alien Greys body, inside their gray colored bodies, their anatomy is very different from the animal. They do not have a digestion system, and they do not possess intestines. They do not require food to replenish their strength. However they do require to certain items to keep those bodies, mostly a type of liquid or formula to sustain the needed liquids, enzymes and similar ingredients.

Their system is beyond belief.

They do have a blood system, but it is not like the human or animal red blood, their blood is a yellowish/greenish liquid. They have a very quiet pair of sort of heart/pumps, but those odd hearts are not used the way a human or animal. Instead, those 'pumps' are active and for cooling the brain, not to pump, not to distribute blood in the body. The yellowish liquid is not kept in veins, but perhaps in four short 'veins' in the upper body and goes directly to the brain.

The Grey's body is NOT similar to the human body.

You may say their body is more like the body of a sponge, than an animal. The most of the small Greys do not possess a specific gender, they are without gender, although, several of the larger Greys do possess a gender.

It is worth mentioning that the body of the Greys, and they do not possess regular bones in their body, but they do have cartilage in several places in their body, including their skull, shoulders, a thick collarbone type frame that serves as a chest. Too, the same cartilage is used for parts of their feet and hands. There are two types of hands, one type has three digits and opposing thumb, and the other hands have four equal length fingers with suction-type digits with no thumb. The feet too differ too. One has three toes, the other possess two long toes, uses for balance in walking and to grasp around a branch or similar item. Both life forms have noticeable webbing between the digits.

Their bodies are cooler than the human body. They do not usually react to heat or cold, although the temperatures drop to frozen levels, their bodily reactions seems to be slower. The eyes of the Greys are not made for brilliant lights, such as sunlight. Their eyes are sensitive and require two protective shields. One to protect the delicate sensitive very thin eyelids, the other to shield the eyes against ultraviolet found in sunlight, that damages certain parts of their cones and rods in the eyes. The human race also shields their eyes from UV, (ultraviolet) and wears sunglasses.

There have been so many fraudulent claims, some writers claim they have bodies like humans, other writers claim the bodies of the aliens are 100% robots. There information stated in this report is as accurate as possible, and will correct any known mistake. I prefer to tell the truth because this information is real and it is vital that the public knows the real facts.

50

THE WORDS OF MANKIND – A POEM

Some of us were born with an unstoppable nature,

We refuse to give up our need to

Share our words of wisdom,

It doesn't matter if we are female or male,

We find a way to communicate.

If we can't fly, we drive,

If we can't drive, we walk,

If we can't walk, we talk,

If we can't talk, we write,

If we can't write, we read,

And share the wise words we like,

With family, with friends, with strangers.

One way or another we find a way,

To reach out and help others,

To give our time,

Our thoughts, our needs and finally,

We share our joys, our hopes, our love,

Because are not the words of mankind both our past and our future?

51

THE NAME IS "I AM"

I suggest you be very careful each time you open your mouth and start talking, my friend. There is a couple words you should avoid them, if you could. Be careful what you say - because a couple of the common words cause constant trouble - if you use them the wrong way.

The two words to avoid is "I am" - two tiny words, but did you know that those words are not yours to use?

Did you ever hear of the Ten Commandments? They are explained in the bible. (Exodus 20)

They are rules or commandments for all humans - and one of those commandments is a big one, because it claims: "Thou shalt not take the name of the Lord in vain." Look at those words closely.

(The dictionary says to use a word "in vain" means don't use it lightly, or to don't use the words for no reason.)

It doesn't say don't talk, or don't talk about god, instead it says do not use the NAME of the Lord for trivial reasons.

So what is the Lord's name? The bible clearly states that the Lord's name is "I am."

In the Holy Bible in book Exodus 3:14, Moses asked God his name. God clearly answers Moses, and tells him his name, and he states his name is "I am, that I am".

(If you asked me, "who are you? What is your name?" and I responded: "Cherry, THAT Cherry.")

The commandment is do not use the term "I am" lightly. God said "don't use my name in vain" because when you use his name, it becomes a command and all the powers above always uses a command from God promptly. Have a valid reason when you use the words "I am" for reason.

So ~ every time you say "I am broke" or "I am a poor man" you are asking the Powers Above to make sure you remain broke and poor. Don't say those words, instead be positive, and say "I am happy" or "I am wealthy" - every time you say "I am wealthy" you are reminding the Powers Above to send wealth to you, and it WILL happen.

No matter what you do, never say "I am ill" because it is a command from god to be sick. Think I am mistaken? You better think again.

For example, although history the ancient world leaders, such as royalty (kings, queens, etc) knew that rule - they never, never used the "I am" in vain, instead they used a plural terms. They did not say "I am ill" - instead they always said "we are ill" they knew the God Within commanded they not use the name of the Lord in vain.

Every time you say "I am ...." you are using the words 'in vain' because you are commanding the Power Above to manifest the terms you command. It is a fact, if you want to command power; you better know the correct way to command.

Be careful with the words "I am" - and remember the wise ones throughout history always stated "thoughts are things, and when you think it, that thought goes out and tried to make it happen." THINK about those words - thoughts are things - ALL words are thoughts. Before you utter those words to think about them, maybe not consciously, but you always think before you speak.

Be careful when you say "I am.....", and think carefully before you say something anything. Use positive words like "I am happy" "I am wealthy" (those words positive commands, and if you use them often, it will be true) and don't even *think* words about sickness, poverty or sadness.

Always think carefully before you speak.

52

WHAT IS THE SPEED OF DARK?

Don't laugh - it is a legitimate question and deserves an answer. All advances in science started with a silly question" - it was considered "silly" until someone answered that question with a fact. Everybody knows that.

Years ago, I wrote a letter and was published in Fate Magazine in early 1993. That letter generated a ton of letters from all over the world.

My letter in Fate was about the question I formed and wanted a serious reply - my question was "What is the Speed of Dark?" Like I pointed out in my letter everybody knows the speed of light - it something that everyone learns in school - but nobody teaches us the speed of darkness. I wanted to know if there is a way to judge the speed of darkness *without* comparing it to the speed of light - but most comments claimed that 'darkness is the absence of light' but that does NOT answer my question. (I KNEW that, but I want a 'real' answer.)

If I ask what is the speed of light about a gazillion people would correctly answer that question in a heartbeat. But NO one can answer what is the speed of dark. If there is answer to the 'speed of light' question - (and we all know that answer) then there is an answer to my speed of dark question. It is the same question in reverse, so it is a legitimate question. (if you ever studied science you know that is true.)

So I am asking you - in your opinion, what is the speed of darkness? Is there a way to judge the speed of darkness WITHOUT using light as the standard?

(Side Note: the first few lines of Genesis in the holy bible - it says God was in the darkness - he WAS in the darkness - and then he created light. I hope at least a few readers will understand what that means.)

Since that letter to Fate Magazine, I have found out my letter generated a lot of interest. I found many articles about the speed of dark, and at least a novel with the title as same words.

53

INTELLIGENT FORCES
BEHIND THE RACES

Did you ever think about the intelligent forces that may be behind the UFO phenomena?

Did you ever think that perhaps ALL of those forces came from one singular force?

Think about it – Greys, Reptons, Sasquatch, Leprechauns, Ufonauts, Nessie, even the Jinn and other evil demons – are they all generated by the SAME one driving force?

What if all that driving force came from they are the same source?

So the ultimate thought is *who* is the Controlling Force behind them?

Who - or what - is behind that force? Is that force good or evil?

(If we don't know that drives a force, there is no way anyone could list it as evil force or a good force.)

Could it be the driving force behind the UFOs or Extraterrestrial could be the same force the human race calls God?

Or - are the Ultra-terrestrials or Extraterrestrials the same force the human race call as the Devil or Satan?

Are they connected? Are they the same force? Are they created by the same God? Are the little Greys, the Leprechauns and Sasquatch blood cousins?

I don't know the answer to these questions, but I hope the near future someone will provide and answer.

54

TESTING THE SOILS – IS IT
A WILD CONCEPT?

How many of you remember the first few space efforts back in the early 1960s? Way back in the 1960s, no one knew if a human could survive a ride into outer space, and return. Remember the fear the scientist went through? The scientists *thought* a man could make the incredible stress on a human body when the pull of gravity is magnified by speed and weight, but no one knew for sure. Going into outer space could mean certain death - at least that is what the scientists feared.

The top men in charge hesitated to send a man into space, maybe to his certain death; it was a serious problem until someone thought about sending a trained animal into space. That solved the problem; first, they sent a dog, then a monkey, and the animals survived, so finally, they chose a healthy brave a human. A man took the ride into outer space and returned – alive.

That is all history - but that is my point - lets seriously think about the space program. The human race hesitated to send a man into space - a simple up and down ride - but scientist feared for the life of any man. The human race is doing the same thing the equipment they create, first just simple rides up and down, recording everything, tracking every possible aspect until they knew what happens in near space. The next step was a trip to the Moon - only the equipment on those first Moon trials, then they landed the simple lunar probes, testing the soils until they knew a man could safely step on the Moon and return to Earth. The logical next step would be sending equipment to Mars, and test that planet's atmosphere, then its surface, testing its soils. On both the Moon and Mars efforts, they left equipment in orbit, sending information to Earth's scientists. Some of that early equipment is still in orbit of the Moon and Mars.

I want you to think about that early space efforts. Is that exactly what a few of the aliens did on Earth? Did the aliens first orbit Earth and watch the activities, and later, did the aliens send equipment to land on Earth and test the soils? When it was safe, didn't they have an intelligent being to walk on Earth?

Let's imagine you are an astronaut, and your mission is to land on a distant planet. You know it is against interplanetary laws to interact with the population of that planet, your mission is to observe - nothing more - just study the soils, the plants and at all cost, you avoid allowing be captured by the living creatures on that planet.

You are a trained astronaut, you know how to survive in the wilds, you know how to find something to eat - perhaps you watch the animals on that planet and you quickly learn what plants the animals eat, and which plants the animals avoid. So far, no one captured you, you know the living creatures on that planet knows about you - they know you exist, and they have tried to capture you. Does that idea sound possible?

Think about the creatures the human race call the Bigfoot - is that his mission? Is Bigfoot an astronaut on a mission to study the soils and the planets of Earth and avoid capture?

What about the other living creatures that first orbit Earth, then studied the life on Earth, captured and autopsied a few cows, horses and other species, including humankind so they could understand the living creatures on Earth?

Is that what a few of the Greys are doing?

Are the Greys on an information mission to understand the intelligent life forms of planet Earth? Does that idea sound impossible to you?

The bottom line is what happens when all the testing is over, and the aliens are satisfied that Earth matches their needs?

Will they erase a few living species from planet Earth?

Is that what is happening to the honeybees? Is it possible honeybees the aliens already erased not only bees, but also many other insects and animals? Or – did the aliens relocate the honeybees to their planet? What species are next?

What happens if the advanced race finds Earth and wants to claim it?

What happens if that advanced race lives for centuries, or maybe they are immortal, while the human race lives only a mere few decades?

The aliens can afford to take all the time they need, but the human race is always on a race for their life, humans do not have time to spare.

What happens if an advanced species studies the human body, understand the reproduction system, and knows it is very easy to prevent a pregnancy? All they have to do is add something to the water and that ends the human race.

If that happened - the entire human population of Earth would be gone in less than 100 years. If an alien race has a life span of a few thousand years, they wouldn't hesitate to spend one century to rid the human race from Earth without the violence of a war.

Is that why the Bigfoot, the Greys or other aliens is here on Earth?

Perhaps your days are numbered and you are living in the last generation of the human race.

Do you think that idea is too farfetched to consider? Think again.

If a peaceful alien life form is already preparing Earth for their take-over, I suspect Mother Earth will rejoice because she will be given a chance to forget the constant wars, the destruction of garden lands, and a chance for cleaning the polluted Oceans.

55

62 ISOLATED FACTS ABOUT CHERRY HINKLE

1. My father, Charles Lloyd, was an inventor, and when he was young, was a friend to Nicola Tesla and Thomas Edison.

2. I can quickly mention the many times and angel helped me. I became aware of the angelic visitation when I was only four years old. We were traveling across the nation in a car, and I kept listening to angelic voices that sang to me. I was surprised to find out I was the only person heard the angelic choir. Shortly after my fifth birthday the angel visited me inside a cave on Mt Shasta, California. After that encounter, I knew I would become aware of angelic presence many times in my life.

3. I know I crossed the United States eleven times, from the Atlantic Ocean in Florida to the Pacific Ocean in California, and I made the trip without the need of a map. I couldn't get lost if I tried, because I think I was born with a GPS built into my brain. I just know where I am going and I never need a map to go anywhere on Earth.

4. I admit my favorite constellation is Orion's Belt, but I like any of the stars. From the smallest dim star to the brightest star if the sky, all the stars are beautiful - especially the crowded Milky Way!

5. One night in the deepest forest in northern California, I was less than a mere four feet from a nine foot Bigfoot. The odor is something no one would want to smell twice in their lifetime.

6. I'll never know why I have experienced the strange occulted things I have encountered in my long life, but I consider them a Gift from the Gods. I guess life may consider me as both star-crossed and blessed, I know I feel lucky to have had Fate touch me many times, and survived it.

7. I once lived in Orlando Florida, I was lucky enough to meet the famous Liberace at one of his concerts. After the show he allowed me to play a few chords on his beautiful ornate piano. Oddly enough, many years later, he and I both lived in the same town - but we both lived across the entire nation from Orlando where we first met, oddly enough, we both ended up living in Las Vegas, Nevada. He was a pleasant kind man to me.

8. I gave birth and raised four children – their hair color ranges from blond hair to raven black hair, and despite the fact my mom was a natural redhead with freckles, none of my children are redheads.

9. Although I was married three times, my third husband, Bill Hinkle, was my only true soul mate.

10. I once visited Puerto Rico in the Caribbean Sea. Those cruises included several other smaller islands, including Jamaica and Cuba.

11. One of brother-in-laws had the name Hoot Gibson Hyde - he was named after the old western cowboy movie star, Hoot Gibson. He was the husband of my sister Francie Hyde. Hoot was a native man of Honduras, Central America.

12. When I was barely 14 I shared my first romantic kiss with an older Latin man in LaCeiba, Honduras. He was the classic tall, dark and handsome guy.

13. When I was 17, my parents shocked me by entering me in a beauty contest. I didn't want to do it especially after I found out what I had to do, and that means talk in the public; but I never wanted to speak to anyone. I never wanted to do that; speaking in the public is a terrible experience for me. I didn't know anything about these plans until two days before I was supposed to be there for the talent section. I was terrified and didn't want to do it, I cried and begs them not to force me to enter a contest, but they thought it would be a pleasant experience for me, (it wasn't) but I managed to get through it. My parents thought it would make me more confident if I went through a rush of parades and other beauty contests. I didn't like any of that type activity. To end the endless contests, I married an older man. I stayed married to that man for 8 years and gave birth three of our children.

14. When I was eight years old, I met a bird-like fairy inside an evergreen tree in the town of Denmark, Oregon. She was a delicate creature and stands about eight or nine inches high. She wore a gossamer dress, and had her hair pulled back on the back of her head. Her voice was

surprising loud, like the way a bird's voice is too loud for the size of their body. The sounds she made reminded me of birds chirping when she spoke. She seemed to be angry because I was inside her tree. She indicated I should leave her tree. I've never seen another bird-like fairy, but whenever I hear the birds getting loud, I look in the trees, just in case I'll find another creature like her.

15. Shopping is something I dread, if fact, I loathe shopping for anything – however, I admit I have a fascination for thrift stores, mostly because you never know what you find. In one thrift store, I found a large beautiful mirror with carved flowers painted on the black frame for $5.00. I discovered that mirror carried the value of at least $250.00.

16. I love to watch any kind of birds, but I am violently allergic to them, but - I like to watch them and listen to their chirps.

17. I am very fond of Himalayan Cats – my favorite cat was Queen Penelope. She died in 1999, in November, if she had lived until January, she would have lived 29 years! Her favorite treats were turkey and gravy and loved pickled beets. Any any time I open pickled beets she would meow and let me know she want some too. If I didn't offer pickled beets fast enough for her, she would jump on my lap and put her paw in the edge of the table and meow. She was one of a kind!

18. I have family all over the USA, from Atlantic City, New Jersey to Yakima, Washington, to Bismarck, North Dakota to Orlando, Florida, and all points in between!

19. I love to laugh, I'd rather laugh that eat, and I can tell you that many nights I enjoy watching some silly sit-com and laugh before I go to bed. It is a great way to go to sleep, with laughter still in your mind.

20. If the truth must be told, I only tell people I am five feet tall, but now I started shrinking due to old age, I lack more than two inches to be five feet tall. To help me look taller, I stand straight when I walk and wear lifts in my shoes. I wear the lifts in my shoes because I can't wear high heels because I have a bad back, and I can't wear anything except flats.

21. I like country music, the blues, some early some rock, and classical piano music, I never learned to enjoy Jazz, but I admit I respect the musical talent required to play Jazz. I was a professional musician for over 12 years. I played a white electric Fender bass guitar with red cherries painted on it, and was the singer in my own band.

22. Since I mentioned it, I'd explain that I once had my own band, (I didn't, but I always wanted to call my band: "Cherry and the Pits" just for the fun of it.) I have sang on the stage with some of the best country music singers – I am proud to say I shared the stage with Kris Kristofferson, Buck Owens, Loretta Lynn, Merle Haggard, George Jones, Johnny Cash and Wynn Stewart and many others, I was friends with cast of the TV show Hee-Haw.

23. My talented mother, Frances E. Lloyd was a professional artist and President John Kennedy himself accepted the portrait my mother painted. That painting hung in the Kennedy memorial library until Jackie Kennedy passed away. The monotone portrait of John & Jackie is now in the hands of the Kennedy family, as it should be. (But I would love to see that painting again!)

24. I have a growing collection of Sci-Fi toys and aliens & flying saucers, including a three-foot grey alien in a tube. A few of my sci-fi toys are as small as a half-inch alien with grey skin and as large as four-foot green alien. I guess I am still a kid at heart.

25. No one in my neighborhood knows I study UFOs and Dulce Base, because it is only if I invite someone into my home my studies become obvious. I am reclusive, and rarely allow anyone enter my home.

26. I love Mensa books - I have a stack of Mensa puzzle game books, because I once was a member of that group. To keep my mind busy, I read those Mensa game and mentally solve the riddles, I never write in the answers in those editions. I am no longer a member, but buy their books when I find them.

27. I've been a fan of metal detectors since 1976. I when to Radio Shack, bought a kit and built my first metal detectors. (I enjoy building gizmos from kits.) That first metal detector worked well, and with that hand-made detector, I found enough rings, earrings and coins buried in the ground to buy a good White's Detectors! One year I found enough jewelry to enjoy a three-month vacation!

28. I am aware that a few people consider me an expert on Dulce Base; maybe I am just the most accurate vocal person on the Dulce Base. Personally, I do not consider me an expert on anything. But it makes me feel happy to know people read my words and know I am telling the truth.

29. I never display photographs that look into your eyes, and keep all family portraits on one wall only. I don't like any photos that stare into the eyes, but just about everybody else do. I think if a person has gentle eyes, I like them. But I don't like 'cold eyes' and today many people today have icy cold eyes with little kindness in their eyes.

30. I do not like dirigibles, hot balloons or blimps. I get very nervous if they cross my path. But I do like rockets, jets, airplanes, gliders and unidentified flying objects.

31. I do not like clowns, the so-called joy of any circus, but I do have three clown paintings, created by the actor Red Skelton, I do not display them because they scare me. I freely admit I do not like them. I never know what the clowns are hiding behind their mask. Too - I do not like clown because I know they are not really happy.

32. Before I was too young to go to school, I wanted to write books. I was a precocious child, and started to read and write at age 2-1/2.

33. At the age 10, I created handmade sets for my short plays. I used shoe boxes or cereal boxes to create my sets, decorated them with curtains and furniture cut from catalogs, glue them on the walls of the sets. To this day, I hate to throw away an empty box.

34. I have a collection of Crystal Balls, Tarot Cards and esoteric books, last time I tried to count; I had over ten thousand of books. Every room in my home contains bookshelves, except bathrooms – the moist atmosphere is not good for books.

35. My great-grandmother, my grandmother, my mother and me, and now my daughter and my granddaughter, great-granddaughter – (and others in this family) we all learned to ancient method art of reading the Tarot Cards. My most delicate tiny deck of Tarot Cards is less than one inch square; my largest deck is eight inches high. I also have playing cards too. The first Tarot Cards were written by the biblical scholar Enoch. As a wise man, Enoch wrote the first book with moving pages, those 'pages' are now called Tarot Cards.

36. Between 1961 and 1991 Thomas Edwin Castello was my best friend! Tom and I began releasing the Dulce Base in 1987. The information is currently known all over the world. Tom & I are the original sources of the real Dulce Base material.

37. I took classes to learn to function in the public, but I remain painfully shy and private, but I learned try hide it enough I can talk to people in the public. I took classes taught by Dale Carnegie and Earl Nightingale those classes are still available. Earl Nightingale wrote the greatest motivational books ever written. (He wrote The *Strangest Secret* that book was the first spoken-word book to sell over a million copies. This recording book was the first spoken-word to achieve Gold Record status.) Nightingale was one of the fifteen survivors when the military ship the Arizona when the Japanese army hit Hawaii. Nightingale passed away in 1989. Dale Carnegie, an author, (*How to Win Friends and Influence People, 1936,* and others) he spent many years of teaching self-improvement to countless salesmen and corporate training. He passed away in 1955.

38. I have been involved with UFOs, flying saucers and aliens - literally - all my life.

39. I have sailed the Pacific Ocean, the Atlantic Ocean, the Caribbean Sea, and the Sea of the Cortez. I also swam in the Salton Sea, in California and the Great Salt Lake, in Utah. I did swim in those oceans too. Swimming in rivers rather than lakes appears more pleasant to me. Even put my feet in the water of the Panama Canal. I have swam in more rivers I could ever list.

40. The first time I visited Havana, Cuba (era: 1952) it was clean and beautiful, and I swam in that harbor, but now it is too dirty and no one swims there. These days it is a dirty harbor with trashy debris visible everywhere.

41. The Central American small coastal town of LaCeiba, Honduras was once my home. I still have fond memories of that picturesque coastal town.

42. From the beach near LaCeiba, I once witnessed three mysterious dome shaped flying saucers when they left the sea and flew over Caribbean Sea, dripping foamy water, and watched the large saucers fly north, towards the USA.

43. I have a little gray mouse made of mink fur, his name is Magoo. I bought Magoo in Long Beach in 1966; he was the first thing I ever bought in California. Twenty five years ago, I bought a female mink-clad mouse dressed in red cape for him! I named her Minnie. (Yep, her name is Minnie Mouse, not very original is it?) They are a cute mouse couple.

44. My late husband Bill proposed marriage on our first date. I said 'yes' six months later.

45. Bill and I were married, on Valentine's Day in 1983. We chose a small Las Vegas chapel - The Chapel of the Little Flowers - to celebrate our wedding. That day, he had a fever of 102, and ended up being 20 minutes late!

46. Some friends have asked me if I am part vampire because I am allergic to garlic, and because for 69 years my body did not produce tears and I have never perspired, not even in the hottest summer in Las Vegas, Nevada. Then - suddenly at age 70, I was shocked to discover I started to perspire. (I do not like way it feels.) At least now I can produce a few tears, not only a few tears, even when I mourn. I still have no idea what took my body so long to sweat, but I can tell you I sure *do not* enjoy it!

47. I have a fascination for round buildings, triangle shaped clocks and heart shaped rings. I still like to see American Indian Teepees, Hogans and Wikiups.

48. My father, Charles Westcott Lloyd, was a Judo instructor for the U.S. Army. By the time I was a teenager I knew how to protect myself from human predators. I have always appreciated the fact he took time to teach me how to protect myself. I have had to use that knowledge twice, and I am so glad I can protect myself.

49. My goal is to publish three books, or more before old age over comes me.

50. My beloved husband Bill Hinkle passed away 6 June 2013, at age 58. We enjoyed 30 years of marital bliss.

51. I stood face to face with too many different reptilian life forms in my lifetime. There are at least three forms of Reptons in Dulce Base: the

DraconLeaders were born with wings, tails or both; the Reptons, to be eligible to work side-by-side with humans in Dulce Base, must have a Golden Face; the beige tall reptilian, sometimes called the Draco, are the undisputed leaders of Levels Five, Six and Seven.

52. With two older sisters and two younger sisters, I stand in the middle of the family seesaw. I never had any male sibling, but I always wish Fate gave a real brother.

53. I do not waste time, if I am not writing, I am sketching or taking photos, or reorganizing my files and books. My mind refuses to just sit down and relax without doing something. Even when I watch TV, my mind keeps busy thinking, planning or creating.

54. No one will starve if I am the cook, but I am not an exceptional talent in the kitchen. I love to cook Mexican food, especially green chili and tortillas! I have never been able to bake cakes or cookies, and that is a documented fact.

55. William Wynn Westcott, the founder of the Golden Dawn, is my ancestor.

56. Keno is my favorite game in any casino; I spent a few years as a Keno Writer on the Las Vegas Strip.

57. One of my wristwatches includes a calendar, the time and a biorhythm chart. Casio Watches are the maker of the biorhythm watch; all my other watches I purchased are Seiko. My other wristwatches or other watches were gifts from friends or family.

58. Tom Castello and I became close friends after my dad introduced us. In 1961, we both drove Packard's with straight eight engines; Tom's Packard was a 1950, my car was a 1949, however, both cars had the original black paint and tan upholstery. They were hard to find in 1961, but we both love that big-nosed car!

59. I have faced little Greys aliens with black eyes, seven feet tall reptilian Reptons, the Jahel (bluish/grey) with golden eyes, nine feet tall Bigfoot, angels and a female only a few inches high that I can only consider as 'fairies.'

60. To me, the strangest life forms I have met in my lifetime must be the dimensional beings that phase in and out of reality, and can disappear from vision faster than you can blink.

61. By the time I was 21, I had already traveled most of the western hemisphere, had been a beauty contestant, professional model a lecturer and was the mother of two children.

62. I have been asked how I managed to meet the famous people I know if I am a recluse. I can tell you it was nothing I chose to do, I really am a natural recluse, and do not go out of my way to meet anyone, and yet I have met countless celebrities, movie stars, and several world leaders including royalty. I did not seek any of them, it just naturally happened. Fate or perhaps the angels decide who I meet. I never try to meet anyone, I just happen to be in a certain place and Fate puts the famous people in the same place, and we meet. It is nothing I plan or arrange.

56

IS IT YOUR TURN?

"I love animals and would never hurt a wild animal I wish they would stay around so I can really watch them run. Meanwhile want venison for dinner?"

Ever think about that? Anybody notice the obvious crossed wires in that statement? Nope. The human never catch on.

So WHY did I mentioning this? I am sure you will know AFTER I tell you, but you won't know until I point it out. (Some of you already know.)

Let's pretend the human race is an advance race, very wise and logical. Let's pretend the human race have mastered space travel and decided to visit another planet and see what type life forms exist on that planet. They test several animals, especially the more advanced life forms that have created a shelter and these shelters all live near other shelters. They are not human, so it is OK to capture a few and cut them open and see what is inside their bodies. Or is it really OK?

You - as a human, get upset if an alien race picks up you, terrifies you by puts you through bizarre medical tests and drops you home as if nothing happened - you do get angry and upset. Sometimes you "forget" about the event but after a few months or years you remember it after a few nightmares jogged your memory.

Is there anything different with what the human race to animals to what the aliens do to the hapless humans? Nothing different - it is the same thing - the human race has no right to complain if an alien does the same the humans do. The aliens pick up the humans, track them, and place an implant in their body, the same thing the humans have been doing for many years.

Now it is the humans turn.

57

SPIRITUAL LAWS – OR HOW TO BECOME A BETTER HUMAN

(and it not as difficult as you think)

• Spend at least 15 time alone, *__in silence__* every day just thinking. NO MUSIC. In silence, think and concentrate on your goal, to be a peaceful and better person.

• Go out of your way to offer a sincere compliment to a stranger, (not a friend) at least once a day, if you can, give three compliments every day. Make sure you smile when you give a compliment. Make sure it is not the same person every day, if you do that, you gain nothing.

• Learn to be grateful for everything, even unpleasant events. If you disagree with me, it may because you think you are better person, and believe you are superior to most people, perhaps you think *you* shouldn't have to feel grateful for anything. Many think they have no reason to be grateful for being alive, and that is so wrong – you are alive, and you have another chance enjoy your life. I just you want to remember that unless go through bad days, how do you know the benefits of a wonderful day?

When you get up in the morning, take time to smile and be glad to be alive. There is a lot of people didn't make it through the night, so be happy you are capable to enjoy the rest of your day!

- Go out of your way to say 'Thank You' for everything another person does for you. It cost nothing, but you receive incredible benefits, both to the person did something for you, and you. If you have a spouse, remember that that person should be the most important person in your life – think about that. When you go to a store and a person opens the door for you, do you say 'thank you'? If you bump into a person, or step on their toe, don't you say I'm sorry? These people are strangers – you will never see them again, never-the-less you remember to be polite to them, but do you say thank you for everything your spouse does every day? This person is your chosen life partner – do they not deserve the same courtesy you give to strangers? You buy coffee at the café, you say thank you when the server brings your coffee – do you say thanks to your life partner for a coffee too?

- Accept whatever life gives you, and sometimes it is not easy. I want you to remember that life is what you make it. Make your life beautiful and strong. I want you to think about that concept. Try to remember that no matter who you are in this world, even if you happen to be the king of the world, remember that no one wins every battle every day. Learn to lose with a smile.

- Take time to be glad for your blessings. Sit down and list every small blessing you have, when you are finished, count those blessings. Even if you think you have no blessings – think again. Can you walk? (Many can't!) Can you speak and tell someone you have a pain somewhere? Many people lost the ability to speak due to a stroke. Count your blessings! Do you live in an apartment or house? (Thank god if you do.) Are you hungry? Can you eat? Do you have food to eat? Remember that many people do not have anything to eat. Count those blessings! Be grateful for every blessing you have in this world.

- Please remember that your soul and your mind – remember that your thoughts – are YOURS. Only you think your thoughts and you can enjoy the freedom of thinking about anything you choose, no one can change your thoughts unless you LET them.

- What you sow, is what you reap. If you want to be happy – all you have to do is make up your mind that no matter what, you will enjoy life. Trust me – you CAN change your life, and all it takes is determination. It all starts with ONE THOUGHT! "I want to be happy!" Trust me – if you can think about it, you can do it.

- Here is one of the biggest secret on happiness: If you want to be happy, make someone else happy. (Believe me, it really works!)

- Are there good days? Are there bad days? No my friend – they ALL are just days. YOU make them good or bad by YOUR own reaction to life.

- Control your thoughts – – yes you can! Is there somebody inside your thoughts with you? Nope – just you, YOU and only you controls what you think. Are you happy? It is because you wanted to be happy. Are you sad? It is because you allowed your thoughts to be sad.

- This is a fact of life: You are what you think you are - no nothing more – nothing less. Think what that means in your life.

- When you do something that is wrong, correct it. It is not an esoteric secret – it is obvious, you did something wrong, so go and make it right. Sometimes all it takes is the words "I'm sorry."

- Your habits are yours, and only you can control your habits – do not blame anything or anyone except you. If you are caught in a habit – quit it. It is just stop doing it. No excuses, no 'maybe later' – just do it.

- If you want to change, you must take that first thought.

- If you want something, first you must THINK about it. Look at the chair you are sitting on – someone first thought about how this chair should look like, soft or hard? Blue or beige? Are you sitting in a recliner or a dining chair? Everything you do in life starts with thinking about it. Whatever you want in life starts with the thought "I want…." Think about that, the words "I want…" is a command to get it. All you have to do is keep thinking of exactly what you want, and the mysteries of life will help you get it. It is a fact. Thoughts are things, when you think a thought, it goes out and tries to make it happen.

- So - to attain your desire, you must want to know what you want, then make the steps to reach it. "All things are possible to him who believes." (Mark 9:23)

- You must have the faith to make it start – and it all starts with "I want…"

58

MEETING ALIENS FOR
THE FIRST TIME

The first time you meet an alien face-to-face can be one of the worse encounter you will ever experience. Nothing is your life has prepared you to meet an unearthly visitor. It is very exciting, and a little scary.

As a youngster, your parents taught you that it is rude to stare at anyone for any reason; it is not acceptable behavior to stare at people that are a little different than the average. But not once did your parents mention the rules about staring at aliens. Maybe the same rule is still applied, but it is hard to remember that rule when it is the first time you stand in front an alien being. What do you do when you suddenly find yourself standing in front in being that leaves you breathless in wonder? You are both afraid and curious as your eyes take in the spectacle of a humanoid creature that you know are not human. In the first few seconds, your heart pounds, your mouth is dry and your hands tremble uncontrollably. Meanwhile, your brain searches its memory banks for anything that matches the being in front of your eyes. Finally the brain-scan stops, and your memory cells screams back one word – "ALIEN!" You want to run to escape the alien invader, but you just stand there, frozen is position.

Let me offer a few suggestions that you may find helpful when and if an alien visits you.

· Do nothing, just look at them and do not look away. When the aliens visit a human, they will have a reason - maybe he has to check to see if you are medically acceptable for their studies. Perhaps he is there to give you an implant. It doesn't matter why he is there, in this case, I assure you it is OK to stare in this case. The alien wants you to look at him, if you are staring into their eyes, because if he is looking at his eyes he is not about to run away or throw something at him. Also, when you looking into his eyes, it shows them you are not afraid, and you are willing to allow them work without fighting them. Most of the little Greys with big black eyes are without emotion and will fulfill their order no matter what happens. It is easier for you if you do not attempt to attack them, because if you try to fight of them, they will stun you. ('Stun' means they will render you unable to move, and it doesn't hurt in any way.) Please to not try to argue or fight them, they strength is amazing and you cannot win in a physical struggle against them.

· What to do: Slowly lower your arms and open your hands, your palms forward. This shows the alien you are not armed and will not harm them. They have instructions they must follow too, and one of those orders is to instantly stun you with a flashgun if you try to fight them. When they must stun you, it means either you are carrying an object, or you are physically struggling with them - or you thought about a weapon. (They can understand your mental thought of a weapon, and to make sure you cannot use a weapon.) Too, they recognize a human smile means 'passive and cooperative.' When the alien enters the room, stand still and say nothing. Try not to cry if you are afraid. Crying or fighting will only upset you more, and the grey is not impressed or understanding. They do not possess emotions and it is impossible for a little Grey to understand how you feel.

· If they are in your home, allow them investigate different items, remain silent and so not attempt to tell them what the item means to you. They will not damage your items.

· Do not attempt to touch the black eyed Greys and do not reach out to shake their hand. They consider the human race an assignment, and do not understand that humans are living entity. It is like trying to be friendly with your car. Your car does what you order, but do not understand why you do it. The little Greys with large black eyes have a computer driven brain system, and they are biological living creatures, they are not 'alive' in the way of a human. They are more robotic than sentient.

· If the alien is reptilian, they are living creatures with emotions and empathy. However, when they enter the room, use the arms down, palm of your hands exposed towards them. They too, have order to complete their assignment and will finish their job regardless the chore. If a repton enters your home, you have a chance to enter a conversation. No matter what, they will fulfill their designated chore, but again they understand all languages on Earth and they are capable to ask questions and answer your questions.

· The repton race are curious about the human race, and as long as you stand still and look straight into their eyes they will tolerate your nervousness. Don't move around, just stand still and don't attempt to touch them, even if they have been there and have talked you for a few minutes. They consider the human race as smelly and they do not appreciate perfumes and other products the human regularly use. Their sense of smell is much stronger, and they get irritated if you perspire profusely. Reptons do not perspire, and they find it uncomfortable and threatening when humans body emit liquids from your face and body. Try to remain calm and stand still. If you must sit down, simply state "I have to sit down," and do not do any else other than sit down, like close a door, or straighten a stack of magazines before you sit down. They expect you to do exactly what you said, and nothing else.

· They do have a sense of humor, but it not the same as humans. Reptons they do not express humor with a smiling face. When a repton laugh, their eyes get larger, and laughter comes from deep in their chest, their laughter sounds similar to a growling. Their mouth will open wider and the eyes blink a lot and they lower their head when they laugh. They just don't smile like the human race.

This is a few suggestions on what to do when you are faced with little Greys or Reptilians. There are other types of aliens, like the Tall Whites, the Jahel Race and many others. The little Greys are 100% business, and nothing else. Some of the Reptons (reptilians) are friendly and curious and welcome a conversation, some of the reptons are not interested in conversation and will strictly do whatever is required to complete their assignment and leave.

59

FOURTEEN STATEMENTS ABOUT ALIENS & REPTONS

*1. Intelligent college trained petite women with blue eyes are more likely to be alien abducted.

*2. People with at more than 2 years of college are apt to be abducted by reptilian aliens.

*3. Muscle bound men and muscular women are rarely abducted by aliens.

*4. World governments and other worldwide secret organizations have known the true identity of the so called 'aliens' since 1933 and their goals have been known since 1954.

*5. Female Reptons can stand over 7 feet tall and could defeat 5 human men with no problem. Their strength is incredible, and her intelligence too can leave humans in the dust.

*6. The human race knew there was another intelligent civilization on the surface of Earth long before man learned to write. Their artistic efforts to record the unidentified flying objects and alien awareness can be found in the ancient caves all over the world.

*7. Men with long hair are more chosen by aliens for abduction. The female reptons have been known to snip a small from a man's long hair. It appears to become a conversation piece with the other females.

*8. In the USA, government and military carried out autopsies on alien bodies. Those aliens were Greys, and at least once the "cadaver" was not dead when they started their autopsy.

*9. Reptons prefer young dark haired human boys aged 5 to 12 years old and again at age 15 to 18 years for abduction. The reason is logical; boys at that age are growing faster at any age in their lives.

*10. The entire world knew about the "cover-up" of the alien situation since 1947, however, the military, the government and the news media of Earth believe hope if they don't talk about it, they can hide alien facts forever.

*11. Reptons consider eating one of their sacred rites; they do not as often as humans, and can be comfortable and healthy if they eat every few weeks. They prefer not to eat in front of humans, but will eat with humans if a dignitary is visiting one of the underground facilities, such as Dulce Base in New Mexico or Area 51 in Nevada.

*12. To this very day, several humanoid reptilian hostages are being held against their will by several government organizations. One of the alien hostages has been at the same facility, underground since 1954.

*13. The aliens have been known to do choose human children as young as 4 years old for their injecting implants studies.

*14. The most common days for alien abduction are Wednesday and Saturday.

SIDE NOTE: Two repton visitors confirmed that they do read online comments about UFOs, underground bases and other related materials. They surprise me when one of the two reptons quoted words direct from my Facebook pages. That happened back in 2013, shortly after my husband passed away. The repton quoted something I wrote and posted regarding my hubby's death. I was shocked when he told me he really liked those words. Until that event, it never crossed my mind they might read anything in social media form.

60

THE NEW SPOOKY INSECTS

We live in a spooky world these days these days. When was the last time you just brushed away a fly without thinking, or looking at the insect to make sure it was a regular fly - and not a man-made creature?

Did it ever cross your mind you mind maybe a fewer insect is smarter than the rest of the insects?

Think about the people that happen to be smarter than average - no one can tell which human can be smarter than the rest of the human race at one quick glance.

It is the same with the new man-made smart insects that have been created with human DNA, at first glance they look just like the rest of the flies, perhaps these new smart insects are also immune to the insecticides, so the 'bug-spray' doesn't work.

After all the studies are finished, it seems the best spy would be an insect. They would be ultimate spy - insects - everyone sees them, and usually shoo them away. Flies - they are everywhere, but the man-made flies are certainly different. They have the ability to record conversations and have cameras to record everything they see. Or perhaps man made mosquitoes that can inject poison and fly away? That is a horrid thought, but already created.

What about the sneaky roaches that spy and record every word in a room, and then return to their master. That sounds like a sci-fi story, but the scientists have already created them. These new insects are man-made, usually created by DARPA or similar groups. The newest insects are hybrid insects highly intelligent, created with human genetic materials and include built in camera and recording devices.

Why in the world would scientist be foolish enough to create a smarter intelligent insect? Did it ever cross their minds that these hybrid insects may retain the human smarter DNA in ALL future insects?

Are they 100% sure only the few special insects will stay smart? What if all the future generation of intelligent insects remains smart after the scientists are finished with their studies?

In the future, the next time a fly decides to inch a bit closer to you, it may be smart to take a better look at it, before you push it away.

61

A FEW "FIRST TIME" IN NEVADA

The first of anything is always nice - Nevada has been the first on several things. Here is a half dozen "first time" things that happened on Nevada. (By the way – the word Nevada is Spanish and means 'snowy.' Nevada became the 36th state on 31 October 1864. Twelve of the world's largest hotels can be found in Las Vegas, Nevada.)

1. It was May 20, 1873 when a pair tailors created the first pair of blue jeans with metal rivets. And it was in Nevada. The name of the tailors was Levi Strauss and Jacob Davis, and they lived in Reno.

2. The first metal hard hats for construction workers were in Nevada, and it was when they built Hoover Dam in1933. It made sure the construction workers were safer in that deep canyon.

3. The first time they convicted a murderer because they found his fingerprints at the scene, it happened in Nevada in the year 1916.

4. The first time black men were granted the right to vote it happened in Nevada on the historic date March 1, 1869.

5. The first time they prospectors found major silver mine, they found it in Nevada in 1859 and it was called the Comstock Lode in north Nevada. That silver mine is the richest silver mine in American history. The Comstock Mine was named after Henry Comstock, but oddly enough he did profit from that silver mine. He died from suicide when he shot himself with his own pistol, in 27 September 1870 in Bozeman, Montana.

6. The first time three thieves decided to rob a train, it happened in north Nevada on 4 Nov 1870. Three men stole over $41,000.00 in gold coins. Ultimately, most of the gold was recovered.

62

I OWN THE MOON!

While thinking back into my childhood, I remembered a special day and remember that on that day, I was given the deed of the Moon many years ago!

I remember that special day and why the Moon was given to me back on February 7, 1952. I was only the tender age of 11 years old. But a special gift like that happens only once in a girl's life.

The person that gave me the Moon was this handsome blond guy, and he was an 'older guy' at the age of 12, and at the time, Keith was my favorite boyfriend. Just being just a boy, he lacked funds to buy a fancy gift for my birthday.

However, on that special day, Keith created a fantastic gift that in reality, I really doubt anyone would ever forget a birthday gift like that - if someone was kind enough to give something like that.

Keith wrote "legal ownership" for "One Moon for Cherry." It is one of the most original gift - and one of the unforgettable gifts - I ever owned. This young man knew I have always loved the Moon, so he created an incredible gift that remains very high on my list of favorite gifts.

I must admit that this deed of the Moon may lack a little bit in the legal ownership, but a gift like that really touched my heart at the time. Too, as you can see, I never forgot Keith and his wonderful gift. A few days past my birthday, we moved out of Lordsburg, New Mexico, and I never again heard from Keith.

I wonder if he ever remembers that special gift?

63

HOW MANY UNKNOWN CIVILIZATIONS LIVE ON EARTH?

How many races exist on Earth? My opinion differs from many other researchers but my opinion is based from 65 years of study. I found a basic recognized 12 races; the others are just varieties of the same races.

Here on this planet, Earth, the human race is considered the controlling species – and the human race is a mortal being. Too, a wide variety types of life such as well as animals, birds and marine life and other creatures call Earth as home.

Here on Earth, humans have five different skins colors of humans, and regardless the color, each color still represents the same race, the human race.

Also, other species such as the Reptilian race and a few of the different Greys, they is the sampling of colors in their species. For example, the reptilian race has the Golden Face, the DraconLeaders, Shott Freyy and Sheyy Freyon reptilian races and others.

There are reptilian, humanoid, aquatic beings, multidimensional beings, bacterial beings, insectoid beings, translucent beings, ethereal beings, immortal beings, spiritual beings, light beings and dark beings. (Negative beings from the shadow world) In each division or 'worlds' in their own race, dimensional levels, there are multiple levels in each 'world,' like the one human race on Earth, as well as animal, marine and insectoid life.

Of these many races, there are only a few people consider as well versed on the reptilian and a couple of the Greys. I do not consider myself an expert on any of them, because I am not a scientist, I am a mere writer and a woman with a life-long keen interest in the paranormal, UFOs and underground facilities and many other interests!

The aquatic races are one of the ancient races and the easiest way to describe them is to equate them with the ancient gods, such as Poseidon. He was the god of the seas, he and his mate, as well as their sons and daughters populated the oceans, and according to the legends, he and his offspring live on Earth as immortals. The stories include heroic fables of their deeds, and mythic romantic encounters with human race, leaving stories of demigods such as Hercules.

There are exciting stories of domed cities beneath the Pacific & Atlantic Oceans and these cities are populated with a mixture of these cross bred demigods and human race.

There are legends of Lemuria or Mu in the Pacific, and the legends of Atlantis in the Atlantic. Some people consider these legends to be part of the lost civilizations when those continents slipped under the surface of the oceans and were lost forever.

There are wonderful books written about those lost civilizations, and one of the best author had the name of James Churchward (27 February 1851 – 4

January 1936) he was known best for his books, *The Lost Continent of Mu, the Motherland of Men* (1926), *The Children of Mu* (1931), *The Sacred Symbols of Mu* (1933), *Cosmic Forces of Mu* (1934), *Second Book of Cosmic Forces of Mu* (1935.)

Sometimes it is both a blessings and a curse to know the ultimate truth, and that is a fact. There are times when the weight of knowledge of these hidden civilizations becomes too heavy a burden for any one person to endure, on those days, those that know long to slip off the weight and truly forget, at least for a few hours. However, no one can erase knowledge as if it is a maledict document, once you learn a fact, it is your knowledge forever, and you are responsible for that knowledge.

You know no one can't go back and say "wait, I don't want to learn this." It is too late, you already know it, and you can't simply unlearn it. What you do with the knowledge you learn is a serious responsibility too. There is some knowledge that you can share with everyone, but a few frightening facts, you must carry alone.

You dare not share those facts - not only because the information is classified, but because you know how it affected you when you first learned the facts, some information is to so horrifying that is wrong to force others to carry that burden too. That kind of knowledge is always a curse, and until you carry that burden yourself, you can't understand how alone you can feel in a crowd.

After said that, I can offer only one more piece of advice - for the sake of your peace of mind – do not try to seek out the fantastic facts behind the Dulce Base legends and UFO community, it is best that you merely be contented with reading science fiction stories.

64

FIVE TIDBITS ABOUT ALIENS OR UFOS

1. Most people think the aliens arrived in 1947 – but the aliens didn't arrive at all, they have always been here. The aliens were an ancient civilization thousands of years before they created the human race.

2. There are many unknown civilizations on Earth; however, they choose to avoid the hostile human race. Who can blame them? The human race kills anything/anyone without thinking about the possible benefits of keeping a person, animal or alien alive. The human do not mind that they are the most hostile creatures in this galaxy. They would rather kill first, without hesitation, and later they regret their decision.

3. The little Greys possess complex eyes, they have 41 separate lens in each eye, although they can see everything within one mile, their distant vision is not well focused clear. They must be within ten feet of a person to see a person.

4. Although they do have a problem with their vision, the little Greys have other superior senses. They have the ability to 'read minds' – that is not an accurate way of explain their ability; it would be more

accurate to say they can pick up the human's mental thoughts via a wide 'broadcast' frequency. The human mind is similar to a broken radio, and the radio refuses to stay on the same station, but keeps scanning all the stations.

5. Because the human mind is in constant change and never focuses on the same subject more than a split second. For that reason, visiting aliens assume the human race is not intelligent enough to understand alien communications. That is because most aliens communicate through a form of mental telepathy.

When an alien attempts to touch a human's mental mind, they find total mental chaos. That is because the human mind thinks in constant changing cycles, and the human mind never tries to focus or control their thoughts. The human mind is in need to learn the art of mental control.

65

THE TEST

From a letter from late Tom Castello, dated 1990. We were friends between 1961 to 1991.

Hi Cherry,

When you asked me to tell you about the first time I saw an alien, close up, I hesitated, trying to remembering if that was in Dulce Base in New Mexico, or was it in Virginia, U.S.A. or was it in California. It took a few minutes to remember it, but then I remembered it clearly when and how it happened.

As part of the Leadership Lessons, in California, just before I transferred to Dulce Base, all the students took part of several bizarre surprise lessons. The point of these lessons was to prepare you to face anything – and I mean anything. The instructor told us we will be have surprise lessons, but didn't tell us when. The instructor reminded us that we need to be for ready for anything. He stressed that if we stay prepared when the surprise arrived, and we won't fail. If we fail, we would be removed from the class. The lesson sounded easy enough to me.

The first surprise happened when two armed officers walked into the class, grabbed one of the students and roughed him up, and dragged him out the room. Everyone remained silent, and went back to our studies. A few minutes later, the student returned, said nothing, just back to his studies. I wanted to ask questions, but I didn't want to fail.

The next day, in the middle of the lessons, we heard a soft knocking on the door, the instructor said 'come in' and to the shock of everyone in the room, a grey alien walked in, wearing a black jumpsuit. An alien, mind you, the first one I saw, and this thing was as real as a heart attack! I could feel my heart pounding like crazy! He walked to the front of the room, and just stood there, looking around at the students. Every eye in the room stared in shock, taking in the spectacle of the huge eyes, tiny nose and thin opening as a mouth.

The instructor asked if he could help him with something, but the grey just walked straight to me and took my arm and looked into my eyes. I felt distinct wave nausea when he touched me, and that nausea felt stronger when he 'spoke' to me mind-to-mind.

Mentally, he told me to relax and the nausea would go away. I could feel the muscles in my thighs starting to shake from the tension. His presence so close to me, I felt like I couldn't breathe, it felt like the strongest sense of being too close into a person's personal zone, only stronger. I willed my body to stay calm, concentrating hard, trying to visualize my body in a relaxed position. Hard as I try, I knew that four foot alien kept touching my mind, plundering my thoughts – I didn't like it. I knew I had reached the moment of truth. From that second on, I knew that a mere human not keep a secret from that alien - no matter how hard I tried. I silently felt betrayed or maybe it was more like being violated, whatever it was, I mentally struggled off the strange anger in my mind.

From that second on, I knew it was no longer just a theory that powerful aliens live, this was the apex of "what if," there was zero doubt at this point. Grey aliens exist, they can touch your memory banks without any form of effort, and I had personal knowledge of that fact.

Part of me wanted to retreat; I wanted to run out of the room. Maybe I wanted to lash out and stop the mental marauding of my thoughts and at least escape from this stark reality. I sat still in my chair, willing my body to remain calm, to stop the shaking in my legs. I stared into those large dark eyes, and felt of wave of peace when his mental assault ended, I sighed knowing it was over and I was safe.

He turned and left the room as quietly as he arrived. Three men suddenly laughed, and one of them asked "what was *that* about?" They talked a few minutes, but the rest of us, went back to our studies. Minutes later, the instructors removed the three talkers. The rest of us passed.

At the time, it was the most difficult test I had encountered. Much worse tests did followed, but that test will remain as the biggest shock when I first met an alien, face to face. ---

As ever,

Tom

66

THE SERPENT KING

I sometimes wonder the why human race denies the reality of the Reptons control of this world. In failing to read spiritual ancients, the human race does not recognize their own Creator.

Most people have heard of Jehovah, the Creator, but they didn't check on the meaning of God's name. Perhaps is it due to mankind's natural fear of snakes but mankind backs off and once again and he recoils if they think about snakes. Maybe that is why mankind considers all snakes as "evil."

Never-the-less, the oldest spiritual books identify Jehovah as the Creator of the human race. These ancient books also identify the meaning of Jehovah's name - the name Jehovah can be translated as the "first-born of snakes" or "one who leads snakes" when you break down the meaning of his name into English, it would be simply translated into: "The Serpent King."

Jehovah created and employed the human race to tend his huge gardens deep inside the globe known as Earth. This immortal reptilian God has a hot temper; all the spiritual books testify his fierce anger. I want to remind everyone what happened when a god gets angry. Don't you remember the legends of the world wide flood when Jehovah killed every man, woman and child, including newborn human infants and wild animal, simply because they displeased him? Admittedly, the human race had become animalistic and cruel is any possible way. Mankind had started creating hybrid people and animals. So in my opinion God had the right to be angry, but to destroy everyone and every living creature seems harsh.

I want you to remember that flood when I mention that this Creator got angry at a few gardeners, and to punish them, he didn't kill them, and he just banned them from the garden.

Jehovah kicked them out of the garden, and for the first these innocent humans first experienced what it means to be alone, afraid and exposed to the harsh solar rays. Can you try to imagine this first generation of humans? They were so innocent they knew nothing other than this lush garden Jehovah created for the Sons of God. In the protected garden, food was everywhere, and the gardeners they were allowed to eat the fruit that grew everywhere in the Garden of Eden.

The first born humans were created inside a sheltered garden, never experienced anything other than this perfect garden – until someone ingested the wrong food – they ate the food that was reserved only to the Sons of God – the so called the Tree of Knowledge and the Tree of Life.

For the first time the poor gardeners experienced the temper of an angry God when he made the gardeners leave the paradise of Eden. The first surface dwellers entered the long journey of walking through a tunnel up to the surface of the surface of Earth.

On this new strange land they found no fruit growing, instead they found a bare desert. These innocent people were accustomed to find fruit growing everywhere, but when the exited the cave and found the surface of Earth, and had no idea how to find fruit on this harsh area, they were alone and afraid. A person would imagine they were hungry from their long walk from Eden but they had no idea how to find food out in this barren desert.

Once they found they were the surface of Earth, nothing looked beautiful and peaceful. They longed for the Garden of Eden. Instead of a lush garden, the terrified first humans discovered a harsh and hostile world await them. They were afraid to leave the entrance of the cave.

Other reptilian men found the first surface dwellers and took pity on these innocent beings; the taught the humans how to survive on the surface of Earth. They taught them how to find food, how to avoid the wild animals, how to survive the storms by living inside the place they called the Cave of Treasures, because the reptilians supplied all the things the humans needed to survive until the humans learned to live on the surface world.

67

ANATOMY OF THE GREY ALIENS WITH BIG BLACK EYES

Part one:

The small Grey with large black eyes:

1. Body frame: approximately 36 inches to 65 inches tall, with an infantile shape.

2. Skin Color: although a few Greys have the skin color of a pale gray or off-white gray, others have a slight yellow/green tinge to the skin; a few Greys have deeper skin-deep beige or a warm tan. (The taller Greys are the unique beings. You might say they are 'natural beings' because they have a brain similar to humans. The little Greys are different, have an artificial brain, and all their thoughts were downloaded from a reptilian master.)

3. Eyes: Large almond shaped black eyes. The eyes of a Grey are similar in size as size a turkey's egg. (Average turkey egg is almost three inches wide) The eyes of the Greys do not blink because they do not have eyelids.

4. Fingers: the Greys have three fingers with an opposing thumb on both hands; fingers are long and very flexible, with three articulated sections of each digit, plus a joint at the hand. Their hands are more flexible than a human's hand. (Human has three joints (phalanx,) plus the hand is flexible.)

5. Hands: A Greys hand appears to be too narrow and long for the size of the fingers, the palm of his hands deeply cupped.

6. Feet: the Greys possess two wide toes. Those long toes are half the length of the foot. The toes have three joints in each toe. Greys feet are very flexible and capable to grasp a tree branch. There is a different type Grey, and their foot is mostly the same except they have three toes on each foot.

7. Arms: two very long and slender with one double-jointed elbow, abnormally long arms and fingers reach beyond the middle of the knee.

8. Legs: two short, attenuated legs that appear too sinuous to support their body. Although the noticeable lack of muscular texture in those limbs, Greys legs do possess the usual flexible ankle, knee and hip. Those limbs are surprisingly fast.

9. Torso or physique: Greys have a heavy torso within the bulk of the weight in lower abdomen, giving the upper body appearance of a weak or unhealthy unbalance body. (When compared to a human's body.)

10. The skull appear to be too large for the size of the skeleton. The hairless skull appears lumpy front, too bulbous in the back.

Part Two:

A) Small Greys are very different from the human race. Those who do not have emotions, they do not understand the fear, empathy or sympathy. Nor do they understand the imagination of mankind.

B) Their brains are not able to create theoretical scenes, when they are with you; they are here to complete a chore. They will complete that job no matter what they must do. If you are afraid, I assure you they cannot imagine how you feel.

C) They have the innate intelligence; try to imagine that their minds are more like a robot or the computer's brain.

D) The Greys understand virtually all known human languages known on this planet, but do not understand what those languages or words mean the human race. The Greys understand that if a human cries, and if tears are seen on a human face, the Greys recognize may expect a physical struggle from the human. Greys can they can only hope to convince humans to follow them, by force is necessary.

E) If you can control your fear when a Grey approaches, you can simply defeat them by commanding a nonsensical order. They do not understand what "pretend" means, (they do not play games of any kind) to defeat the Greys; simply recite nursery rhymes as if it is a command. The Greys must return to their home base for new instructions. It will only happen once, if you try the same trick they will ignore you.

F) Do not be fooled by his small stature, the little Greys are five times stronger than the average human male. If you struggle with them, you will lose, and you may get hurt. Don't attempt to fight with them; it is not worth the effort.

G) Gray can walk through solid walls a lot easier than you can walk through water. They have mastered atomic matter, and they can take you through that solid wall with no problem. It is suggested that you try to attempt to hold your breath until you get through that wall. Walking through a solid wall is an odd sensation, it is difficult to describe, you might say it feels as if water is moving 'through' your body, not around it.

H) Medical examinations by a Grey are never fun, and the biggest problem is because you are afraid. Do your best to stay calm and remember one big fact: "that if they wanted to kill you, they would have done that a long time ago." Typically, they return you to their home or car when the tests are completed.

I) The Greys do their best to block the memory of your kidnapping in your memory. They blocked it from your memory for a reason, to protect you and allow you to continue your normal life. It is best you do not attempt to remember those events; all it does is upset you for no reason.

J) J.) Be wise, do not visit a hypnotist and try to remember what happened, it was an unpleasant memory, why work hard to remember something unpleasant when they tried so hard to make sure you don't have to remember?

68

DULCE BASE: THE HIGH SPEED MAGNETIC TERRA-DRIVE SHUTTLE

Dulce Base can claim the title as most important underground facility in the western hemisphere. Both human and non-human beings consider Dulce Base's international transit station is vital. This high speed system of shuttle/trains use a combined network of connected subways that circles the globe, and is that system carries the name as The Sub-Global System. The interconnected tubes reach all five continents, and cross both the Arctic and Antarctica polar areas.

Although the individual countries on the surface world seem to have a problem with Passports, Visas and identity problems, these problems do not exist in the Sub-Global System. Since the late 1960s there been a few countries that adhere to the old customs of physically photographing each passenger, and for that reason, those countries are not part of Sub-Global System. Four different international shuttle/trains cuts through and usually stop at Dulce Base Second Level, from the four corners of the world.

When the shuttles are in is motion, information screens turn on, and each rider can watch the educational screen. Tom Castello states he got tired of seeing the screens, because the distance from the Base to Los Alamos is just a few minutes, and rarely had a chance to see anything other than the educational warnings not to attempt stand up or walk when the shuttle is in motion.

The shuttle between Los Alamos & Dulce Base is a 'local run' and it follows a specific route. But the larger international high-speed shuttle/trains, do not stop at small stops, such as cities like Los Alamos, Las Vegas, Seattle or Denver, they go directly to Area 51, Dreamland or the Nevada Test Site or Telos City. (Mt. Shasta, Ca.) They all go to Dulce Base, and from there, they take a smaller shuttle to other smaller bases under the cities.

The shuttles are similar a longer and wider Amtrak train car without, of course, windows. There is no need for windows a high speed shuttle; there is no pleasant scenery to enjoy, the only thing you could possible see would be the blur of very dark walls of a bare rock tunnel.

When passengers approach the station, the education film suddenly ends, and a live view from camera of the station becomes visible on the screen. Although there is an attendant in each shuttle car, the need for an engineer or driver is an obsolete concept, because these magnetic shuttles are truly fully automatic. There is no need to worry the machinery will allow the shuttle leave the station while the doors still open, or suddenly accelerate with the passengers entering or exiting. The activation of an ignition or starter found in internal combustion engines - standard engines – is missing in the shuttles. The strength of alternative polar magnetics alone will power to shuttle smoothly along the tubes in high speed.

The international shuttles use magnetic drive. (Opposing magnetic poles that constantly attempt to repel the walls. That same power impels the shuttle and forces it forward in high speed.) I know they can travel from Dulce Base (New Mexico USA) to New York City, USA in under one hour, (almost 3000 miles) from Dulce Base to Paris, France under 3-1/2 hours. There is nothing to touch, so there is no friction to slow the craft down.

When asked to list the cities familiar with and use the underground shuttle/trains – in reality, time alone makes it an impossible chore because most every major city – world wide – uses or is aware of the possibilities. Although only four international interconnecting tubes circle the globe, there are thousands of smaller tubes. Researchers discovered these subways – always connected – either interconnected by Magnetic Drive (Sub-Global System,) Terra-Drive System, Mag-Lev System or Railroad System. One way or another, these underground tubes reach every major city on Earth.

69

A FEW PIECES OF GREY
INFORMATION

Dulce Base – The Greys, plus a mention of Repton facts. Bits of information:

* The large eyes of the Greys cannot handle brilliant solar light, those eyes are accustomed to dim lights of caverns.

* The vertical pupils in the eyes of the Greys can be seen in dim light.

* Certain Greys have webbed and clawed fingers, the same as their creators – the Reptons.

* The Greys are considered hostile and evil, but it is not their fault, their programming is to be hostile via mind control.

* None of the little Greys have red blood cells in their bodies. Their blood cells are yellowish.

* A few of the Greys are actually 'Blues' or at least their grey bodies appear to blush blue, and their blood cells are a bluish green due to the silver in their blood cells.

* It appears a few of Greys want to be friendly or at least pleasant towards humans, but their programmed fear prevents it.

* They subterranean realms are the natural home for both Reptons and some Greys. According to the Lost Books of the Bible, Adam and Eve exited the underground Garden of Eden via tunnels and feared for their lives when they saw the sun for the first time. The Greys and Reptons took pity on them and taught a few required skills to survive.

* A few of the Greys have been seen to try to smile, but their tiny lips were not made for friendship.

* Author John Keel suggested the Greys bodies may be made of Ectoplasm and not third dimensional at all. But that is simply his theory.

* Some of the visible UFOs are holographic images controlled by the Greys.

* The Repton in the Garden of Eden walked like a man, talked like a man and Eve and Adam were not surprised by their ability, they treated him as a trusted advisor. It has been said there were many of the reptilian humanoids is that era.

70

FAIRY IN AN EVERGREEN

In 1948 I lived in a few miles outside the small town of Denmark, Oregon. We didn't stay in that town very long for a few months. It was a pretty area, lots of streams and plenty of evergreen trees and those trees is where I loved to play at age 8. I used to play under a strand of evergreen trees with beautiful sweeping limbs that touch the ground.

These trees were wide with lots of room if you were a petite young girl. I got used to the sound of the different birds that sang their songs from the top of that tree. It was such a peaceful area, and the lush dark green limbs provided welcome shade from the summer heat. Without hesitation I settled down on the soft padding of years of old evergreen needles, and found a cozy spot where the limbs formed a back rest.

I had a book with me, and I thought I was ready to enjoy the story of Robin Hood under this evergreen tree. I barely opened book and turned a few pages when I heard of a different bird call. That 'bird' was insistent and noisy; it kept 'chirping' and the voice sounding like the scolding of an angry little bird. I turned my head and looked up to a branch about a couple feet above me.

To my eternal shock there stood a tiny humanoid dressed in a white translucent gown. The other features of her angled face were barely noticeable because of her very pointed nose. It accents her sharp beak-like nose. That nose of hers, started from the middle of her forehead. The only way to describe her face is to say nose was similar to the beak of a bird. And yet it was a face with skin, a nose, eyes and lips and pointed chin and not a beak - it was just that her nose was the largest feature. She had a very light tan skin and dark brown eyes. I was surprised at her thin long bare feet; those thin feet were designed to grasp branches. She was really different, but beautiful in her own way.

Instantly I decided this female could be a real life fairy! I remember my mother telling stories about fairies, and their tiny bodies only a few inches high, but they appeared to be quite human, despite their delicate size. There was no doubt in my mind that fairy was angry at me, because she continued berating me and gesturing her arms and hands. She frowned and chirped and pointed her fingers towards me and although I couldn't understand what she said, it was obvious she was furious that I dared to enter her tree without permission.

I must admit I was bewildered as to why she was so upset with me, it finally crossed my mind that maybe I accidentally 'invaded' her tree, but I didn't try to choose her tree to invade, it was the only tree I saw that had an opening in the limbs. I wondered if she had a nest not far from where I sat. I looked around for her nest, but saw no obvious nesting area. Then I considered maybe this tree is her territory or maybe this tree her home. I knew that female was upset because I disturbed her peaceful home. Bringing the book with me, I slowly I back out of the tree, I stood up but didn't leave because she was still scolding me. I didn't want to be rude and leave while she was still talking, so just stood there listening to her scolding until she finally calmed down.

To this day I have no idea what she said, but it is obvious she quite angry because I entered her tree. This delicate creature could really chirp loud and from the tone of her chirps she was more than a little angry. Like most birds, her calls were loud, I am sure all the birds is the entire forest heard her scolding me. She was so little, but her voice was sharp and strong, she reminded me of the calls of the birds, her vocalized calls could be heard from a long distance, despite her tiny throat and beak. She was such a tiny humanoid, She was a little smaller than a Barbi doll, but back then, there weren't any Barbi dolls.

I don't know for sure what she was, maybe a fairy, maybe an elemental – but in my mind I can still hear that sharp chirps she used to run me out of her tree.

For the next few days I brought little items for her, a few little beads, a pieces of fabric, even a gumdrop - I left the items on the same branch. For the second day I returned and looked for the beads but they were still there. The following day all four beads were gone, so I added the fabric. It too, was gone the next day. I continued bringing peace offerings to her every day until we left that state, and each time the items disappeared. I never saw her again, but I like to think she accepted the gifts.

I'll tell you one thing - you never forget an event like that, you just hope that someday you might encounter another creature like her. So far, she has been the only experience like her. Because of her, when I hear birds scolding, I go to the window - just in case.

71

FIFTEEN SIGNS YOU HAVE AN IMPLANT

1. You feel moody, or suffer from quick mood shifts.

2. You find you are unable to maintain your normal weight, no matter what diet you try.

3. You suffer from unable to reach restful sleep, no matter how many hours you sleep, you still feel tired.

4. You discover you are trying unusual foods you never wanted to try in the past.

5. You find you awake during the night and want food, but you are not hungry, but want "something."

6. You discover you are unable to concentrate on your job, hobby or other normal interests.

7. Suddenly, you find the subject UFOs is fascinating.

8. You discover you and your family is dreaming of UFOs, aliens and alien abduction, and it is too often to be coincidence.

9. You notice items in your home have been moved to a different location, and you know you didn't move them.

10. You notice you have many 'wrong number' phone calls, usually no one speaks, but you remember a 'hollow' sound in the phone. Later you have the desire to 'go somewhere' – anywhere, for an unknown reason.

11. You have noticed strangers with odd eyes are looking at you recently.

12. Recently you have seen cars, van or pick-ups seem to follow you, but when you try to defeat them, it appears to a coincidence, because they turn away, but the minute you decide to prove they are following you. You feel silly, but still, you know the feeling of being followed stays with you.

13. At night you hear odd sounds in another room, when you investigate, there is nothing can explain the sounds because they want away.

14. You begin feeling slightly feeling paranoid, but you don't want to talk to a doctor or not even a friend, you keep it the thoughts bottled inside.

15. You discover you suffer from headaches, intestinal problems and a low backache, sometimes your feet and knees ache as if you ran a mile in your bare feet.

72

ANGELIC TIDBITS

Chalkydri --- Flying Archangels, they are linked with the Phoenixes; their caste is between the Cherubim and the Seraphim. Each Chalkydri possess 12 wings. According to legends, they sing beautiful songs when they approach their home planet – Sol, the Sun. The human ear cannot hear their melodious voices, but their songs can be translated into colors in the sky known as the Aurora Borealis. Their home is in the fourth heaven.

Auphanim --- (Ofanim) Their name and title means "Wheels," and these angels known to be the highest caste of Seraphim. According to the ancient legends, they can be recognized as the "many eyed ones." They are one of A few authorities identify the Auphanim (or Ofanim) as a caste of angels higher than the rank of Seraphim, but most authorities rank them as sixth is position in power. They reside in the fourth heaven.

Aralim --- (Erelim) The Valiant Ones, in the celestial hierarchy these angels rank third in power, and their title is called as "Thrones" and they reside in the fourth heaven.

Messiah --- he is equated as Christ, Metratron, Savior and God. Messiah is designated as a cherub and guardian angel of Eden. He is always armed with a flaming sword. As the title of Head of Days, he sits at the right hand of God, and Resides in the Ultimate First Heaven. He is known as El Soph, wise emanations from the mystical Right Side of Shemhamphorae.

A question to ask - and the answer – what and where is fourth heaven?

According to some legends, heaven is different levels of purity of 'good souls' that humans hope to reach before they die. When a human dies, the soul of humans must be judged by advanced souls. All the 'good and bad' acts a soul when through in their life will be seen in a 'split second' before they are allowed to advanced to their eternal reward.

Depending on how on you look at it, the best place to hope to reach in heaven is the ninth heaven. However - other writings tell the story of heaven from a different point of view, they point out the 'cycle of life' is an endless series of eternal circles, the beginning and the end over-lap in the cycle of life. The highest point of purity stands side by side the lowest point of purity. In other words, purity is pure, no matter where you see it.

A few other writers have pointed out that the different levels of 'heavens' are similar to solar systems, The brilliant Sun is God, and the nine planets are the nine 'heavens.' If you choose to consider that point of view, the 'fourth heaven' would be the planet Mars. The 'Third Heaven' would be planet Earth. (Personally, I would be hard pressed to accept the idea of planet Earth as part of the heavenly line up.)

"The Music of the Spheres" - many people have heard those beautiful songs, it is the song of the Sirens. No the human ear can hear the songs of the Chalkydri, but - like I said - the human eye can see the beautiful Northern Lights. Color and sound is the same thing in different frequencies.

73

ALIEN FOOD - DO REPTONS EAT HUMANS?

I've read the reports that state "if the public knew the alien race is here on Earth, there would be pure chaos because the public would panic."

That is pure nonsense.

Nobody would get excited and discover there is 'panic in the streets' just because they found out a few of the aliens life forms consider the human race 'food.'

The human race wouldn't panic if they found aliens are carnivores and eat wild or domesticated animals. Why would the public panic? Maybe the public would sit in front of their TV's wanting to know more about this new life form; but there wouldn't create panic. I think the human race is a little more intelligent and they remember the human race is another form of animal.

The human race have four limbs, a head, and a torso – each cow has four limbs, a head, and a torso – even the lowly mouse has four limbs, a head and a torso – even fish have heads, torso and their limbs are fins instead of legs and arms - most animals on earth have the same description – but the human race eat other animals, so does the canine, so do the felines and a few species.

Do you remember anyone started panic start screaming and running in the streets around when they heard that lions and wolves sometimes eat humans?

Of course not.

Every living thing on Earth eats something – sometimes people eat plants, sometimes people eat other animals. Sometimes animals eat humans – it is no big mystery – when an animal is hungry, they will eat anything they can find. And that includes human.

It's not odd – it's just life - the human race have always been part of the food chain, and it just the inflated ego of a few humans to think they are immune to the food chain. Do you think a hungry lion cares if you are a vegetable loving man that never ate meat in your life? Nope. To that lion, you are "just a meal."

If there are aliens that are stocking their freezers with human meat, it is nothing personal - any more than it not personal when you eat a meat sandwich. When you are hungry – you eat, and some of you eat meat. Maybe the aliens eat meat too.

The human race has always considered themselves as the highest-ranking animals on Earth - but maybe the human race is mistaken – maybe there are much more intelligent beings in the universe other than the violent human race. A truly intelligent race would not be violent, like humans. They would not kill their own race – they would not murder their own offspring, nor would they would indulge in war for centuries.

There is not an intelligent race in the universe that would be considered endless war and daily murder as "intelligent". Think about that fact for a minute and you know that is true.

Perhaps but maybe there are scavenger races that do not care if a race is intelligent or not – perhaps these savage aliens only see a human is 'meat.' Think about it - to a savage alien race from across the universe, the humans are just another meal. So – think about it – if an alien eats a human – it's nothing personal, he is hungry and this time you are the meal.

74

THE ARK VS THE TITANIC

Something to think about...

In 1912 - many years ago, a team of professional wealthy ship builders decided to make the world's first unsinkable ship, the named the ship that gigantic ship the Titanic. The giant ship was 882 feet 9 inches long. The ship was 92 feet 6 inches wide and had nine decks. The ship carried a total passengers and crew was 2229 humans.

On the maiden voyage that massive metal ship sank and went to the bottom of the Atlantic Ocean. When the ship sank, only 712 people survived.

Thousands of years ago an amateur boat builder named Noah had to save the world. Noah and his sons built the world's only floating zoo.

Noah named the wood ship "The Ark." The wood huge ship was 440 feet long, and was 72 feet wide, plus the surface of the ship. The Ark had three roomy decks to carry his family – Noah's wife, and his three sons and their wives, and countless animals. Plus all the food the humans and the animals would eat for over 150 days that covered the entire world.

That huge wood ship weathered the worse flood planet Earth has ever thought about, a worldwide flood so bad that it covered every mountain on this planet with water. Great Flood (a worldwide rainstorm and flood the entire Earth) an unheard of fiercest storm that dropped water from the sky for months. After all these storms on the water and after many months afloat, that ship settled gently against on Mt Ararat in Turkey. When the flood was over, all the paired animals survived, and all the eight humans survived too.

To this day, the petrified wood of this ship still stand as a monument to what determined people can achieve when they are determined to complete a mission.

The moral of this story: Wood floats. Metal sinks.

Too, just because a boat is made of wood doesn't mean it is easy to sink. At the same time no one human should be so vain as to claim their boat is 'unsinkable'.

The Hand of Fate would reach out make sure you are wrong.

75

THE ART OF LISTENING

Have you noticed that each time a person interviews a man or woman with 'natural charm' that internal peaceful approach to life makes you feel comfortable and welcome, even though you never physically met them?

Too, have you noticed that a person with personal charm seems to be very intelligent, even though he or she didn't say much? Have you ever wonder what is the secret behind their natural charm? Their secret charm is very simple - they listen more, and talk less.

Did it ever cross your mind that the person with 'personal charm' is the same type person that really listens when you speak? People with an abundance of personal charm are the same people that will truly listen to the words of the other speaker, before they speak.

In addition, learn to be a more interesting person. Read something new every day. That doesn't mean you must read a new book every day, if you are too busy to read a lot, you may consider buying a book on trivia, and read one new piece of trivia each day. You will learn a lot, and it will make you a more interesting person.

Learn to leave your phone alone and talk to a living person in person. The same thing with your computer – laptops can be a fascinating device, but talking to a real person, face to face, can be far more rewarding.

These days you can't even catch your eye to a living person because they have their face buried into the pages of their phone or computer. No one *can't* learn to be a charming person when you are too busy tapping constantly on your phone/computer.

Everyone appreciates a sincere compliment – take time to offer a compliment to anyone, it cost nothing to say "I like the shape of your eyeglasses, they look good on you." Or maybe "I like the color of your necktie." Or maybe "what a lovely ring you are wearing!" If cost nothing and the comment is appreciated, if nothing else, you can always just smile and say "Hi there, don't you love this weather?" It makes you for an interesting person, and maybe you just opened the door to a new friendship.

Are you aware that you can develop the art of personal charm too, and it is not that difficult either? It is very easy to develop the so called 'natural charm' by simply learning to really listen to the words other people say – before you form an opinion and speak. Too many times people are thinking what they plan to say to the other person as soon as they stop talking, instead of pay attention to the actual words are said. Why don't you stop talking and learn to really listen?

76

SHOULD YOU BE AWARE
OF SERPENTS?

Throughout history the civilizations have talked about the powerful serpents that overpower the human race.

The holy bible has many references about serpents and their connections with humans. One of the serpentine beings was one of the rulers of Heaven until - he was cast down to the underground by a powerful rival. The loser of this battle was cast not only to Earth, but cast to the underground of planet Earth. The Great Serpent - Jehovah – AKA: the Serpent King is also known as Sabazius. The most powerful angelic castes are known as the Seraph, or Seraphim these divine fiery serpent were the original serpent-spirits on Earth.

After mankind had been on Earth for a while, and Moses was in the middle of the Exodus, one of the constant problems was flying serpents that would bite the people. God informed Moses he can cure the bites of fiery serpent by making a brass T-shaped brass rod. Legend has it the T-shaped brass also has a Serpent coiled around on the brass rod. The people had to look at the serpent on the rod and any bites were instantly cured. (The King James Version of the holy bible has the story on Numbers 21:8.)

Another powerful serpentine man was the father of the biblical son - known as Cain. The name of that man is not listed in the bible, but the story says the naive and innocent Eve "knew" the serpent man (had a sexual encounter) they produced a powerful son, Cain, however that son was born with an unpleasant temper and a jealous nature. Later, Adam and Eve produced a gentle kind son, his name was Abel. The brothers were different, one had a hot and quick temper, and the other was gentle and loving. Cain was jealous over Abel's offers to God, and finally Cain's temper took over, and in a fit of anger, he killed his brother Abel. Cain made history as the first murderer in the Adamic or human race.

Other serpentine connections can be found in the history of India you find out that the "secret name of God" is Uraeus. (Meaning: snake.) The Egyptian "Mistress of Serpents" was Isis or Nephthys. The Palestine clan, the Levites (meaning "sons of the Great Serpent") they had several names for these one of these serpent rulers, but usually it was known as Nehusatan, Nahash or Nahusha. Other serpentine names: Ouroboros, Sata, Leviathan, Taaut, Thoth, Ophion, Geras, Kundalini, Chinoi, Kadru, Nagas, Kadi, Derhermes, Peruarchet, ananta, Isis, Ninhursag Ishtar, Lamia, Kali, Pazuzu. All those names indicate reptilian names.

77

THE ALIEN MONETARY SYSTEM AT DULCE BASE

At Dulce Base, the alien residents do not use money, gold or silver. Instead everything simply as true share everything. The reptons do not bank paper money, gold coins or silver, there is no need for it, because their values are different from the human race. The reptons still have stores and items in the markets, but they select the items they need and choose nothing else. They have no use for impressing each other because they all possess the same items in their homes.

They do not have fancy clothing or working clothing, simply because they the same uniforms or simple tunics. When they must work with powerful humans, they will wear the proper clothing to make the human feel more comfortable, for example if there is a dignitary visiting and a party is suggested but after the function is over the garment is returned to the exchange. Reptons have no use for such garments in their own closets. The female reptons (and a few of the males) express themselves by placing gemstones on their claws. Their claws are similar to fingernails, and they do grow fast, so they do not keep the gemstones long. Too, they use delicate chains on their ankles and those chains sometimes are connected to their claws.

To the human race, money is everything – you better have money in your hands, or money in the banks, or that human is almost considered as worthless. I don't know when it started, but I wouldn't be surprised to find it started about a month after Cain murdered his brother, Able.

Ever since that time, the human race has been trading gold, gems or services. The more the gold or gemstones a person they have, the more important they are in the eyes of the other humans. It has always been like that – and will remain that same system as long as there are humans on Earth.

No other animal on earth use clothing or ornaments. It is only the human race that attempt to impress other with their wealth. The reptons, the Greys or the Nordics do not use money, they do not use banks, investments or the gathering of gold, silver or gems – that is limited to the human race. That is the exact reason the repton race is far ahead in advance in technology, because they do not waste their time and efforts collecting money and gold.

78

A LIST OF UFO CRASHES, LIVING OR DEAD

22 July 1947, Roswell, Desert, New Mexico, dead bodies, 2 living entities, 1 serious hurt

13 Feb 1948, Aztec, New Mexico, 12 dead bodies, 3 living entities 1 serious hurt

7 July 1948, North Mexico Area, South of Laredo, Texas, 1 dead body

1952, Spitzbergen, Norway, 2 dead bodies

14 Aug. 1952, Near Ely, Nevada, 16 dead bodies, 4 living entities

10 Sept 1952, Near Albuquerque, Desert, New Mexico, 3 dead bodies

18 Apr 1953, South West Arizona, no living bodies, but found 2 severely damaged robotic humanoids

20 May 1953, Kingman, Arizona, 1 dead body

19 June 1953, Laredo, Texas, 4 dead bodies

10 July 1953 Johannesburg, South Africa, 5 dead bodies

13 Oct 1953, Dutton, Montana, 4 dead bodies, 1 living entity

5 May 1955, Brighton, England, 4 dead bodies

18 July 1957, Carlsbad, Desert, New Mexico, 4 dead bodies

12 June 1962, Holloman Air Force Base, New Mexico, 2 dead bodies, 1 lived briefly

10 Nov 1964, Fort Riley, Kansas, 9 dead bodies, 2 serious damaged, both died after a few hours

27 Oct 1966, North West Desert Arizona, 1 humanoid dead found

1966-1968, Indiana/Kentucky/Ohio area, 5 crashes, 3 dead bodies, 3 living entities

18 July 1972, Morroco Sahara Desert, 3 dead bodies

10 July 1973, North West Desert Arizona, 5 dead bodies, 3 living entities, 1 serious hurt

12 May 1976, Australian Desert, 4 dead bodies

22 June 1977, North West Desert Arizona, 5 dead bodies

5 April 1977, South West Ohio, 11 dead bodies, 3 living entities, 1 serious hurt

17 Aug 1977, Tobasco, Mexico, 2 dead bodies

May 1978, Bolivia South America, No bodies found, but three seats possible. (Entities survived?)

Nov 1988, Afghanistan, 7 dead bodies, 1 living entity

July 1989, Siberia, Russia, 7 dead bodies 9 living entities survived

79

DESCRIPTION ON THE ANCIENT REPTILIAN WATCHERS

Reptilian Dracon species have a visible tail and wings, some of those traits may have atrophied from lack use. Never the less, they are still the off spring of their saurian ancestors.

There are a few people that believe these Reptons the living descendants of the original fallen Angels of Heaven. Back in biblical era, it was a common event for the Reptilian Watchers to cross bred with the attractive human females, and the resulting off-spring became several notable patriarchs, including Moses and the famous of Noah, known as the builder of the Ark.

Physical Shape: Saurian or Draconian Repton

Three ridges on the elongated skull, pointed chin, ridged cheek bones

Webbed Fingers & Toes: 3 webbed toes, 6 webbed fingers each hand

Average Wing Span: 16 - 20 feet wide

Average Height: 7-9 feet tall

Average Weight: 400-700 pounds

Body Temperature: 89.3 (human body: 98.6)

Pulse/Respiration: 2 breaths per minute (human 60-72 per minute)

Skin: of various colors tan, dark yellow/beige, with a greenish avocado, dark green

Eyes: Mostly golden or amber in color, some beige color eyes

Life Expectancy: average 800-1000 years

Other Physical Information: Reports of visible long and broad tail with large feathered wings of certain Reptons. Some reptons have wings with no feathers, they resemble leather. Their wings have no problem with maintaining altitude and distance in the sky.

Origin: Originally from a planet found in a constellation in the Draco star cluster. The Draconian Life Forms descended from a branch of bipedal saurian that existed on planet Earth thousands of years ago.

Witnesses Describe the Reptons as: Witnesses as well as the abductees stated the reptilian life forms resemble a humanoid lizard.

80

THINGS I WANT TO SHARE BEFORE I CROSS THE FINAL DOOR

1. A wish all the governments of this planet would finally step forward and admit they know about the Unknown Civilizations that coexists on Earth.

2. I also wish the governments would divulge the unvarnished truth about exactly why/what this civilization may be. I firmly believe the public would prefer being terrified for a short period of time, but would adjust their though patterns and adjust the new awareness.

3. I am one person - I learned to adjust and accept new concepts. I do not consider myself unique or the only one that can accept different ideas - far from it. I think everyone has the RIGHT to know the truth about the unknown civilizations hidden on this planet. If I can handle the truth, so can you.

4. I think it is deadly wrong to withhold UFO knowledge that rightly belongs to the entire world, just because a few greedy people want to *sell* that information for their own purpose....to make their name

famous. (Do they not realize that they also may gain a fleeting fame as one of the inconsiderate and greediest people on earth?)

5. I firmly believe that the mistaken fools that KNOWS the truth and knowingly lies and claims there are no aliens, and claims there are no non-human intelligent race hidden on Earth - is one of the lowest form of human on Earth. (Shame on them.)

6. The unknown civilization lives in cities hidden inside caverns on Earth. This race was an ancient intelligent race when they decided to create human. This secretive race lived hidden on Earth as long as the human race lived on this planet. At one time, it was not a hidden fact - but centuries of years ago the religious groups found a way to hide that information and use that information to control people. It was a time when very few people knew how to read or write.

7. For centuries the rulers of this planet knew the truth, and now they are live in fear the truth will be exposed and their lies will cause the largest backlash in history. Currently, these "leaders" (the controller) find it easier to murder anyone that knows the truth - but in today's information world, they live in fear the day will come when there will be too many people with that knowledge, and they will lose their control.

81

ANYONE SPEAK BIRD?

You hear the songs and chirps of birds; I think just about everyone would agree the birds seem to have a language of their own. Some birds songs are complex, others, like the Dove, their song is appears to be three repeated tones, that is all the human hears. But maybe there are other sounds the human ear cannot hear.

What about the dolphins that co-habit this planet - they speak in their own language, and that language is complex, with individual words. I believe just about each intelligent human on earth knows the dolphins have some kind of language, but after more than 50 constant years of study, not one human has been able to understand one word of the dolphin language.

Think about that - dolphins are on same planet as the humans but they have not learned to understand each other. Perhaps it is because the human never tried to learn language. It is the same with all animals – No human have learned to converse with a horse, an elephant or even a dog. They human race have never learned any of the languages of any of the hundreds of animals that share the same planet. May I point out that many of the animals understand when a person tells the animal to do something, the animal quickly does. It appears the animals understand the language of humans.

Now think about a visiting alien - they traveled millions of miles across a universe, and crossed galaxies to reach the planet Earth - do you think the human race would able to communicate with an alien?

Not a chance - the human race have never understood the language of any animals - and they have had thousands of years to learn any other language. Not even the "man's best friend" the lowly dog. Dogs understand the human language, but not one human ever learned one word of the canine language.

Not one scientist on Earth can even guess what forms of communication an alien may use. No one knows if an alien would choose vocal communications, perhaps a written communication, or a different frequency. Maybe they communicate like the ants do, or like a jellyfish, or maybe they communicate with chirps. We do know the birds talk, so does the dolphins - and we all know the human can't communicate with dolphins. If a human can't understand a dog, bird or a dolphin, what chance do we have to understand an alien from a distant galaxy?

The human race have been trying to sending messages to other alien worlds, and if they do hear the human's messages, they better talk like a human or the communications will break down in a hurry, because the human race can only understand another human language. Perhaps the aliens have been monitoring the human language for centuries waiting for the first time a human understand another animal language. Perhaps the aliens will make no effort to contact humans until they learn the animal languages?

82

MY SCISSORS RETURNED FROM ANOTHER DIMENSION?

A few years ago, as I sat in my recliner, I leaned over to pick up my small neon green 6 inch scissors. I always keep those scissors I keep in a round box with pencils and pens and a small ruler. When I picked the scissors they flipped out of my hand - and literally silently disappeared! I thought they just fell and maybe hit the carpet. But the scissors were nowhere to find.

I searched every inch of a 7 foot circle, determined to find them. I searched in places I decided was silly, like under the phone, and searched the deep sides of my recliner, even turn that heavy chair upside down just in case the scissors fell and bounced deeper under the chair. I even searched the contents of the small trash-can beside my chair, but those neon green scissors were not to be found. I was baffled. Things do not just disappear.

On the next day, I searched for the brilliant green scissors in the same circle but didn't find them. Determined to find them, I decided to expend the search to the entire 33 foot room. The following day, thinking I might have missed something so I searched the entire area again, but the scissors are gone.

Confident the scissors simply disappeared and will never be found, I gave up for the search and bought new scissors.

After four complete months - I opened a small I drawer in a small box (8x6 inches) that I use every day, maybe 3 to 10 times a day, but today I opened the same drawer – to my shock - there were are my neon green scissors! The scissors barely fit in the small box. That box has three drawers and I use the middle drawer for little items, like a finger nail file, a few different erasers and finger nail clippers. I never use those drawers for scissors, but there they were, right on the top of the erasers.

I have to admit I suddenly got cold chills, because the scissors abruptly appeared out of no-where. I used that same less that drawer an less than an hour ago, I had been sitting in that chair for three hours, I know I used that same drawer several times that morning, and each time there were no scissors were in the drawer.

I was totally alone in the house, and no one else entered this home for over five months. (I am very reclusive.) I choose to be alone, and do not entertain neighbors, family, no sales people are allowed inside. I have been alone simply because I am reclusive and enjoy being my own company.

So - into what dimension did the scissors disappear to four months ago - and better question - who returned them? Too, don't mind admitting that ever since that event, each time I use those scissors feels a little uncomfortable.

Do you think it is possible an angel borrowed and then return those scissors to me?

Perhaps a ghost found a use used these scissors and when they were finished with them, they returned them again? Or was it an alien life form that borrowed them for four months?

I guess I'll never know the answer.

83

MONEY FROM SOMEWHERE

According to reports I found, back in 1995, in Scotland, it seems there was a rainfall that included living frogs, a lot of them. Come to find out on that date, the heavens rained thousands of little green. At least one family found their car was covered with countless green frogs.

In the year 1877, a farmer in South Carolina witnessed a rainfall of living alligators. Some of the one foot baby alligators were a little stunned after their fall from the sky, but quickly recovered and started slithering around the farm.

More than once on a stormy day in New Orleans, Louisiana, it rained alligators. There was a rainstorm, with severe lightning and thunder, during that rainfall, alligators were seen falling. With luck, no one was seriously hurt during that storm, but St. Paul's Church was hit with lightening. (*Times-Picayune newspaper. 11 July 1843*)

Who would expect a rainfall of small fish in the Australia Tanami Desert? Nevertheless, in the year 2004 two separate rainfalls that included live little fish that fell from the sky. Too, that same phenomenon - fish from the sky - same location, was reported in twice in the month of February in 2010.

According to the local citizens of Salta Province in Argentina, in the month April in 2007, everyone was shocked to witness a rainfall of multicolored spiders. A person can only shutter to imagine to the shock of looking out of your window and see colorful spiders fall from a normal sky. Most people would not want to see something like that in my life time.

Back in 1968 in England, (in Ramsgate) that December day was far from mundane - on that day, the store clerks listened in shock when pennies from heaven clinked onto the sidewalks for about a quarter of an hour. Oddly enough the coins fell from the sky hard enough to bend the coins when they hit the sidewalks. No doubt the coins fell from the sky, that small town does not possess any tall building, so no one tossed the coins from high windows, there are no tall building there.

Speaking of money - back in the year 1975 in Chicago, Illinois, can you imagine the surprise to witness hundreds of one dollar notes floating from the heavens on a public highway? But that December day the heavens rained a total of $588!

84

THE MOST POWERFUL ARCHANGEL - MICHAEL

Archangel Michael Metatron - has many names, and as an immortal being has lived on planet Earth many times. For example he lived on Earth and used the human name Enoch, and as known on Earth as Enoch Metatron.

Enoch he was a very wise man, and the author of many books. They say he penned over 366 books, but some writers say Enoch wrote over 800 books. Many of them were about nature; other books were about the types of life on Earth. Most of his books discuss spirituality.

It has been written that Enoch never died, because God himself took that patriarch from Earth, without ever tasting death. However, in other another spiritual book, it was suggested it was not God that took Enoch, but it was the angel Anpiel, that physically transported him to Heaven. Either way, both ways, Enoch left Earth without dying.

In one of Enoch's book he explains that there are actually two forms of Paradise - one in God's Heaven, the other remains on Earth - it is called Eden. (The Garden of Eden.)

Michael, the Archangel is also called El Shaddai and sometimes called the 'lesser god', in this position, he is not only known as the Son of God. There are over 100 names to indicate the name of Michael Metatron.

In the holy bible, it was Metatron was the angel of God that stopped the hand of Abraham when he was going to sacrifice Isaac.

As an angel Michael used the name Metatron. He is also known as the angel Jehoel, Joel, or Jahel. As Metatron, he became the angel with a flaming sword that guards the entrance of Garden of Eden.

Metatron/Michel/Enoch is also called as of the "Head of Days," or the "King of Days." Michael as Metatron is also known as the King of Angels and is always in charge of all the angels on heaven and Earth.

Metatron has a twin brother; he and brother are considered the tallest angels in heaven. Metatron's twin brother name is Sandalphon.

Like many other archangels, Michael Metatron is a shape shifter and can appear to a human in other forms.

*As one of the seven leading archangels, Michael sometimes takes the form as a lion when visiting a human.

*The angel Suriel sometimes visit a human, and he takes the shape of an ox.

*To visit a human, the powerful angel Raphael takes on the shape of a dragon.

* When the angel Gabriel visits a human he takes the shape of an eagle.

*The angel Thautabaoth takes the shape of a bear.

*The angel Erataoth usually takes the shape of a dog or wolf.

*Onoal, the angel, chooses the gentle shape of a donkey or ass when visiting humans.

These seven ruling angels (potentates) are the rulers of Heaven.

85

THE PHILADELPHIA EXPERIMENT MISTAKE

They military had a many problems to solve when a person attempts to transport something the size of a military ship to a different location/weight/space/location. The alleged experiment took place at the Philadelphia Naval Shipyard in approximately 28 October 1943, in Philadelphia, Pennsylvania. The plan was to render the USS Eldridge invisible. Back then, the scientist kept trying, but they simply didn't know enough about changing atoms to a different location to use them safely. Nevertheless, they tried. I will give credit for their efforts. However, there were many unknown facts so they were experimenting blind because they didn't know what they were doing. (The U.S. Navy, USS Eldridge, launched 25 July 1943)

One of the problems with that Philadelphia Experiment is not all dimensions travel at the same speed as the third dimension. The third dimensional world travels at a specific speed in space, and other dimensions may at a travel faster or slower.

They attempted to simply cloak a military ship, (they hoped that cloaked ship would be "invisible" the enemy ships and planes in that era,) if it was successful, that would have been an amazing event and the world would be shocked by the unheard of invisible ship. However, sometimes the best efforts are not enough. Instead, the experiment they created was a created dimensional time lag, and that ship not only was distorted in time, but space or location also, was distorted. When they attempted to returned, to the same location, they miscalculated the position simply because they didn't know about the time/space lag. When the war ship returned to the same location, they found many items slightly 'out of place,' including the men on the ship. Simply because the atomic matter of each item on the ship is slightly different.

The atomic weight of iron is not the same as brass; the atomic of glass is not the same as plastic. Every single item on a military ship has a different atomic weight. For example, the atomic weight of metal is not the same as the atomic weight of a human being. That atomic weight makes a vast difference when you are trying to "send" a military ship across time and space. But back then, they were still learning the basics of the unified field theory, and no one knew they violated the physical laws of nature. The scientist involved in the Philadelphia Experiment didn't know the problems they would face when they 'play around' with displacing different weights of atoms in time/space. They found out the hard way, and many brave men died a horrible death, trapped in a metal/human atomic mistake.

One can only hope in some distant date in the future the human race can correct their mistakes, go back in time, and make sure the men in the USS Eldridge live through the Philadelphia Experiment mistake.

86

HIDDEN FACTS - ALIENS & REPTONS

* In the USA, government and military carried out autopsies on alien bodies. Those aliens were Greys, and at least once the "cadaver" was not dead when they started their autopsy.

* Intelligent college trained petite women with blue eyes are more likely to be alien abducted.

* People with at least more than 2 years of college are apt to be abducted by reptilian aliens.

* Muscle bound men and muscular women are rarely abducted by aliens. (But there are exceptions).

* World governments and other worldwide secret organizations have known the true identity of the so called 'aliens' since 1954. However, a few of the world governments knew about the aliens in 1933. Less than a dozen countries knew the secret treaties with the secretive hidden civilization prior 1660. Thousand years ago only three countries had treaties with the hidden civilization inside this planet.

* Female Reptons can stand over 7 feet tall and could defeat 5 human men with no problem. Their strength is incredible, and her intelligence too can leave humans in the dust.

* The human race knew there was another intelligent civilization on the surface of Earth long before man learned to write. Their artistic efforts to record the alien awareness can be found in the ancient caves all over the world.

* Men with long hair are frequently chosen by aliens for abduction.

* Reptons prefer young dark haired human boys aged 5 to 12 years old for abduction. The reason is logical; boys at that age are growing faster at any age in their lives.

* The entire world knows about the not so well known "cover-up" of the alien situation, however, the trained military, the governments of Earth, as well as the news media of Earth believes and hopes if they don't talk about the alien situation, they can hide the alien facts forever.

* Reptons consider eating one of their sacred rites; they do not need food as often as human race. The Reptons can be comfortable and healthy if they eat every few weeks. They prefer not to eat in front of humans - but will eat a small portion of vegetable or fruit, if a dignitary is visiting.

* To this very day, several humanoid reptilian hostages are being held against their will by several government organizations.

* The little Greys do not eat, and their bodies do not have a digestive system. When their body is in need any nutriments, they soak their hands in a liquid form of supplement requirements.

* The Dracon race can live several thousand years, and cannot relate to the short life the human race. The Dracon consider humans an unnecessary disposable race.

87

CLUES TO IDENTIFY HYBRIDS IN NEIGHBORS & CO-WORKERS

The hybrids might wear the wrong seasonal clothing. In the summer they can be seen bundled in sweaters or even wear a heavy overcoat, or in the winter they wear a polo shirt and jeans. Their bodies have trouble adjusting to weather changes. Too, they are not aware of the passing of clothing style; in the year 2022 a female has been seen wearing 1950s era poodle skirt, a cardigan sweater and small scarf around her neck.

It would appear Hybrids need to rest often, as if the weight of a human body is a heavy burden. The hybrids gulp air, similar to human with emphysema or asthma; they are out of breath after walking a short distance. Hybrids require medication, eye witnesses state they have been seen to take green or off-white capsules pills or drinking thick opaque liquids from bottles or flasks from their pockets or briefcases. The liquids appear to be iridescent.

The recording of data is vital to the hybrids. They make notes in small notebooks as well as mumbling softly into a recorder. Too, many hybrids are not good drivers, and ignore the safety rules of the road. For example they fail to turn on their headlights at night, grossly exceed speed laws and rarely use turn signals. The hybrid beings to not appreciate human humor; nor do they understand the proper use of timing in humor. They might giggle during a funeral, or during a serious speech they laugh as if the material is hilarious.

They do not understand the use of table manners or how to use the correct flatware. Over the years eyewitnesses have seen hybrids stir their coffee with a fork. It is not usual for them to attempting to use a spoon to drink a glass of soda-pop. In household appliances, they might try to toast bread with a microwave, or place a frozen dinner in the oven – including the outer box.

The hybrids do not understand the need for privacy. They ask personal questions and do not hesitate to ignore the normal clues that the person does not want to discuss the subject.

They do not understand human customs, such as religious holidays. They do not understand a simple thing like a 'moment of silence' and continue talking when asked for silence. They ask personal questions but refuse to answer simple questions such as 'are you married' or 'do you have any hobbies.' They are secretive regarding their past. That its self is not too odd, because many people do have a desire for secrecy, but since most hybrids do not have a past, they might have been created a few months ago.

The average hybrid requires practice to fit into the human life style. They may appear to be pacing back and forth, but they are reminding themselves how to walk. Also they appear to be talking to himself, but in reality they are practicing appropriate speech patterns.

88

QUESTIONS & ANSWERS ABOUT BREATHING UNDERGROUND

QUESTION: With the amount of people inside Dulce Base, how do they manage to keep the air fresh and breathable?

ANSWER: In Dulce Base, deep underground there are always air monitors that make sure the air is in motion. Look at any large city on the surface, from a distance anyone can see the dirty air, from vehicles and companies, on the surface they call it "smog." On the surface, those cities are at the mercy of the natural winds to blow away the smog and bring fresh air.

The population at Dulce Base understands that problem and makes sure the air inside the Base is in constant motion. People breathe in oxygen and breathe out the used carbon dioxide. Every human on earth have their own built in air monitors - but we call it breathing.

The air is everywhere, and the trick is simple - just make sure that air moving. One of the easiest ways is to make sure live plants and trees are positioned in each level. Plants, especially trees, provide oxygen that is the reason they planted trees on several key locations. Quite a few trees on the second level at Dulce Base are third generation trees, and that means those trees were planted in the years 1930 to 1935. It is not difficult to gently keep the fresh air moving, they have many small air vents that sends the fresh air through several levels.

I have talked about the acres of trees thriving underground, and mentioned them before, but there are many trees underground, and one of the most popular trees are pecan and walnut trees. Underground it takes around 8 to 12 years before pecan trees produce edible nuts, compared on the surface they can start harvesting their nuts after 10 years. It takes longer underground, but the trees will provide healthy large pecans for many generations. The oxygen these trees produce are more vital than the delicious nuts they produce.

As long as the fresh air from the trees and plants are kept in gentle motion, the air monitors do their job well. If it becomes required, additional oxygen is pumped into the air conditioners on the lower levels, but as always, many small fans are more efficient than one huge fan. These thousands of fans are small, quiet enough that few people and reptons do not even notice them. They use a system of ventilation that is similar to the air conditioning in your home and similar the system the space labs use in orbit. They need to keep the air circulated and fresh oxygen is pumped in constantly. As long as the air is circulated, and ventilated constantly, there is not a problem.

Stagnant air is a problem in any closed building, rather or not the rooms are on the surface or underground. At Dulce Base the air moves gently, but constantly, and the healthy breathing abilities are superior to the smog producing cities on the surface.

89

HIDE THE FACTS

1. After successfully shooting down unknown flying objects, the U.S. Government acquiring advanced alien technology.

2. Third dimensional flying craft from unknown dimensional sources have been flying in the skies of Earth for centuries. They still do. The U.S. government is powerless to prevent these talented flyers to fly over any location they choose. I understand why the military is not willing to talk about the skills of these alien flyers. The fact is mere human pilots cannot match the talent of the alien pilots, or the incredible abilities of their flying machines.

3. Unknown advanced civilizations from other planets have been shot down on Earth. Most of alien pilots did not survive very long because the military do not understand what is required them alive. Humans have no idea what types of food to offer alien pilots, but aliens do not like most food humans enjoy. The humans only found out that the aliens yellowish-green blood finally stop flowing long before the alien dies. If the alien is captured and is held in an underground facility, the "lucky" survivor is held hostage for the rest of their life.

4. Since 1941 living alien hostages from unknown civilizations is currently the "guests" (held hostage against their will) of the U.S. Government in underground facilities in Ohio, New Mexico, California or Nevada.

5. Governments of three countries have knowingly conducted autopsies on alien cadavers. The alien victims were alive when the autopsies started, and no anesthetic was used while the alien life forms. The autopsies were required what makes the alien alive. To hide those crimes against alien species, the government agreed to never admit they knew about the alien life forms. The governments of the world pretend they know knowing about the aliens, to hide their own crimes against life.

6. After 1947, several military branches of the United States, agreed to cover the knowledge that an unknown civilization is in charge of the skies over the USA.

7. Human victims have been abducted, held hostage, tortured and mutilated, and ultimately murdered to cover up the alien situation. It has been alleged the aliens still are allowed to torture humans to death because the government was the first to autopsied live alien cadavers.

8. It is a fact that a non-human civilization has always been at the controls on planet Earth. One being - the so called "King of the World" controls the destiny of the human race.

9. Long before the human race attempted to walk on the surface of Earth's only natural satellite - the Moon - an unidentified life form controlled activities on and inside the Moon.
    (The Moon also known as Luna)

10. An unknown civilization has the ability to cloak or hide their silent large crafts. The smaller disk-shaped UFOs cannot be cloaked, but can be disguised as an airplane, a helicopter or a flock of birds. In some countries these unusual crafts move in the sky disguised as large swarms of flying insects, such as locusts.

11. The story of Mother and Child - the story of Terra and her son, Lune, the goddess in Babylon Semiramis with her child Tammuz, the story of Mary and her son Jesus, and been told and retold many times.

90

COUNT YOUR BLESSINGS!

My friends - It is time to take time to really look at your blessings. This morning I was reading online and was surprised to read a young man stated he didn't have any blessings. He had a terrible case of "poor me." His silly problem happens looked foolish because his only real problem was he felt bitter because he had an 'old' computer. His 'old computer' was created 14 *months* ago.

I laughed and I looked at my own computer, it is the computer I use every day. It is the computer I used to write this article. Today the date is 2023. But my computer was created in 2007. It the time it was new when I first purchased it all those years ago. However, my 16 years old laptop is an antique as computer go. I am happy to use this laptop, simply because it works. To me, a computer that works is a blessing.

All computerized equipment is antiquated the minute it is made. In my case, over the years I remembered my laptop crashed a couple times and a few years ago I had to replace the original hard drive about eight years ago, but my old laptop is so old it bare spots when the surface of the finishing where my fingers have worn off the finish. I am certainly not complaining,

I am very happy I have a computer of any type, and I thank God for the countless times I have been blessed. My laptop has more problems that I dare count. But it is all I have, and I thank my lucky stars because I do have a computer I can use every day!

Think about it, where does it is written in the spiritual books "thou-must-have-the-best-and-the-newest-stuff"? I do not remember finding anything like that in any spiritual book, do you? That young guy needs to count his blessings and be happy with he DOES have.

Everyone should try to be happy with whatever you DO have! I know I do!! It is called 'counting their blessings.' I highly suggest everyone should count their blessings every day of their life.

There are many people that forget to count their blessings. The way I think about it, how can *anyone* forget to count your blessings? As long as you are alive, you have the blessing of hope for a better day. Think what you *do* have in your life. When you have anyone you can call you 'friend' you have blessings! If you have someone that you can love, then you have the biggest blessings! Always remember that you must *give* love someone if you hope to be loved.

Also - remember that you must love yourself first, before you can love your neighbors. Do you want to know why?

Because it is a fact, love starts within your own heart. Remember the old ten commandants from the bible? The biggest commandant is you must love your neighbors like you love yourself. The Son of God, Jesus stated the Kingdom of God is *WITHIN*.

That means the Kingdom of God is inside *you*. God is not hanging out on a cloud, or sitting on an ornate throne somewhere, he is *inside* each human. He is *not* an entity wearing a fancy robe.

When you took your first breath the Kingdom of God entered *you* too - and that is called prana, that soul, that holy breath is inside your body. *THAT* - is a *REAL* blessing!

I want you to really look around you and realize there are homeless people everywhere - are you homeless? Or do you worry because you live from paycheck to paycheck and barely make it? Just about everybody it does that these days, so don't feel isolated of think you are alone in your problems. Just be happy to be alive and able to enjoy another day. I know I do.

Here where I live, Las Vegas, Nevada - like everybody else in the world - the casino workers live from paycheck to paycheck. There are people with problems everywhere. It is a fact that I do not know anyone without problems.

So take a minute to look at your life, and be glad you have a family, a friend or two, a neighbor you can trust, and *really* count your blessings!

91

A FEW QUESTIONS FOR LEONARDO DAVINCI

I want you to think in a different way. I like to allow my mind to roam free and think about other possibilities. Don't you? Do you ever consider unique concepts? I mean things that most people usually considered "impossible"?

What if the impossible is a fact? Is that possible? Let's think about something impossible.

Did you ever think you'd like to talk to Leonardo DaVinci?

I know I'd love to talk to him. Everyone knows he invented scores of advanced machines, and if he really wanted to invented things I suspect the first thing he would invent would be a time machine. I am sure he would think about it. (All inventors think about time machines, and what they could do.)

At least DaVinci *says* he invented theses incredible advanced machines. But think about this - After inventing a time machine, all the other 'inventions' were just reporting something he witnessed in that time machine. Correct? (Or perhaps he didn't invent it, instead he found a time machine, and figured out to make it work. Do you think that is possible?)

What if a person from the future visited like DaVinci, and during the visit the real time traveler dropped dead from a heart attack - and suddenly DaVinci becomes the new owner of the time machine. Or - what if the real DaVinci was a violent man and he actually murdered the time traveler? Either way - DaVinci uses the machine or everyone assumes he is "very advanced, and becomes the world best inventor." *(I seriously doubt DaVinci would ever harm or kill anyone, but it is always fun to think of other possibilities.)*

If I had an opportunity to talk to Leonardo DaVinci, here is a few questions I would ask:

1. Mr. DaVinci, how old were you when you invited this time machine?
2. Was that your first invention?
3. Did someone help you? Like - a stranger from the future?
4. If you are the actually inventor of this time machine, would he please give me a working model of that machine? I mean since if it is yours time machine to share with others, I am sure you wouldn't mind, right?
5. Another question to you Mr. DaVinci, doesn't God get a little upset because you miss-use your talent and used your time machine and going back in time to keep you alive and healthy for centuries when so many others must die?
6. Why didn't you tell others in your era about the machine you found?
7. Did you attempt to return the machine to the real inventor?

(DaVinci was born 15 April, 1452, in an area called Anchiano, in the Republic of Florence, Italy. He died on 2 May, 1519, in Cloux, France. He was an Italian painter, draftsman, sculptor, inventor, architect, and engineer whose skill and intelligence was above the other people in that era. As an artist, he is best known for "Mona Lisa" [c.1503-19] and for the "Last Supper." [1495-98.] Even in his own era he was considered a famed man. In today society is DaVinci considered one of the best artist is history, and could only be matched be the also famed artist Michelangelo, a younger peer. DaVinci visualized flying machines, adding machines, radio, tanks and countless other items.)

92

SACRED COMMANDS –
HOW TO USE THEM

Here is something I want you to think about: the words of "I believe," "I know" and "I am…" are those terms could change your life if you are willing to apply them and correctly.

Think of the words: "I believe…"

The term "I believe…" implies there is some not quite solid in the term "I believe…" the words "I believe…" is lovely, but the tiny three letters of doubt "*but*" takes away the powers behind the "I believe but…." is a term killer. "I believe in UFOs" indicates it is your opinion regarding UFOs. The term does allow doubt.

Now then - think of the words: "I know…" The term "I know…" for example the term: "I know UFOs are real…" that statement is powerful. Out of the two terms "I believe…" and "I know…," which words imply doubt?

Words are things called "thought forms."

Every time you say a word, that word goes out and tried make it happen. Every word you utter looks for a way to make the words manifest. Do not allow say the words "I doubt…." is a negative term and should ban it from your vocabulary. Even worse are terms such as "I can't…," because it limits you severely!

I do hesitate to tell the sacred command words because that could change your life, but without change your life remains weak. Without the sacred commands no one cannot be powerful.

You need to learn how to use the sacred command "I am…" – the term "I am…" is a command and the term must be carefully used. If you say the term "I am happy…," or the term "I am lucky…" is a command and you should confirm it every day. Say the words "I am happy" and say it three times in a row, command the words and it will change the way you think, you will become happy.

In the spiritual book known as the Holy Bible (King James Version) Moses asks the Lord for his name, so he could tell the public so they would believe the words of God. The Lord God replies to Moses and tells him his name is "I am that I am." (so to speak, "I am – THAT – I am" the way I would tell you when you ask my name and I wanted you to that it is me, not some other woman named Cherry, I would tell you "Cherry, THAT Cherry.") So God's name is "I am…" and God warns you that you must not his name in vain…. Think about what his name and what happens when you use his name in vain, do not use his name unless you mean it.

The sacred command "I am" is so powerful it instantly commands without hesitation. The command "I am happy" is an instant command that demands that you become happy. Say the command "I am happy" and you instantly feel happier.

So ---- when you say the sacred command "I am happy..." the command tries to start happen, and instantly you are happier.

If you are willing to try the command "I am happy..." and you right away you feel better and feel happy, what do you think would happen if you utter the sacred command "I am wealthy..."? Think about it.

93

ANGELS AND THEIR INFLUENCE

This is a fact - there are no books or scrolls written that were written by the Eternal God. Too, there are no known scrolls alleged written by Jesus or the Holy Ghost. It would be nice if there were any books like that, but the holy books on Earth were written by other humans. Even the most ancient version of the spiritual books, in any language, such as the Holy Bible, was written by another human. However, there seem to be a few books may have been written in the angelic script.

Angel Script -

We all have heard about the so called "Angelic Script," the language of the Angels. So - if there is a Language of Angels, shouldn't there be a few books authored by these angels? But there are no books that were actually written by an angel. Why not? Perhaps they are not in the third dimensional world. The 3rd dimension is the world for the human race, not angels. In this modern world today wouldn't it be nice to get even a little answer such as 'where is God.' The answer seems to be he is busy on his own planet, known as Heaven.

I like to think the reason God or his angels can't write a book for us is because they live in a different dimension. I am aware those words do not really supply an adequate explanation, so I assure you I am not pretending I know all the answers - I am only suggesting that the concept of other dimensions do offer hope of understanding as to why the spiritual beings can't not write books.

However, according to other well written humans, the angels known as Grigori, (also known as The Watchers) these angels are not allowed to write books for the human race because (quote:) "For man was not created for such a purpose." (According to Enoch, the angel Penemue instructed mankind in writing *and thereby many sinned for eternity to eternity and until this day. For man was not created for such a reason.")* (Enoch I: 7:8)

After God banished Adam and Eve from the Garden of Eden, they followed a cave/tunnel to reach the surface of Earth. The fallen mankind was so innocent they had no idea how to find food because everything was provided to them inside the perfect Garden.

The innocent mankind didn't know how to survive on the barren surface of Earth, but it was it was the 'fallen angels' that took pity on the child-like beings like Adam and Eve, when God banned them from the Garden of Eden. It has been written that it was not just Adam and Eve, but several of their friends followed them to the surface of Earth. It was the fallen angels that instructed mankind and taught man how to survive on the harsh surface of planet Earth. This is a few of the names of what they taught Adam and Eve and the other humans. Here is a list According to A Dictionary of Angels that helped the outcast humans. (Author: Gustav Davidson1967)

1. Armaros: Taught men the resolving of enchantments
2. Araquiel: Taught men the signs of the earth
3. Azazel: Taught men to make knives, swords, and shields, and to devise ornaments and cosmetics.
4. Baraqijal: Taught men astrology
5. Ezequeel: Taught men the knowledge of the clouds.
6. Gadreel: Introduced weapons of war
7. Kokabel: Taught the science of constellations
8. Penemue: Instructed mankind in writing and taught children the bitter and sweet, and the secrets of wisdom.
9. Sariel: Taught men the course of the moon.
10. Semjaza: Taught men enchantments, root-cutting etc.
11. Shamshiel: Taught men the signs of the sun.

The angels still reach out and help humans the same way today.

Angels do not author books, but according to a few human writers, but the Other Races can't appear in the 3rd dimension because the angels can appear out of no-where, we see them, we hear their spoken words, and sometimes the angels find a way to reach the human race by convincing a willing human to complete a mission, all under the guidance of angelic influence.

94

CHOSEN WORDS

1. The name Sheba means seven, and the name Abednego means 'the god Mercury.'

2. The word "Mish-mash" has the meaning of 'something hidden.'

3. Cherub means 'the keeper of God." Cherubs are angels of the air.

4. The words "Ubi terrarium summus" is Latin, and in English they mean "Where in the world are we?"

5. Lucifer means "light bringer" or "bright morning star," it name also means "Venus, the morning star."

6. In Latin the word is "fraternitus" but in English it means "brotherhood."

7. "Albus" and "white bright" have the same meaning.

8. "Illuminatatis" means to "make light."

9. "Illuminati" means the "enlightened ones."

10. The number three in Latin is "ter."

11. Egyptian god is Ra means the Sun.

12. The ancient name for Earth is "Ter-ra" or Terra. Ter means 3. So, Earth Terra shows it position in the solar system – Terra means "third from the sun."

13. Subterrasire – can means "the lower world" or "under the surface is another world."

14. Lucifer's parents were Aurora (mother) and Ceyx. (father) Lucifer is the son of illuminated parents - he is the son of the brilliant golden dawn, and also the bright evening star. Lucifer is both the morning and the evening - the beginning of light and the end of light - the alpha and the omega. {the word alpha means 'the first' or 'beginning' - the word omega means 'the last' or 'ending.'}

15. Aurora means "golden dawn" and she is the goddess of morning. {think about it}

16. In ancient Babylon there was a seven story temple, and each level had a color. The name of the Temple was: "The Temple of the Seven Spheres." (In Dulce Base there are seven layers or seven levels, and each level uses a different color uniform too.)

17. The names Esther and Venus means the same. {think what it means}

18. The name "Og" - he was a deformed giant that stood over 9 feet tall, he was from the race of Rephaim. (These Raphaim were members of the native race of aboriginal beings or previous inhabitants that lived in the valley before the smaller human race entered and destroyed the giants.)

19. Hades or Sheol means "hollow" and was sometimes called the "lower realms." (Natural "hollow pockets" inside the Earth, or caves.) In ancient times it was thought that after death to souls of evil humans spend eternity is Sheol, it was considered Sheol was hidden in the bowels of Earth, while the souls of the pure return to their Creator in the sky.

20. The name "Babel" means "the gate of God." Before God destroyed it, the "Tower of Babel" was a large building, and builders were trying to build a tower that would reach God's kingdom. These builders almost made it, but God didn't the idea, so he destroyed the building, changed the languages of the builders so they couldn't understand each other, and to make sure, he relocated the builders to different places on the earth so they could no longer find each other. Today, the word 'babble' (Bable) comes from that ancient profound event.

95

ANGELS, ALSO KNOWN AS MULTIDIMENSIONAL ETHEREAL BEINGS

Beautiful Angels that worship God is "beyond numbers" and these incredible creatures that only answer to God himself, but appear through ancient scrolls such as the Holy Bible. One of these angels is known as Malach. (The angel Malach also honored as Malachi, the last book of the Old Testament.)

Others are considered as angels and they include Irinim (Watchers/High Angels.)

Here are a few:

*Cherubim (Mighty Ones),

*Sarim (Princes),

*Seraphim (Fiery Ones),

*Chayyot ([Holy] Creatures),

*Ofanim (Wheels)

*Powers (Dynamis)

*Dominians (Lords)

Collective terms for the full array of numina serving God include:

* Kedoshim (Holy Ones)

They are known as an Adat El, a divine assembly (Ps. 82; Job 1)

A select number of angels in the Bible have names. Names such as Michael, Joel, Set, Malach and Satan.

*Tzeva, (Host),

*B'nei ha-Elohim or B'nai Elim (Sons of God),

*Beni-Elohim-Craul (spiritual creatures) God created them on Earth ages before he created the human race. The Beni-Elohim was the real beings that were made in God's Image. They are also known as the Son's of God. They were created on the 6th day of creation. (Human race was created on the eight day of creation.)

Genesis Chapter 2: 5. On the Seventh Day of creation, God rested. After God created the trees and other living things, as well as the animals, God created the Son's of God. - But God had NOT yet created the human race. This is what he said: "….for the Lord God had not caused it to rain upon on the Earth, and there was *not a man* to till the ground." (Chapter 2: 6) "But there went up a mist from the Earth, and watered the whole face of the ground" (Chapter 2: 7) "And the Lord God formed man of the dust of the ground, and breathed into his nostrils the breath of Life; and man became a living soul."

96

CITY OF SECRETS

Like many small western desert towns, the dusty streets are far from seething with activities during the week. It is the same in the town of Dulce, New Mexico. Weekends are different for the country stores and taverns. The businesses are packed with local cheerful patrons. They are anxious to catching up with the news of cutting-edge ranching methods, or the hottest gossip.

These people are hard working desert ranchers; their families and ranch hands drive their small trucks and pick-ups into town in search for a well-deserved diversion. They are looking for a bit of innocent fun, maybe a game of pool, or a few beers.

Occasionally, they check out the newest films at the theater or take a chance with Lady Luck by local game of Bingo. Like most small western towns, about the only changes are the faces, their personalities or the name of the citizens.

That pleasant scene changes from innocent to sinister when you enter the Native American community Dulce, New Mexico. It is not the residents of

Dulce in New Mexico that feels sinister, it is an unnamed aura that is hard to explain. In fact the exact cause for the difference in hard to pinpoint. The local residents are friendly, they are willing to chat with strangers.

Alternatively, I guess it could be the aura of unrest in furtive glances the some Apaches give to outsiders? I can understand that, there have been too many outsiders, too many government agents asking questions and a small army of UFO enthusiasts taking photographs without asking permission. Should the Apache Nation ignore Television camera crews from foreign countries that climb fences and trespass on private land and scramble on the sides of Mesa without bothering checking if it is legal?

Too, the town of Dulce suffers from a well-documented history of strange animal mutilation, not just a few, but dozens of bizarre bloodless deaths that plague the ranchers. The first known case of animal mutilation happened Alamosa, Colorado back in 1967. That case happened roughly only about 100 miles northeast of Dulce, New Mexico. That was mutilated animal was an Appaloosa horse. The body of horse was bloodless, all the flesh of the head and neck was removed, so it appeared it was 'cleaned.' The bare bones of the head appeared clean and bloodless. There was not a trace of blood was found in the area. This was the first of many animal mutilation in the same area, same town.

Nestle near the base of the tall Archuleta Mesa; the desert community of Dulce is inside the Jicarilla Apache Indian Reservation. An unnamed foreboding preys on the minds of the two thousand Apaches. In small clusters, the debate rumors of silent aliens that kill off the cattle in the area. Some say it a paramilitary organization that mutilates animals in the near-by ranches, but no one knows for sure.

In this area, countless pale green sagebrush and stately pinion trees and cedar trees dot the reservation. Dry washes meander across the valley when rain arrives that water helps to add to several small lakes. Not only rain. but also the winter snow melts in the spring, that too, adds to the water that trickles into those lakes. The area boasts a large population of both wild and domestic animals, including an abundance of fowl, deer, horses and both dairy and range cattle. And of course, a few coyotes or wolves howl here and there, moaning with their eerie lonesome from hillsides. It is enough to wonder why these animals were mutilated in that area. A person is bound to also wonder if it the mutilations were strictly animals, or were humans mutilated too?

A few well-known UFO researchers claim the intimidated villager's whisper of is an unknown race of beings that sneaks into the area at night. The aliens select healthy cows and perpetrate unspeakable mutilation acts on the hapless cattle.

Is it more than the slaughtered animals at the hands of unknown beings that bring terror to the residents? Do the citizens avoid walking alone at night in Dulce? What other secrets are whispered behind locked doors of the homes of Dulce? Do the local clergy know the truth, but cannot talk about underground base said to be under town? The local residents quietly admit they wonder who is behind these unspeakable mutilations. They also wonder who or what is underneath their churches, their stores and their homes.

97

ILLUSIONS, TV & COMICS
OVER THE YEARS

The size and the location of a flying saucer is an illusion. When we see something, it becomes real to us. Much like a movie, the illusion of seeing the picture moving becomes very effective. In reality the many photos that we call a 'movie' is just a lot of still pictures that creates that effect of a moving.

Years ago, no one dreamed that television could be possible; several people thought TV was a worthless invention. However, time has proven TV is a fantastic invention. Soon (if not already) it will be easy to create a moving image anywhere, any time and the original source will be difficult, if not impossible, to locate.

Are moving images a link with UFO? There could be. What about water - is there a link between water and UFOs? Many UFOs have been seen leaving or entering large bodies of water, like lakes, bays, even a large rivers or the oceans. Is there a tube or tunnel of water in the ocean that somehow divides and shapes the water and the result would resemble a tube?

Is that the way Moses divided the Sea that allowed his people to escape? When it is not used, the tube would be no longer visible. But in action, the tube may look like a swirling vortex in the water.

I wonder if that water-tube could explain the Bermuda Triangle mystery? Could it be that when the water-tube is activated, it disturbed the surface and any ship near that disturbance would be pulled under the surface? Is it possible the atmosphere or the air above that tube is also pulled into the moving vortex underwater and any airplane in the area would fall from the sky? Could that explain part of the Bermuda Triangle Mystery?

After images:

Could it be that by we see a UFO, it's already gone, and all we see is the after image? Like a visual echo.

Silent Boom:

We have all heard those mysterious sky booms, could it be possible that it is an echo from an explosion in another dimension? If there is a major explosion in another dimension, could it be heard it here in the 3rd dimension? Or – are there atomic testing going on inside our hollow Earth, too?

Comics and Real Life

Did you ever check old cartoons for a link with the UFO's and Space Brothers? Could there be a connection? There could be a connection.

George Adamski (1952) claimed the Space Brothers and Sisters wore a pageboy hairstyle that matches the character "Prince Valiant" in the same era. (1937—1950)

How about the changeable shape of UFO's? You can compares to the comics character named the "The Shmoo" (Lil Abner, 1935—1950) The Shmoo changed shape too.

Early the 1947 to the late 1950s we could find the beautiful space women, and several of the space brothers also had beautiful women, it compares to the comics character known as "Brenda Starr." (1947—1957)

Late fifties we can find military type with CIA stuff action in the comics (1947 to the present) compare it to the "Sad Sack" and "Terry and the Pirates," the "Phantom." Those comics included military, and unusual para-military characters. That matches with the bungling MIB and the warning laden Space Brothers.

In the 1970s dogs were popular on the cartoons with "Snoopy" and "Maraduke." Canine characters that are almost human un their demeanor. Also, was the mysterious "Devil Dogs" that kill other animals, but were never caught.

What about "Bigfoot" and "King Kong" and "Swamp Thing"? What about the comics about the wee-people or elves and the little green men from Mars? Genetics and hybrid life forms are really easy for us to accept because we all read or saw talking animals like "Donald Duck," "Pogo" and the hero like the "Mighty Mouse."

Our childhood heroes were frequently space born, like "Superman," a character that was born on another planet, or characters become fantastically strong and wise thru a lab accident or some strange elixir.

Think about of all these comics – were they just preparing us for the reality Day of the Alien when they walk among us? Maybe it is time to think about it.

98

DISINFORMATION AGENTS OR SLEEPERS IN THE UFO WORLD

To understand you need to comprehend the meaning certain words and terms. Here are the four terms you need to really understand: There are four "de" words - to "de" anything means to "remove" or "un-create" anything already made.

*1. The word "deceive" - the word comes from Latin "decipere" that means to 'catch, ensnare, cheat'. The original word to deceive is used to indicate to create a false credibility.

* 2. The word "deny" comes from Latin "denegare," from to say 'say no'. The word deny means to refuses to admit the truth or existence or the reality of something.

* 3. The word "destroy" - the word comes from the Latin "destruere," meaning to reverse the original form, in other words to "de- struct or un- build."

* 4. The word "defeat" comes from medieval Latin "disfacere" 'undo'. To defeat a person is to "undo" that person by any possible means.

The U.S. Army uses three terms "Deceive, Deny, and Destroy" to defeat the enemy.

The government uses all four terms freely to block any efforts to clearly explain anything they want to hide.

Please be aware there are hidden agents that hide inside the UFO community, and their entire reason to exist is to deceive, to deny, to destroy and defeat the truth about the unknown civilization that has co-existed with the human race for centuries, or longer. These agents are known as disinformation agents.

The UFO community has been infiltrated by disinformation agents whose complete intent is to destroy any work that gets too close the truth. These government agents have the ability to hide their connections to the government.

Not all these agents remember who they are, because they have been first trained, then hypnotized, and then taught a new name and a new life history. These agents are no longer aware of their original position because they went through deep hypnosis and forgot their original name or their position in the government. These under-cover agents are known as "sleepers," and although they are well hidden the information about the sleepers were exposed via movies and TV shows.

Through programs such as the MK-ULTRA Programs, these agents went through mind-control hypnosis, and now believe they are no longer with the government. Sometimes they firmly believe their own lies. These hypnotized agents believe they have never been connected to any government agencies.

According to their knowledge, they do not realize they are undercover agents. Nevertheless, they are under-cover agent, (deep cover, and no longer remember their previous position) and several of them firmly believe doubt anyone that tries to tell them they worked together for more than a year.

The deep hypnosis is very effective; sometimes these agents become assassins for the government and do not even remember the murders they committed. This type of work is very frightening and is enough to make any intelligent person want to avoid anyone deeply into the UFO community.

Their work is similar to the work seen in the movie The Manchurian Candidate. If you haven't bothered to see that older movie, I suggest you look for it. The original movie was released in 1962, and starred Angela Lansbury, Janet Leigh, Laurence Harvey, Frank Sinatra, James Gregory & Henry Silva. (there was a remake of that same movie in 2004.)

[That movie is NOT about UFOs, but in watching that film you can see the connections.]

99

TWO INSIDE STORIES

This is a true story, and aside from the names of the president of the United States involved you won't read the specific names if the people in the story.

The story is only partly accurate, because the dates, the reasons and the events are not accurate. According to the popular story of the 1947 New Mexico event has the alien craft happened in June of 1947, and an alien craft crashed and several humanoid beings were injured when the craft was demolished by the crash.

The story says that by the executive order by U.S. President Harry S. Truman, facilitated the recovery and investigation of a fallen an alien spacecraft. Within a few days President Truman formed a secret committee of scientists, military leaders, and government officials, and named that committee The MJ-12. There authentic story did not include the true reason for the alien crash.

The leaked story of an alien craft is only part of the story. The alien craft didn't 'fall out of the sky' - it was shot down by military personnel in Los Alamos, New Mexico. In 1947 project Magnetic Journey was instigated in Los Alamos, New Mexico after a flying saucer was shot down by U.S. Army soldiers. The crew of the saucer included 5 humanoid being; two beings died instantly when the Army shot down the alien craft, and a third died a few hours later. The two aliens that survived were treated for their wounds and were transported to an underground medical facility in or near Los Alamos, New Mexico.

But that was not the first incidence with an alien craft.

Years before, 1933, in New Mexico, a government study group (the NSC/MJ-12) was formed after an event involving an alien craft landed. In the event, the alien craft landed inside a fenced field in the high desert, in the edge of a cedar forest.

The U.S. Army soldiers were on standard maneuvers in the desert of New Mexico, when the alien craft developed unknown problems. The near-by soldiers noticed the alien craft when it flew over their camp. The soldiers witnessed the landing motion and immediately investigated.

The soldiers watched while the three humanoids carried a small box, one of the alien opened the box and saw he only carried tools and the alien began working an unknown problem that involved the bottom of the craft near the landing legs. For reasons that were never fully explained, a team of several U.S. Army soldier fired on the humanoids.

At the same time the soldiers noticed the alien craft was trying to take off. The soldiers used several rounds of anti-tank weapon, and succeeded to prevent the alien craft to take off. All three aliens died in the attack, two inside the craft survived.

The Army used three large tarps and totally covered the alien craft and transported it by truck to the White Sands Facility in New Mexico.

After the scientists entered the alien craft, the researchers opened the working machinery of the flying saucer and discovered how the silent craft actually flies. They found 12 large movable triangle shaped magnets is a specific geographic design. In the cockpit there is a small keyboard with the same pattern of the 12 triangles. It is the specific twelve fingers of the hand shape keyboard of does the job. To change the direction of the craft, they simply move one of the 12 triangles. The average human could not safely fly that craft simply because the average human has only ten fingers. Several of the alien races possess six fingers on each hand.

Only a hand full of people know the inside story behind the MJ-12, and I assure you I am telling you this much at the risk of my life. These government agents do not allow anyone reveal the secrets.

I know I'll get in trouble for talking about it, but I only gave you the basic story and did not provide names of the soldiers involved, or the exact location of the incident. I hope that is enough to keep me alive.

100

THE MISSING WOMEN
OF DULCE BASE

I do not think it is coincidence that the largest group of missing people in the west is in four states that touch; those touching states are Utah, Colorado, Arizona and New Mexico. Locally, the Four Corners Area is home to several Native American Tribes, including the Navajo, Hopi, Apache and other Native Indian tribes. Please be aware these Native American Indian Tribes are NOT involved with the missing women. They are mentioned to let you know this area has been populated for centuries before the white people entered the area. The Native American Indians have talked about beings from underground to the white settlers in this area.

It is a dubious honor but New Mexico can boast of the highest levels of missing people in the United States. I can't help but wonder if New Mexico's high level of missing people happens to be very near the entrance of Dulce Base. In other words, close to New Mexico's largest city, Albuquerque, and near Los Alamos - the main entrance one of the largest genetic facilities in the United States, the infamous Dulce Base. This genetic facility has a work force that includes both human and alien.

These missing very young females are old enough to have already began their monthly periods, however, the mystery deeps, when you discover most of these missing females are usually petite, usually they stand around five foot three, weigh under 110 pounds and most of the young women have dark hair. Many of the females happen to be young Native American women from the Four Corners section, and they become missing at a very high rate. However, females from all five races, as well as mixed races also missing.

There is a specific reason the Greys or Reptons choose petite females that during their most fertile age, and at the age when the females are capable to produce eggs. When the females age and no longer have the ability to produce eggs, the aliens have no use for these females. It has been proven that post menstrual females ages are not taken for their genetic studies. Females with a high IQ of women with an abundance of certain esoteric knowledge are still taken for a different studies, the exact reason is currently unknown.

The Greys or Reptons do not seem to abduct or kidnap postmenstrual women, or elderly men that are no longer sexual active. The exception is always visible - men and women of any age with an abundance of certain esoteric information. Due to the unusual nature of the esoteric information in question, it is best I do not elaborate.

Another question one might ask is they do not kidnap a woman who had already experienced a hysterectomy, or if the female is barren. However, women of any age with unusual esoteric information are abducted, and sometimes are taken for certain studies, and sometimes they become one of the missing women. Nor do they abduct men that have experienced a vasectomy. But once again, there are exceptions for several reasons, but usually because the men in question hold unusual esoteric knowledge. A person is bound to be curious as to why the aliens usually kidnap only fertile men and women.

(The small Greys with large black eyes are genderless androids and without sexual organs. Too, the small Greys cannot originate anything. These Small Greys are similar like a machine or a computer that continues to keep trying to complete their original order. They do not have original thoughts, and their brain depends from orders downloaded from the DraconLeaders. However, without the guidance the DraconLeaders the small Greys require constant help, and the body of the Grey will break down and will no longer function.)

Did you ever wonder why the aliens grab so many young boys between is five to fifteen? I believe it is because those boys are going through rapid growth periods of their lives, and it is during these growth spurts the Reptons can easily manipulate the changing bodies of these boys and turn them into "Advanced Warriors."

Have you searched online and looked at the new modern soldiers of today? Do they resemble the soldiers of the past? Do the react the same as soldiers of the past? New soldiers do not even look close to the soldiers of the past.

Young healthy men of ages 16 to 45 are the most common men abducted. No one asks these men if they would like to volunteer their sperm; the men go through an uncomfortable ordeal while their sperm is forcible removed by machine. Frequently the young men suffer a sensation of shame that bothers them for the rest of their life. They may joke about it, but it is their way to deal with the shame. The same reaction with the women, they usually hesitate to discuss the entire ordeal they went through at the hands of aliens.

The Greys have been abducting the humans; using and modifying the human body since the early the 1930s. It was so easy for them adapt the humans, they created a world-wide financial crunch, and history called that era the Great Depression. While everyone was hungry, and hurting for money, the world was ready for any kind of an easy way out of their problems. The world governments quickly agreed to any treaty that might help the world's population suffering. The government agents sold the human population like cattle and they called it a "Treaty," and never discussed it with the general public. The government agreed to barter off a few thousands of men, women and children, and the aliens, and in exchange, the aliens agreed not remove the souls of these humans from this planet.

The aliens tried to use the human body without separating the human soul from the body. The aliens did know how to separate the soul from the body, but when the human body removes the soul, the body dies. For years, nothing worked, then the Greys introduced illegal drugs, they tried everything they knew. But it was not enough. To this day, the human race have become an enslaved drug dependent zombies – humans without a soul.

101

40 CLUES OF ALIEN ABDUCTION

1. You have become aware of RH negative blood, and attempt to check your blood type.

2. Since your childhood you have felt you have been chosen to complete an important task, but you do not know what that task involves.

3. As a child, you had an invisible friend, and that friend talked to you, taught you things and that invisible friend was important to you.

4. Family members also remember your vital invisible friend and recall certain "strange events" connected with that 'friend'. Many of the family members were also convinced the invisible friend was a real being.

5. You feel anxiety when someone is discussing aliens or UFOs, but you remain fascinated and listen for hours, but choose not to talk about aliens yourself.

6. More than any other period in your life, you feel a strong need of protecting Mother Earth.

7. You in a safe home, but sometimes you have a fear of being kidnapped.

8. You are often check your surroundings, and each time leave your home, you always check your home for "intruders." Before you go to bed, you check the locks of doors and windows.

9. Certain sleep disorders such as insomnia or sleep walking has bothered you all your life.

10. You are aware you are more comfortable with your bed sleeping against a wall.

11. You recall strong dreams of being paralyzed in bed and sometimes you feel as if someone else is in your room.

12. Often dreams of flying in the sky, or dream of jumping over mature trees, jumping the distance of a block or two and it feels normal.

13. You can't shake the memories of being taken through a solid wall by small Grey aliens.

14. Memories of UFOs, halls and rooms in alien craft, or remembering being with UFO occupants.

15. Too, you can't forget your odd memories of medical procedures that are not handled by humans.

16. Vivid nightmares of total destruction of the world have bothered you all your life.

17. Odd memories of receiving instructions of educating the world, they do not feel like "dreams."

18. Repeated memories of interacting with UFO occupants, but you feel "guilty" if you talk about them.

19. Constant feeling of being watched or monitored, especially at night.

20. Having unexplained lights in your bedroom in the dark room at night.

21. Hearing unexplained tones and sounds, frequently hums and clicks.

22. Frequent unexplained nosebleeds, especially at dawn.

23. You awake to discover unexplained marks or bruises on your body.

24. Sometimes you awake with soreness in your genitals which cannot be explained.

25. X-rays or other procedures reveal strange, objects in your body and you have no idea how they ended in your body.

26. You have constant sinus trouble, or you have a history of migraine headaches.

27. You suddenly hear a loud sound in one ear, or others you notice sporadic ringing in your ears.

28. You have become you aware you have unusual scars, scoops or marks and you have no idea what caused them.

29. Overnight you find tender spots on your fingertips and find a straight line cut, no memory of what caused the new cuts.

30. Other mornings you find tender triangular marks, usually on your limbs, but sometimes scars in roof of mouth, or behind one ear.

31. For no logical reason to avoid medical appointments or standard treatment.

32. More than once in your life you know you have experienced missing time, usually one to four hours you cannot explain.

33. Against your own nature, you find decide you drive to unfamiliar area, you do not why you when there.

34. In the middle of the night you awake and notice a strange haze or fog in your room, against logic, you go back to sleep without investigating.

35. You hear strange pulsing tones, and you could not identify the source.

36. For hours you hear the distant sound of truck idling, the sound appears to seems to based under your house, or near it.

37. You find a pressing need to double check all the locks in your house, that includes every window, but the need is not based on fear, but compulsion.

38. You know you have witnessed at least one unknown object in the sky what was not a bird, plane or jet or star and it is not the Moon.

39. You have a haunting memory of "something happened" - but can't pinpoint that uncomfortable memory.

40. Certain images trigger instant "uncomfortable feeling," that image may be the image of a sketch of alien face, or an examination table.

102

BASIC QUESTIONS &
ANSWERS ABOUT UFOS

1. I think the term 'UFO' is an acronym, but what do those initials mean?

   ANSWER: The United States Air Force (USAF) defines a UFO as: "Unidentified Flying Object." Anything that relates to any airborne object which by performance, aerodynamic characteristics, or unusual features does not conform to any presently known aircraft or missile type, or which cannot be identified as a familiar object.

2. In plain English, would you please explain what an alien is or extraterrestrial?

   ANSWER: The term "alien" simply means "stranger" or not from this area. That is why when a person enters the USA soils they are considered an alien. In today's society the term "alien" has been included to mean an extraterrestrial being. The word extraterrestrial is a being that was not born or created on a planet other than the planet Earth. Extraterrestrials are not from planet Earth. I will breakdown the term extraterrestrial - "Extra" means in addition. "Terra" - a Latin term meaning "three", in this case, the word "Ra" the sun god, so the Terra means "third in position." (Third in the solar system.) So - the word "extra" means in addition, so a being that was not born on planet Terra (Earth) is known as an "extraterrestrial."

3. I keep reading about the word "Star Child" - what does it mean?

ANSWER: A child from the stars. That child could be a physical half breed of half-alien - half-human, or that child it could be a mental product of mental manipulation. The child never feels comfortable with around other children. Sometimes the child is has been the victim of genetic manipulation by human or extraterrestrial when as a fetus. These children are NOT from the stars, and like all children grow up and become adult, unfortunately most of these "star children" grow up, the adults start pretending they are "special" simply because they miss being the 'main attraction,' these adults would say anything to stay in the middle of attention. It is sad.

4. What does it mean when a person claims they are a contactee?

ANSWER: Real contactees are men and women that have experienced physical contact with an extraterrestrial being. They have agreed to share a limited agreement with the non-human beings. Contactees do not fear their extraterrestrial contacts. There has been an agreement between the human and the non-humans that their memories will be retained and are allowed to discuss their experienced. Contactees are quite comfortable discussing the extraterrestrial experiences. (Like many other subjects, there are MANY frauds and pretend they have experienced alien contact.)

5. Please, can you tell me exactly what an abductee is?

ANSWER: Abductees consider themselves victims. Their alien contact is based of fear and refuses to consider their experience as a learning experience. These people consider themselves as "victims" and usually experience fear when they must discuss their alien contact. These "victims" fear the lack of control they experience, and due their fear, they frequently must be restrained during the initial contact. Most of these people cannot retain any memory of their contact. As a kindness, their memories are blocked so they need not recall alien contact. Later, these same "victims" go out of their way to try to remember what happened. They know 'something' happened to them and they use hypnosis to remember. When they do recall, they are once again horrified and fear again controls their lives. There is no one to block the memory and they spend the rest of life in abject fear.

6. Is there a difference between a contactee and an abductee?

ANSWER: The contactee willingly experiences an alien experience and has a "limited agreement" with non-human life forms. An abductee considers them self a victim and chooses to consider their alien experiences as unpleasant. These victims claim they have suffered from "involuntary contact" with the aliens.

7. I read the term 'Keeper' what does it mean?

ANSWER: Keepers experience an open and established relationship with non-human life forms. They do not fear the extraterrestrial beings and sometimes complete missions for the non-humans, such as educating the public on the extraterrestrial situation. These Keepers sometimes occasionally become shadowy government agents, and become untrustworthy.

8. What is the most vital information required when reporting a U.F.O. sighting?

ANSWER: Vital facts when reporting a U.F.O. sighting:

** Compare the craft to something you are familiar with, such as a large as an 18wheel truck, the size of a house, or larger of a department store.

** If possible, get closer to the craft, to view the object clearly, without risking physical danger.

** Take photos if it is possible, or as soon as possible write everything you can remember about the craft. Use paper and a pen/pencil and sketch what you saw, or a recording device to tell what happened. It is vital you write your encounter as soon as possible, including any possible witnesses. Make sure your report includes the date, the actual hour and minute of your sighting, the location of your sighting, list any witnesses, the color of the craft, shape and any odors, sounds or emotional reactions (fear, excitement, happiness etc) The path the craft took (west to east etc) and rather the path they took was a straight line or a zigzag path, when recording the event include any stops, turns and landings.

** Also when recording, note how long you had the craft in sight, note any missing time or related thoughts. Notice any planes, jets, helicopters or any other vehicles in sight or near at your sighting. Did you see any other people or living beings outside or near the craft, write anything you saw about it, did anyone use a phone, a camera or a Geiger Counter or objects like them in your sight?

9. How can you find a finding a reliable organization to report your UFO information?

ANSWER: Use your phone book, ask friends, go online and search for UFO groups, ask them about the size of their organization, how long they have been helping people. It is YOUR information, but it is worthless unless you share it with others. Report your sightings!

103

UNUSUAL PATTERNS IN ALIEN ABDUCTION

* 1. All victims experience a sense of danger.

* 2. Most of the victims experienced the awareness of being immobilized.

* 3. Victims remember recall being inside an alien spaceship.

* 4. It is not just being there, but the physical examined by something that is not human.

* 5. The Greys often examine the victim's genital organs, but it is not just the exam, but many victims remember "some type of sexual activities."

* 6. After the initial contact, there remains a strange ongoing communication between the aliens and their victims.

* 7. In several cases, the victims were given a limited tour of the insides of craft. They sometimes see the communication rooms. Sometimes a victim are shown the room that room.

* 8. A few victims were shown a book that appears to be the plans of the alien agenda, but that book is not in a human language.

* 9. At the end of the limited tour, a few victims were shown the alleged hybrid offspring. The nursery includes newborn infants, toddlers, and preteen hybrids.

* 10. The victims are aware of the implantation of a device that appears to be just under the skin, that implant is flexible.

* 11. Victims are often told the small implant is used for tracking the Grey's victims.

* 12. A few isolated cases the memories if the victims are clearly remembered. Other victims struggle to recall any vivid memories of the alien event.

* 13. Almost all victims know they experienced missing- time, the missing time can be from a few minutes to a few days.

* 14. In a few cases the events are permanently blocked from the victim's memory cells.

* 15. More than a few cases the victims became victims of rare diseases, and doctors cannot cure these bizarre disorders.

* 16. After the abductions, many victims experience a total change of their normal life style.

* 17. Many victims feel like part of an ongoing experience, and believe the victims now have messages for humanity.

* 18. After the abduction, a few victims have a feeling of being on a vital mission, and they are responsible for the entire human race.

* 19. Following the abduction, the victims find unexplained physical scars. The victims cannot remember what caused the scars.

* 20. Many of the abduction victims now have new abilities, such as healing abilities, perhaps emphatic abilities or new psychic talents.

* 21. Several of the victims of alien abduction believe they are no longer the same person, and they believe they are a "walk-in" or "partial human."

104

TRIPOD OF REALITY – A POEM

In reality, my dear friends -

A bird cannot build a nest in is the moist banks of clouds,

Nor a fish cannot swim the dark and dry labyrinth tunnels known as Agharta's Deep.

Human - the frail mistake of some long forgotten God – can only stumble through life - blindly,

Knowing he cannot comprehend the mysterious clockwork of Gods, he can only hope for a gift,

That once in a while is bestowed to mankind – the gift of understanding reality – and at least briefly, before once again,

Mankind forgets their place in the cosmos zoological garden.

105

SUPERSTITIONS ABOUT NUMBER 13 & NUMBER 7

Are you superstitious about numbers? Do consider the number 13 or 7 as bad days? Or perhaps do you think of those days as evil?

Don't harbor negative thoughts about any number; remember it is just a number. Instead, focus on the positive - and that includes the number 13!

If you are religious, try remember that Jesus had 12 disciples, and Jesus made the 13th member of the group. Jesus didn't think the number 13 was evil.

If you are pagan, try to remember 13 it the same as the members in witchcraft covens. (So witchcraft can't be that too bad if Jesus chose that number for his group too!)

If you are patriotic, remember the first colonies for the USA's first 13 states....and there were 13 beautiful stars on the first flag.

Ancient lore hints there were originally 12 planets around the Sun. (just like coven's & Jesus' disciples)

Do you never step on crack on a sidewalk, but always make sure to avoid the 13th crack on your sidewalk?

Do you avoid black cats?

Do you throw away the 13th penny?

Do you remember that hotel elevators rarely have the 13th level? You are at either 12th level or 14th, but never on 13th level. It is because a lot of people still believe the number 13 is still evil.

How do you feel lucky about number 7? Or do you think it is an unlucky number?

What do you feel about the number 7? Could that a simple number could be evil? I was born on the 7th day of February. But I am just as lucky or unlucky as every other people. I wasn't born on a special day – I was simply born just like everybody else.

Do you think the number 7 connected with bad luck or good luck? Or maybe you remember the old rule that says if you break a mirror you will have 7 years of bad luck?

If you are a gambler you may think about the number 7 if you see dice. Do you think the number 7 will bring you good luck?

Only a few folks are aware the word "shiva" means seven.

In ancient time the historians thought there were only 7 planets in this solar system.

In some ancient religion based theories the high priest believed the seven days of the week were literally stacked in history, and they thought that the number 7 was magical, because no matter what day of the week you are standing, there were always six other days, and the seventh day it's self was very magical.

Or perhaps you have religious point of view of the number 7?

Think about the different religious connections. The number 7 is the total days it took to complete the Creation - God worked for 6 days, and rested for the 7th day.

In the Book of Revelations you will find 7 Holy Seals that will be broken.

The 1500s the High Priests thought the Earth was created for a specific time of time, and they thought the Earth began 1500 years ago and the world will end after the 7000 years all the End of Days were completed. They couldn't consider other ideas. If that idea was accurate, the Earth would end last year. (Hmm, after all there have been humans on Earth, they were always counting down to the end of Earth – so far all the countless times the humans thought this year would be the end of Earth. But we are still here aren't we?)

Remember in Egypt the Pharaoh suffered from 7 years of famine, but don't forget there were 7 years of plenty too!

There are countless numbers – and all the numbers and none of them are special. When you think about of the numbers from 0-1-2-3-4-5-6-7-8-9 that is all of it. All bigger numbers are simply but multiple copies of the same numbers. There is nothing special about numbers. Other than they exist.

106

MISSING PEOPLE: 1,096,095 GO MISSING EACH YEAR DID THEY END UP AT DULCE BASE?

Quite a few years ago I wrote this article (in 2012) – it is still as important as ever – nothing change except in that last five years another 5 million people disappeared – think it is impossible? The numbers continue growing higher each year.

Read on ....

The amount of people that literally disappear in the U.S.A. – every day – is flabbergasting!! What is the world is going on? Reports of missing persons in the last 25 years have increased six-fold! In 1980 the statistics were 150,000 each year – this year we were astonished to discover the missing rolls jumped up to 900,000! But the numbers also indicate that law enforcement treats the cases more seriously now, including those of marginalized citizens.

If we assume the adults left in their own power, that still leaves more than 58,000 children that were not victims of family dispute, but were kidnapped by strangers. Here is a small mention of the statistics of a sampling missing of the missing children:

According to National Center for Missing and Exploited Children and the U. S. Department of Justice the number of children that go missing every year is staggering.

How many children are reported missing each year?

Be prepared to be shocked:

The U.S. Department of Justice claims that 797,500 children (younger than 18) were reported missing in a one-year period of time studied, resulting in an average of 2,185 children being reported missing each day.

203,900 children were the victims of family abductions.

58,200 children were the victims of non-family abductions.

If we assume the largest amount of the 58,200 missing children are kidnapped by people with twisted perverted sexual needs, there the remaining children are nowhere to be found.

Were they taken to Dulce Base, or a similar underground facility?

Since there are no real statistics on Dulce Base (it is classified material) let's just guess that out of the 58,200 missing children let pretend it is 365 children that are Dulce Base victims – we are talking about of one child each day of the year.

If we start our count the year Tom Castello left Dulce Base, and count down the 33 years since Tom left – we are talking about of 12,045 – that is a small city of missing children. Let's assume too that one adult was kidnapped every day and taken to Dulce Base too, another 365 adults – then we are talking about 24,090 kidnapped people. That is one child and one adult – but Tom claimed the amount of men, women and children that enter Dulce Base were the average of 13 people every day, all year round. So now we are talking about of 4745 people a year, and the amount of people missing for the last 33 years since Tom left Dulce Base is a whopping 156,585 – and that is Dulce Base alone – and I am aware of 7 underground bases in the USA.

I'm sure there are a lot of more than just the few I found. Two other very large bases are Telos City in California, (under Mountain Shasta) and Arizona, Perica rival Dulce Base is size. (It is under Page, Arizona.) If we guess the other bases also kidnap the same amount every year – the missing number jumps up to 1,096,095 missing people since 1979.

Who are these missing family members? Why did they disappear?

Why were they chosen for their one-way ticket to Dulce Base? What is in their DNA important enough to kidnap them and take them to Dulce Base? Just about everyone knows someone with a missing family member – that doesn't mean they were certainly taken to Dulce Base – but if they are not at Dulce, where are they?

Do you think it is not something that will never happen to YOUR family? You think you are 'too careful?' Think again – it can happen in ANY family. Also be aware that not every missing person is a child, but adults go missing, grown men and women can disappear with no clues. Maybe they left for their own reasons, but then again, maybe not, perhaps they were 'taken' to a place like Dulce Base, in New Mexico.

Every year over a million people disappear – that is a huge amount of people. It is the size of a city like Dallas Texas, or Las Vegas, Nevada – now imagine to wake up and find out the entire population of Dallas suddenly disappeared! It is shocking to realize the missing people in the USA every year are enough to populate a large city!

This happens to ordinary people, people just like you and me.

It can happen in your family too.

107

SIX THINGS ABOUT THE ANGELS

1. The angels can sin, just the same as the human race:

   "For if God did not spare the angels who sinned, but cast them down to hell and delivered them into chains of darkness, to be reserved for judgment;" - 2 Peter 2:4.

2. The angels eat and enjoy the same food humans eat:

   "The two angels came to Sodom in the evening, and Lot was sitting in the gate of Sodom. When Lot saw them, he rose to meet them and bowed himself with his face to the earth and said, "My lords, please turn aside to your servant's house and spend the night and wash your feet. Then you may rise up early and go on your way." They said, "No; we will spend the night in the town square." But he pressed them strongly; so they turned aside to him and entered his house. And he made them a feast and baked unleavened bread, and they ate." – Genesis 19: 1-3.

3. The angels were created before the human race:

    "*Thus the heavens and the Earth, and all the host of them, were finished.*" – Genesis 2:1

    The human race was created on the 8th day of creation, because on that 8th day remembered he forgot to create a being to tend of the Garden of Eden. So on the 8th day God created the human race.

4. There are five different types of angels

    A. *Archangels* – 1 Thessalonians 4:16
    B. *Common Angels* – Hebrews 13:2
    C. *Cherubim* – Exodus 25:20
    D. *Living Creatures* – Revelations 4:6
    E. *Seraphim* – Isaiah 6:1-13.

5. The angels do not marry. "*For in the resurrection they (angels) neither marry, nor are given in marriage, but are as the angels of God in Heaven.*" Matthew 22: 30.

6. Some angels have multiple wings to fly:

    "*Above it stood the Seraphim each one had six wings; with twain he covered his face, and with twain he covered his feet, and with twain he did fly.*" Isaiah 6: 2

108

UFO TRIVIA

1. Out of the 12,618 UFO sightings between 1947 and 1969 reported that was reported to Project Blue Book, (a research agency out of Wright-Patterson Air Force) only 701 remained truly "unidentified." All the other 11,917 sightings were "clearly explained" by government reports.

2. In 1947 the term "flying saucer" was used to discuss the strange objects seen in the sky. But in 1953 the U.S. Air Force started reporting shapes other that were the simple disk or saucer, the official term the Air Force reported was changed to UFO - Unidentified Flying Object.

3. Do you know the difference between UFO and IFO? If a flying object remains unidentified, is stays the term *UFO*. However, after the UFO is identified the object is listed as an IFO, or Identified Flying Object.

4. The term UFO is used to discuss modern unidentified flying objects, but a different term - "Ancient Astronaut" - is used to discuss flying objects in the distant past.

5. Back in 1883 an astronomer named Jose Bonilla from Zacatecas, Mexico captured the first photograph of an Unidentified Flying Object.

6. The first sci-fi book that clearly discusses an alien invader was titled "War of the Worlds". The English author, H.G. Wells penned that famous book in 1898.

7. By the year 1991 more than 4 million men or women reported they were abducted by an unknown civilization according the Roper Polls. Aliens continue kidnapping people for their own reasons. The U.S. government refuses to discuss the subject.

8. In the year 1965 Queensland, Australia claims the first known Crop Circle.

9. If an Earth-bound UFO travels across land, the object is called Extraterrestrial Vehicle or ETV. That term is used to distinguish from the flying unknown objects.

Made in the USA
Columbia, SC
11 August 2023

21516487R00204